A TEXT BOOK OF

INDUSTRIAL ORGANISATION AND MANAGEMENT

For
Semester V

THIRD YEAR DEGREE COURSE IN ELECTRONICS ENGINEERING

As Per New Revised Syllabus of
North Maharashtra University, Jalgaon, June 2014

M. S. MAHAJAN

B.E. (Mech.), M.E. (Produciton Engg.)
Ex-principal, Govt. Polytechnic, Jalgaon
Ex-I/C Principal, Govt. College of Engineering, Jalgoan

N2290

IO&M (T.E.) SEM-V (ELECTRONICS) (NMU) **ISBN 978-93-5164-109-4**

First Edition : August 2014

© : Author

The text of this publication, or any part thereof, should not be reproduced or transmitted in any form or stored in any computer storage system or device for distribution including photocopy, recording, taping or information retrieval system or reproduced on any disc, tape, perforated media or other information storage device etc., without the written permission of Author with whom the rights are reserved. Breach of this condition is liable for legal action.

Every effort has been made to avoid errors or omissions in this publication. In spite of this, errors may have crept in. Any mistake, error or discrepancy so noted and shall be brought to our notice shall be taken care of in the next edition. It is notified that neither the publisher nor the author or seller shall be responsible for any damage or loss of action to any one, of any kind, in any manner, therefrom.

Published By :	Printed at
NIRALI PRAKASHAN	**Repro Knowledgecast Limited**
Abhyudaya Pragati, 1312, Shivaji Nagar,	**India**
Off J.M. Road, PUNE – 411005	
Tel - (020) 25512336/37/39, Fax - (020) 25511379	
Email : niralipune@pragationline.com	

DISTRIBUTION CENTRES
PUNE

Nirali Prakashan
119, Budhwar Peth, Jogeshwari Mandir Lane
Pune 411002, Maharashtra
Tel : (020) 2445 2044, 66022708, Fax : (020) 2445 1538
Email : bookorder@pragationline.com

Nirali Prakashan
S. No. 28/25, Dhyari,
Near Pari Company, Pune 411041
Tel : (022) 24690204 Fax : (020) 24690316
Email : dhyari@pragationline.com
bookorder@pragationline.com

MUMBAI
Nirali Prakashan
385, S.V.P. Road, Rasdhara Co-op. Hsg. Society Ltd.,
Girgaum, Mumbai 400004, Maharashtra
Tel : (022) 2385 6339 / 2386 9976, Fax : (022) 2386 9976
Email : niralimumbai@pragationline.com

DISTRIBUTION BRANCHES

NAGPUR
Pratibha Book Distributors
Above Maratha Mandir, Shop No. 3, First Floor,
Rani Jhanshi Square, Sitabuldi, Nagpur 440012,
Maharashtra, Tel : (0712) 254 7129

BENGALURU
Pragati Book House
House No. 1, Sanjeevappa Lane, Avenue Road Cross,
Opp. Rice Church, Bengaluru – 560002.
Tel : (080) 64513344, 64513355,
Mob : 9880582331, 9845021552
Email:bharatsavla@yahoo.com

JALGAON
Nirali Prakashan
34, V. V. Golani Market, Navi Peth, Jalgaon 425001,
Maharashtra, Tel : (0257) 222 0395
Mob : 94234 91860

KOLHAPUR
Nirali Prakashan
New Mahadvar Road,
Kedar Plaza, 1st Floor Opp. IDBI Bank
Kolhapur 416 012, Maharashtra. Mob : 9855046155

CHENNAI
Pragati Books
9/1, Montieth Road, Behind Taas Mahal, Egmore,
Chennai 600008 Tamil Nadu, Tel : (044) 6518 3535,
Mob : 94440 01782 / 98450 21552 / 98805 82331, Email : bharatsavla@yahoo.com

RETAIL OUTLETS
PUNE

Pragati Book Centre
157, Budhwar Peth, Opp. Ratan Talkies,
Pune 411002, Maharashtra
Tel : (020) 2445 8887 / 6602 2707, Fax : (020) 2445 8887
Pragati Book Centre
Amber Chamber, 28/A, Budhwar Peth,
Appa Balwant Chowk, Pune : 411002, Maharashtra,
Tel : (020) 20240335 / 66281669
Email : pbcpune@pragationline.com

Pragati Book Centre
676/B, Budhwar Peth, Opp. Jogeshwari Mandir,
Pune 411002, Maharashtra
Tel : (020) 6601 7784 / 6602 0855
PBC Book Sellers & Stationers
152, Budhwar Peth, Pune 411002, Maharashtra
Tel : (020) 2445 2254 / 6609 2463

MUMBAI
Pragati Book Corner
Indira Niwas, 111 - A, Bhavani Shankar Road, Dadar (W), Mumbai 400028, Maharashtra
Tel : (022) 2422 3526 / 6662 5254, Email : pbcmumbai@pragationline.com

www.pragationline.com info@pragationline.com

PREFACE

This book has been written with a specific aim of providing a text book on **"Industrial Organisation and Management"** for V^{th} semester Third Year Degree Course in Electronics and Telecommunication Engineering students pertaining to North Maharashtra University, Jalgoan.

An attempt has been made to provide the specific subject matter through a single source. Typical questions have been added at the end of each chapter.

The author expresses his gratitudes towards Shri. Umakant Nehete (Entrepreneur), Advocate Shri. Bipin Bendale and Shri. Sunil Mahajan (Entrepreneur) for their constant encouragement and valuable suggestions.

The author is thankful to Shri. Dineshbhai Furia, Shri. Jigneshbhai Furia, Shri. P. M. More, Mrs. Prachi Sawant, Mrs. Manasi Pingle and other staff of Nirali Prakashan for bringing out this book in the shortest possible time.

The author is also thankful to Sau. Meena Mahajan for her co-operation from time to time. It will not be out of place to express thanks to Shri Ganesh Dalwale (Quality Book Distributors), Jalgaon for extending his co-operation during the writing of this book.

Although extreme care has been taken to avoid mistakes, yet some of them might have crept in. The author shall feel obliged, if the errors are pointed out by the readers.

Any constructive criticism and suggestions will be appreciated by the author for enhancing the utility of this book.

August 2014   **Manohar Mahajan**
Pune

SYLLABUS

Unit-1: Introduction to Business, Industry and Management (08 Lectures, 16 Marks)

Management: Various definitions, Nature, Importance, Overview of business, Types of Business: service, manufacturing, trade. Industrial sectors: introduction to Engineering, process, textile, chemical, agro industry, Globalization, I.P.R.

Unit-II: Management Process (08 Lectures, 16 Marks)

Evolution of management thought, Concept of Management, Administration and Management, Scientific Management by F W Taylor, Principles of Management (14 principles of Henry Fayol), Levels and skills of management, Functions of Management: planning - types and features, organizing, co-ordinating, directing, controlling, decision making - types.

Unit-III: Organizational Management (08 Lectures, 16 Marks)

Organization: definition, steps in forming organization. Types of organization: line, line & staff, functional, project type. Departmentation: centralized & decentralized, authority & responsibility, span of control. Forms of ownerships: proprietorship, partnership, joint Stock Company, co-operative society, government sector.

Unit-IV: Human Resource Management (08 Lectures, 16 Marks)

Personnel Management: Introduction, definition, function. Staffing: introduction to HR, HR Planning, recruitment procedure, Personnel - Training and Development, Types of training, Induction, skill enhancement, Leadership and Motivation, Leadership- Styles and types, Motivation: definition, Intrinsic and Extrinsic, Moslow's theory of Motivation and its significance. Safety Management.

Unit-V: Ethical and Legislative Management (08 Lectures, 16 Marks)

Ethics: Meaning and Nature of Ethics. Meaning, Moral and Ethics, Types of Ethics, Importance of Ethics, Nature of Ethics. Ethics in management and qualities and social responsibility of managers, Introduction, Objectives and feature of Industrial Legislation: factory Act, ESI Act, workman compensation Act, industrial dispute Act.

❖❖❖

CONTENTS

UNIT I: INTRODUCTION TO BUSINESS INDUSTRY AND MANAGEMENT 1.1 – 1.28

UNIT II: MANAGEMENT PROCESS 2.1 – 2.44

UNIT III: ORGANISATIONAL MANAGEMENT 3.1 – 3.52

UNIT IV: HUMAN RESOURCE MANAGEMENT 4.1 – 4.64

UNIT V: ETHICAL AND LEGISLATIVE MANAGEMENT 5.1 – 5.42

❖❖❖

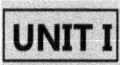

INTRODUCTION TO BUSINESS, INDUSTRY AND MANAGEMENT

1.1 Various Definitions of Management

Management has been defined by different thinkers in a number of ways. For our understanding, management may be viewed as, what manager does in a formal organisation to achieve the objectives.

Some of the important definitions of management are as under:

1. Management has been called by *Mary Parker Follet,* 'the art of getting things done through other people.' This definition throws light on the fact that managers achieve the organisational goals by enabling others to perform rather than performing the task themselves.

   Management, in fact, encompasses a wide variety of activities, such that no one single definition can capture all the facets of management, given its dynamic nature.

2. "Management may be defined as the art of applying the economic principles that underline the control of men and materials in the enterprise under consideration". —*Kimball and Kimball*

3. "Management is the force that integrates men and physical plant into an effective operating unit". —*Keith and Gubelline*

4. "Management is principally a task of planning, co-ordinating, motivating and controlling the efforts of others towards a specific objectives". —*James Lundy*

5. *As Appley L.* in his book has written, "Management is the attainment of pre-established goals by the direction of human performance along pre-established lines". According to Appley L., Management is essentially personnel management. We do not build automobiles, airplanes, refrigerators, radio's etc. We build men and women and these human resources build products. Human resources are our great assets. They have unlimited potential. Hence, it is but natural that management must give special attention to the development of human resources.

6. P. Drucker in his book Practice of Management has defined, "Management is a multi-purpose organ that manages a business, manages a manager and manages workers and work".

Drucker stresses *three* jobs of management — *(i)* Managing a business; *(ii)* Managing manager; and *(iii)* Managing workers and work. Even if one is omitted, we would not have management any more and we also would not have a business enterprise or an industrial society. According to Drucker, the manager has to balance and harmonise three major functions of the business enterprise. Hence, a manager is a dynamic and life-giving element in every business. Without efficient management we cannot secure the best allocation and utilization of human, material and financial resources.

7. "Management is knowing exactly what you want men to do? and then seeing that they do it the best and in cheapest ways". —*EW Taylor*

8. "Management is defined as the creation and maintenance of an internal environment in an enterprise where individuals, working together in groups, can perform efficiently and effectively towards the attainment of group goals".
   —*Koontz and O'Donell*

   According to this definition, management is an art of creating favourable performance environment enabling the group to attain stated objectives and management is the body of organised knowledge, *i.e.* Science which underlies the art.

9. Quoting from *American Management Association*, "Management is guiding human and physical resources into dynamic organisation units which attain their objectives to the satisfaction of those served and with high degree of morale and sense of attainment on the part of those rendering service".

10. According *to Henri Fayol the father of modern management* thought, "Management is to forecast and to plan, to organise, to command, to co-ordinate and to control". It attempts to describe management in terms of what a manager does and not what management is ?

11. The definition given by *James A.F Stoner* covers all the important facets of management.

    According to him, "Management is the process of planning, organising and leading the efforts of organisation members and of using all other organisational resources to achieve stated organisational goals".

    The definition suggests:

    (i) Management is a continuous process.

    (ii) Several inter-related activities have to be performed by managers irrespective of their levels to achieve the desired goals.

(iii) Managers use the resources of the organisation, both physical as well as human, to achieve the goals.

(iv) Management aims at achieving the organisations goals by ensuring effective use of resources.

It is evident that the emphasis is on achieving the objectives by using the inputs like materials, machinery, money and the services of men.

12. A precise definition of management can be stated as: "Management is a social process involving co-ordination of human and material resources through the functions of planning, organizing, staffing, leading and controlling in order to accomplish stated objectives".

There are five parts to a definition of management as a social process:

(i) the co-ordination of resources;

(ii) second, the performance of managerial functions as a means of achieving co-ordination;

(iii) third, establishing the objective or purpose of management process, i.e. it must be purposeful managerial activity;

(iv) fourth aspect is that management is a social process i.e. it is the art of getting things done through other people; and

(v) the fifth is its cyclical nature *i.e.* an ongoing (continuous) process which represents planning — action — control — re-planning cycle.

This definition of management is applicable to all forms of group efforts in all forms of organisations; i.e. profit or non-profit enterprises. It is also applicable to all levels of management in an organisation.

1.2 NATURE OF MANAGEMENT

The important characteristics of management are as follows:

1. **Management is a purposeful activity:** Management basically deals with the attainment of some clearly defined objectives. Objectives differ from organisation to organisation.

   In business, the basic economic objective is to earn maximum profits. While in service organisation like hospital, the basic objective is to provide better service. Management co-ordinates the efforts of the workers to achieve the objectives of the organisation.

2. **It is an efficient management of economic resources:** Management is one of the important factors of production together with land, labour and capital. Management is an operative force which assembles and integrates other factors of production, namely men, machines, materials and money.

3. **Management is a distinct process:** Management is a distinct process consisting of planning, organising, staffing, directing and controlling.

4. **Management is universal:** It is found in every walk of life where the economical and intelligent application of scarce resources are involved. The principles and techniques of management are universally applicable to all group activities performed at any level of organisation.

5. **As a team of managers and system of authority:** Management as a team of managers represents a system of authority, a hierarchy of command and control. Managers at different levels possess varying degrees of authority. Authority enables the managers to perform their functions effectively.

6. **Co-ordination is the soul of management:** Management is necessary in the group activities. Various human beings organised in formal groups are endeavouring to achieve the common organisational objectives. So, various departments in the organisation must work in harmony with one another. In the absence of co-ordination of efforts of different groups, there will be conflicts and chaos.

7. **Management is dynamic:** Management is applied to human groups. Human groups work in society. The ever changing social environment directly and indirectly affects the group activities. Thus, changing environments provide a challenge to management. Efficient management cannot remain static. It must adopt itself to changing conditions.

8. **Management is decision making:** The managers are decision makers; e.g. the marketing manager decides about how to market, when to market, where to market etc. A finance manager takes decision about how much funds will be needed, how to collect funds, how to distribute profit etc. Such countless number of decisions based upon data and analysis constitute management.

9. **Management is a profession:** Management is not only a science but also an art. As an art it refers to innate qualities of managers. As an artist, the manager has to depend on his own experience, intuition and judgment, while making decision on taking action. He has to handle the persons tactfully. (Manage—Men—Tactfully). As a scientist, he relies upon the existing theory and philosophy of management and develops new knowledge, new principles, applies scientific attitude and method in

problem solving. Dean Stanley observed that at present management is 90% art and 10% science. But in the course of time the percent of science will increase. However, it should be noted that science will never eliminate the art part of the management. Born managers can still become better managers if they receive scientific training. In modern times, management is rapidly emerging as a profession. Management Consultancy Services are amply available now-a-days.

1.3 IMPORTANCE OF MANAGEMENT

Management is a universal process in all organised economic activities. It is found in every walk of life where the economical and intelligent application of scarce resources are involved. It is not merely restricted to shops, factory or office. It is necessary for a business firm, Government enterprises, education and health services, military organisations, trade association and so on. In fact, management is an operative force in all complex organisations trying to achieve some stated objectives.

Truly speaking, no enterprise can survive without the competent management, even if it possess huge money, excellent machinery and expert manpower. Because without management it will be all confusion and nobody will know what to do and when to do. Management is indispensable for the successful functioning of every organisation. The slow rate of economic growth of under-developed countries is due to the poor management.

Peter Drucker has rightly remarked that there are no undeveloped countries, there are under-managed countries. According to him, "management is a dynamic life-giving element in an organisation. Without it the resources of production remain mere resources and never become production."

The importance of management can be judged more clearly from the definitions and from the following points.

1) Achievement of Group Goals:

A human group consists of several persons, each specialised in doing a part of the total task. Each person may be working efficiently, but the group as a whole cannot realise its objectives unless there is a mutual co-operation and co-ordination among the membes of the group.

Management crates teamwork and clearly defines the objectives of the group. Managers provides inspiring leadership and motivates the members to make their best contribution towards the accomplishment of the group goals.

2) Optimum Utilisation of the Available Resources:

Management forecast the need of materials, machinery, money and manpower. They ensure that the organisation has adequate resources and at the same time ensures that the resources do not remain idle. They create and maintain an environment conductive to higher productivity.

Managers make sure that the workers know their jobs well and use most efficient method of work.

They provide training and guidance to employees so that they can make the best use of available resources.

3) Minimisation of Cost per Unit:

In the modern competitive age, no business can succeed or survive unless it is capable to supply required goods and services at the lowest possible cost per unit.

Management directs day-to-day operations in such a manner that all wastage and extravagance are avoided. By reducing cost and improving efficiency managers enable an enterprise to be competitive and earn adequate profits.

4) Survival and Growth:

Modern business operates in a rapidly changing environment. An enterprise has to adopt itself to the changing environment. Changes in business environment creates risks as well as opportunities. Managers enable the enterprises to minimise the risks and maximize the benefits of opportunities.

In this way, management facilitates the countinuity and prosperity of business.

5) Generation of Employment:

By setting up and expanding business enterprises, managers create jobs for the people. Managers also create such as environment that people working in the enterprises can get job satisfaction.

6) Development of the Nation:

The development of a country mainly depends on the quality of the management of its resources. Capital investment and import of technical know-how cannot lead to economic development unless wealth producing resources are managed efficiently and effectively. By producing wealth management increases the national income and the living standard of the people. Thus, management is regarded as a key to the economic development of the country.

The importance of management in modern business has increased considerably on account of the following reasons.

1) Increasing competition in the market at national as well as international level.
2) Growing size and complexity of business.
3) Growing specialization of work.
4) Scarcity of resources like materials and power.
5) Increasing social obligations of business.
6) Development of trade unions.

1.4 OVERVIEW OF BUSINESS

Concept of Business

Business literary means a state of being busy. From the dawn of human civilization, human beings have always remained busy to maintain their lives for sustained existence. They have adopted different types of occupations having some economic bearings. However, the true meaning of the term business is given in the following definition:

Diksee defined the business as "the economic activities carried on with a view to earn profits".

Human efforts directed towards the production of goods and services for self consumption though they are economic activities cannot be treated as business activities. Only those economic activities of the production of goods and services resulting into the marketable surplus with a view to exchange them with a profit, are regarded as business activities.

Characteristics of Business Activities

The following characteristics will clarify the proper meaning of the term business:

1. Production and/or Exchange of Goods and Services: Business includes all those economic activities which are directed towards the production of goods like industrial goods (e.g., machines, equipment, tools) and consumer goods (refrigerator, T.V., soaps, cosmetics etc). It also includes the provision of services like power, transportation, bank services, warehousing etc.

The production of goods and services should be made with a view to sell them in the market.

2. Profit-Motive: The marketable surplus of the goods and services is sold in the market with a view to earn profits. It is said that profit is prime mover of the business activities.

3. Uncertain Returns: There is no guarantee that the business deal will always result into profits. It may also otherwise result into the losses. Such business risk sometimes opens the avenues of windfall returns, at the same time it creates the chances of the erosion of the capital invested by the owners.

4. Regularity and Recurrence of Transactions: The sporadic and single transaction does not account to business activity. Business pre-supposes the existence of regular and frequent transactions.

5. Industrial and Commercial Activities: The scope of business is wide and includes both industrial and commercial activities. Industrial activity is concerned with the manufacturing of goods and services while commercial activities are confined to the distribution of manufactured goods and services.

1.5 TYPES OF BUSINESS

The definition of business includes in its scope any service, trade, commerce, manufacture or any adventure or concern in the nature of such service, trade, commerce or manufacture whether actual profit is earned or not.

Further, it also includes any transaction which is incidental or ancillary to such trade, commerce, manufacture, adventure or concern or service.

[I] Service:

Service sector of the economy covers a wide range of activities like trading, banking and finance, real estate, transportation, security management and technical consultancy among several others.

The various sectors that combine together to constitute service industry in India are:
- Trade
- Hotel and Restaurants
- Railways
- Banking
- Insurance
- Transport and storage
- Communication (Post, Telecom)
- Dwelling, Real Estate
- Business services
- Public Administration, Defence
- Personal services
- Other services

There was a marked acceleration in service sector growth in eighties and nineties especially in the nineties. While all the service sectors participated in this boom, growth was fastest in communications, banking, hotels and restaurants, community services, trade and business services. One of the reasons for the sudden growth in the service sector in India in the nineties was the liberalization in the regulatory framework that gave rise to innovation and higher exports from the service sector.

[II] Manufacturing:

Manufacturing industries convert the raw materials into finished products as desired by the consumers. The raw materials obtained from the mine, farm, forest, sea etc. are modified to create and enhance their form utility with the help of various manufacturing processes. Thus, manufacturing industries either create or enhance the form utility with the help of mechanical or chemical processes, e.g., cotton is converted into cloth, sugarcane into various types of petroleum products etc.

Manufacturing processes can further be classified as under:

(a) Fabricating and assembly processes,

(b) Analytical, synthesis and modifying processes.

[III] Trade:

Trade fundamentally deals with the buying and selling transaction. It refers to the sale, transfer and exchange of goods. A person is said to be involved in a trading activity when he buys the goods at the lower price and sales them at a higher price so that he can make a profit. The trader is not a consumer because the consumer buys the goods for the purpose of his own consumption while, the trader buys with a view to resale it at profit. Thus, the trader is an intermediatory between producer and ultimate consumer.

The trading activity is classified on the basis of geographical boundaries as:

- Internal trade, and
- External trade

Internal trade refers to those trading activities which are carried on within the country. They are carried on according to the laws of the land and its national currency. Internal trade is further classified as *(i)* wholesale trade and *(ii)* retail trade.

When the trade is carried on between two or more nations, it is treated as international trade. Unlike internal trade, the complexities of the international trade arises due to different laws, different currencies, and geographical distances. In the modern times international economic co-operation has converted the world into a single market.

Aids to Trade:

The activities which help to effectivating the trading (i.e. buying and selling) are treated as aids to trade or auxiliaries to trade. The following are the main auxiliary functions to trade:

1. **Ware housing:** The time lag between the production and consumption is adjusted through ware housing services. Thus, ware housing eliminates the hurdle of time and they create time utility for the goods.

2. **Transportation:** The inter-regional and international trade exists due to transportation facilities. It helps the flow of goods from the manufacturer to the ultimate consumer through the channel of distribution. It thus creates place utility.

3. **Banking and credit services:** Money is the essence of all business transactions. The trade between unknown parties and involving huge sum of money is possible only through the banking and credit services.

4. **Advertising and publicity:** The dissemination of the information about the product, its quality, price, term, manufacturer etc. is essential for its effective trading. Thus, the hurdle of lack of knowledge is eliminated through the advertising services.

5. **Insurance:** The storing, transportation etc. of the goods involve the risk of fire, accident, theft etc. The insurance services try to cover the risk incidential to such activities and facilitates large volume of business without any substantial losses. Thus, the hurdle of risk is eliminated by insurance agencies.

6. **Agents:** Brokers, agents, deal order agents, forwarding agents, clearing agents, auctioneers etc. provide the essential services for effectivating the trading activities.

1.6 INDUSTRIAL SECTORS

[I] Engineering Industry

India has a large and expanding engineering industry. It has grown not in terms of investment and output but also in terms of structure, composition of products, technological sophistication and self-reliance.

There are *four* major and distinct segments in the engineering industry.

(i) Machine building segment/heavy engineering segment;

(ii) Transport equipment and tractors;

(iii) Heavy electricals;

(iv) Machine tools

Each of these segments has registered good growth. For example, in machine tools India has already become one of the top 20 producers in the world. There are about 150 units engaged in the manufacture of machine tools at present. Hindustan Machine Tools is the largest machine tool industry which manufacture large variety of machine tools including NC and CNC machines. And similar developments has taken place in other segments of engineering industry. The engineering industry plays a vital role for the progress of industrialization and economical development of the country. It is providing the infrastructure required for the continued industrial expansion in the country. It not only fulfils most of the domestic needs but also makes a very sizeable contribution in the field of exports.

[II] Process Industry

Process industries converts the raw materials into finished product by carrying out number of processes. Process industries include:

- Iron and Steel Industry
- Sugar Industry
- Cement Industry
- Paper Industry
- Food Processing Industry etc.

1. Iron and Steel Industry:

Iron and steel industry is one of the basic industries in connection with the manufacture of machinery, electrical, textile, household appliances, metal products, transport equipments etc. India is self-reliant to produce steel. Before Independence Indian Iron and Steel companies were established at Burmpur and Bhadravati in the year 1919 and 1923 respectively. After Independence Iron and Steel plants were developed at Bhadravati, Rourkela, Bokaro, Vijaynagar and Vishakhapatnam etc. India has richest iron ore mines with the highest iron content, which are in the proximity of coal mines. The Steel Authority of India Limited looks after the development of the steel industries.

Today, India is the fifth largest producer of iron ore in the world and the tenth largest producer of finished steel.

2. Sugar Industry:

India is the leading **producer** of sugar, it ranks fourth in the world. About 50% of the sugar factories are in co-operative sector. In 1988 the number of **co-operative sugar** factories were 211 out of total 414 sugar factories. Govt. licence is necessary to set up sugar industry, usually preference is given to proposals from the co-operative and public sector.

3. **Cement Industry:**

Cement production started in our country since 1914 by ICC at Porbandur in Gujarat. There are 20 large and 140 mini-cement plants in India. The public sector ACC and Birlas and Dalmia mostly control the cement production as a centralized control. In cement production India ranks seventh in world; the first six being, Russia, Japan, USA, Italy, West Germany and France. Most of the cement factories are located in southern and western part of India.

4. **Paper Industry:**

The availability of abundant quantity of raw material and forests in India gave rise to the growth of paper industry. At present there are about 340 paper producing units in India out of which large units are only 30. The industry is mostly in private sector, except the currency rights paper manufactured at NEPA Mysore paper mills and Hindustan Paper Corporation are the producers of newsprint.

[II] Textile Industry

It is the oldest and firmly established major industry. Textile industry is unique in the terms that it is an independent industry, from the basic requirement of raw materials to the final products, with huge value-addition at every stage of processing. Textile industry in India is the second largest employment generator. It provides one of the most fundamental necessities of the people. Indian textile industry is the second largest in the world, second only to China. It accounts for 30% of the total exports.

Indian textile industry is constituted of the following segments. Ready-made Garments, Cotton Textiles including Handloom, Man-made Textiles, Silk Textiles, Woolen Textiles, Handicraft, Coir and Jute. India is the largest exporter of cotton fabric and ready-made garments. India is the largest producer of Jute, but still India has to import raw jute because after partition most of the areas producing jute went to Pakistan. Textile industry in India has vast potential for creation of employment in the agricultural, industrial, organized and decentralized sectors and rural and urban areas particularly for women.

Strengths of Indian Textile Industry:

- India has rich resources of raw materials of textile industry. It is one of the largest producers of cotton in the world and is also rich in resources of fibres like polymers, silk, etc.
- India is rich in highly trained manpower. Because of the low labour rates the manufacturing cost in textile automatically comes down to reasonable rates.
- India is highly competitive in spinning sector and has presence in almost all processes of the value chain.

- Indian garment industry is very diverse in size, manufacturing facility, type of textile items produced, quantity and quality of output, cost requirement for fabric etc. It comprises suppliers of ready-made garments suitable for both, domestic and export markets.

However, Indian textile industry is led by small scale companies. Smaller companies do not have the fiscal resources to enhance technology or invest in the high-end engineering of processes.

Secondly, Indian labour laws are relatively unfavourable to the trades and there is an urgent need for labour reforms in India.

The outlook of textile industry in India is very optimistic. It is expected that Indian textile industry would continue to grow at an impressive rate. It is being modernized by an exclusive scheme.

[III] Chemical Industry

The chemical industry involves the use of chemical processes such as chemical reactions and refining methods to produce a wide variety of solid, liquid and gaseous materials. Most of these products serve to manufacture other items, although a smaller number go directly to consumers. Solvents, pesticides, washing soda, dyes, portland cement, industrial gases, adhesives, sealons, coatings, cleaning chemicals etc. are few examples of products used by consumers.

Chemical Industry includes manufacturers of inorganic and organic industrial chemicals, ceramic products, petrochemicals, agrochemicals, fragrances, flavours, food additives, printing inks, polymers, plastics etc.

Chemicals are used to make wide variety of consumer goods as well as inputs to agriculture, manufacturing, construction and service industries. Major industrial customers include rubber and plastic products, textiles, petroleum refinery, pulp and paper and primary metals.

[IV] Petrochemical Industry

Indian Petrochemical Corporation Limited (IPCL) at Baroda was responsible for the development of petrochemical industry in seventh plan. Plastic is the main constituent of petrochemical industry. It covers a wide range of products such as polymers, synthetic fibers, synthetic rubber, plastics, IDPE sheets etc. Which have tremendous application in industrial, agriculture and construction industry and also useful as a cheap replacement material for wood and metallic parts.

[V] Agro Industries

Agro Industries are considered as an extended arm of agriculture. The agro industry is broadly categorized into *three* types:

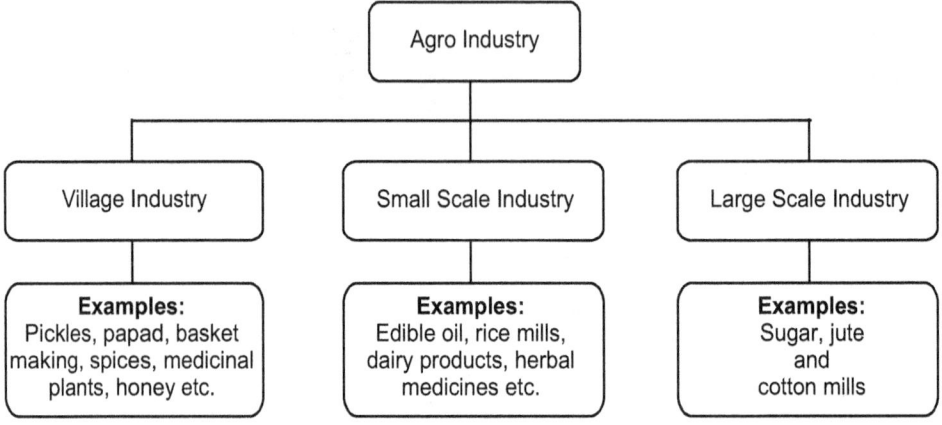

Fig. 1.1

Village industries are owned and run by rural house hold with very little capital investment and a high level of manual labour.

Small scale industries are categorized by medium investment and semi-automation.

Large scale industries involve large investment and high level of automation.

The development of agro based industries started during Pre-Independence days. Cotton mills, sugar mills, jute mills were promoted in the corporate sector. During post Independence days with a view of providing more employment and using local resources small scale and village industries were encouraged.

Agro industries help in processing agricultural products such as field crops, tree crops livestock and fisheries converting them into edible and other usable forms. The global market is enormous for sugar, coffee, tea and processed foods such as sauce, jelly and honey. The market for processed meat, spices, and fruits is equally large. The raw materials and commodities produced and marketed in India are of a wide range such as paddy, wheat, rice, maize, sugarcane, potato, cotton, fruits, vegetables, flowers, spices, fish, poultry, tea, coffee, medicinal plant and honey. All these commodities are processed in one form or other and consumed in large quantities within the country and also exported.

1.7 GLOBALIZATION

1.7.1 Introduction

Globalization is the process of becoming more globally interconnected – the building of ties within and among the peoples of the world.

Globalization is also the process of making our world more interdependent – the growing of mutually dependence among peoples, socially, economically and politically.

Globalization of the economy means free entry in the world market, forcing the organisations to face new challenges and international competition.

Basically globalization is a concept by which the globe becomes one unified entity cutting across the political, economic and regional barrier. In recent years quickly rising share of economic activities of the world seems to be taking place between people who live in different countries. This growth in cross-border economic activities takes various forms:

1. International Trade
2. Foreign Direct Investment (FDI)
3. Capital Market Flows

1. **International Trade:**

    Import: Goods or services are purchased from other countries as import.

    Export: A growing share of what countries produce is sold to foreigners as export.

2. **Foreign Direct Investment (FDI):**

Firms based in one country increasingly make investment, establish and run business operations in other countries.

3. **Capital Market Flows:**

In many countries (especially in the developed world) savers increasingly diversify their portfolios to include foreign financial assets (foreign bonds, equities, loans) while borrowers increasingly turn to foreign sources of funds along with domestic ones.

A *corporation can be said to be global in true sense when:*

1. It provides a product or a service of a brand which is recognized and accepted by the world market, and is export oriented.

2. The entire system of the organization, quality of the product is approved and is up to the level as mentioned in ISO: 9000.

3. It has a overseas marketing and distribution system.

4. It operates a branch of the firm in the operational area with the assistance and finance of the local people but retaining its laid down share.

Globalization Demands that:

1. The product or service rendered by the firm should be at minimum possible cost. The products should also withstand competition with other firms in the national market.
2. World trade is subjected to less restriction.
3. There is economic liberalization. The process of globalization in financial sector i.e., the money and capital market operates globally.
4. The developed countries should invest in developing countries through Multi National Companies (MNC).

Essential Requirements for a firm to become a Global Unit:

1. Establish R&D department so as to develop product and technology and discover new technologies in the field.
2. Product development should be a routine affair. Every effort should be made to develop new products.
3. It should have a strategic response to market feedback so as to know the change in demands, fashion, technology etc.
4. Quick and effective attendance to consumer complaints and their removal in the minimum possible time.
5. Commitment to satisfy the customer by providing the right quality of the product or services in right quantity at right time and right price.
6. Organization should be flexible enough to meet the changes and still satisfy the customer demands. Multi product practices are always preferable.
7. Quick decision making system with enough flexibility.

General Agreement on Tariff and Trade (GATT):

The General Agreement on Tariff and Trade (GATT) was established in 1948 in Geneva. The objective of GATT was to develop free trade among the countries of the world with least barriers. At present about 117 nations are its members, including India.

World Trade Organization (WTO) was established in 1955 with it center at Geneva. The aim of WTO is to deal with disputes of trade amongst its members, reduce trade barriers and permit free flow of goods in the world market. The WTO has established an Institute International Standards Organizations at Geneva, in order to facilitate the standardization of the products and services on global scale.

1.7.2 Advantages and Disadvantages of Globalization w.r.t India

Advantages:

1. It helps industrial and overall development of the developing country like India and may lead to economic prosperity and poverty reduction.
2. It acts as a high elevator of universal peace, prosperity and human welfare.
3. It allows the country to sell its surplus output to other needy countries and also to buy other items which are scare from other countries.
4. Customer can get better quality products at reasonable prices.
5. Our foreign exchange reserves have increased, exports are getting higher and overall industrial growth has also increased.
6. Customers have a free choice to select the products as per their liking.

Disadvantages/Limitations:

1. Domestic industries may suffer due to world wide competition unless protected by the government through its industrial policy.
2. International trade, foreign investment and capital market flows raise distinct issues and have distinct consequences, potential benefits on one hand and costs or risks on the other.
3. Extreme opponents charge globalization that; it enriches the rich and devasts the environments.
4. Indian industries have to face cut throat competition among organizations both at national and international levels.
5. In most of the important determinants of national competitive advantage, India lags behind. There are several factors relating to technology, productivity and quality which adversely affect India's competitiveness. India's industry and its products lack competitiveness not only in comparison with the developed countries, but in comparison with even some of the newly industrialized countries.
6. Wrong policies, lack of foreign exchange resources, poor technology base and lack of international marketing competence had left India behind for years and also exporters of primary commodities, leaving the benefits of value addition to other countries.
7. The Indian products today rank low in global market; Indian brand names are not recognized; and in terms of overall international orientation too, India is rated low.

To what extent should we embrace globalization, is a difficult question. Because it raises many other questions.

1.8 INTELLECTUAL PROPERTY RIGHTS

1.8.1 Introduction

Intellectual Property Rights protects the use of information and ideas that are of commercial value. The term "Intellectual Property" covers Patents, Copyrights, Trade marks, Designs, Know-how and so on. The scope of intellectual is growing tremendously. Intellectual persons who create new creative ideas (invention) attempts to seek protection under the umbrella of IPR. Although, the creation of a trade mark has very little to do with intellectual creativity, however it is clear that patents, designs and copyrights are products of intellectual efforts and creative activity in the field of science and technology.

In our country, the majority of intellectual property rights are today founded in the five enactments. i.e.,

i) The Trade Mark Act, 1999

ii) Copy Rights Act, 1957

iii) The Patents Act, 1970

iv) The Designs Act, 2000 and

v) Geographical Indication of Goods (Registration and Protection) Act, 1999.

The law of intellectual property plays a significant role for the cultural and economic development of the country.

The granting of patent monopoly encourages the competitors in the market to manufacture / invent new product or effect improvement in the existing product or in the process of manufacture.

Similarly, industrial design protection encourages people with the creative mind to utilize their talent in developing new improved or economical designs for the product.

The protection of trade mark is intended to provide for better protection of trade marks and prevention of fraud in using the existing or reputed trade mark.

Similarly, copy right is the right granted to the author or originator of certain literary or artistic production where by he is authorized with a sole and exclusive privilege of multiplying copies of the same and publishing and selling them.

The main purpose of intellectual property rights (IPR) is that no one should be allowed to take advantage of a thing which has been invented or produced by the intelligence, labour, skill, judgment and efforts of others.

Different kinds of intellectual properties can be commercially exploited in different ways.

In case of patents, the patentee may himself commercially exploit the patent or assign his rights or license to the Businessmen/Companies for a lump sum payment or on a royalty basis.

Similarly, the registered designs can be commercially exploited either by assigning or by licensing the rights to others capable of exploiting it on a lump sum or on royalty basis.

Similarly, the copyright can also be exploited.

However, in case of trade mark the commercial exploitation is only possible by way of registration of the license as registered user. Hence commercial exploitation of registered trade mark by way of licensing it to others to use if on a royalty basis is not permissible.

1.8.2 Patents

Patent is a grant of right to exclude others from making, using or selling one's invention. It includes right to license other to make, use or sell it.

It is an official document conferring a right or privilege, securing in writing to an inventor for a term of years the exclusive right to make, use and sell his invention; the monopoly or right so granted.

The 'Patent Act' is founded in the enactment "The Patent Act, 1970". The Patent Act provides protection for an invention which must be new and useful.

An invention, in order to be patentable must be capable of being made or used in some kind of industry. In this context, industry should be understood in its broader sense as including any useful, practical activity, and does not necessarily imply the use of machine or the manufacture of an article.

The expression 'invention' has therefore been defined in the Patent Act, 1970 to mean manner of manufacture; machine; substance produced by manufacture. The invention relates to the skill (art), series of action (process) or the particular way (method) or the way (manner) of making a product or thing. It also relates to machine or apparatus by which a thing is made and also the product which is the result of act of making.

The effect of grant of patent is quid pro quo, quid is the knowledge disclosed to the public and quo is the monopoly granted for the term of the patent. Patents and Designs Act sets out that a patent once granted confers upon the patentee the exclusive privilege of making, selling and using the invention throughout India and of authorizing others to do so. This is quo. The quid is compliance with the various provision resulting in the grant of patent.

In case of Patent, the patentee may himself commercially exploit the patent or assign his rights or license them to the Businessmen/Companies for a lump sum payment or on royalty basis. In this context "Patentee" is he to whom a patent has been granted. The granting of patent monopoly encourages the competitors in the market to manufacturer new products or effect improvements in the process of manufacture.

Since its inception, the Patent Act, 1970 was subjected to a single Amendment in 1999 to the obligation of India under the Agreement on Trade Related Aspects of Intellectual Property Rights (TRIPS) forming part of the World Trade Organization (WTO). For the purpose of integrating intellectual property system with international practices, the Act needed another amendment so that it is modern and in accordance with international practices and consistent with the TRIPS agreement. Thus, the Patents (Amendment) Act, 2002 was introduced making far reaching changes in the 1970 Act. It also widened the scope of non-patentability of substances in the nature. Several other modifications were also carried out.

1.8.3 Trade Marks

Trade mark means a mark capable of being represented graphically and which is capable of distinguishing the goods or services of one person from those of others and may include shape of goods, their packaging and combination of colour.

In our country, the trade mark act was founded in the enactment. 'The Trade Mark Act, 1999'. The Trade Mark Act provides for better protection to the registered trade mark for goods and services, and prevents the use of fraudulent marks on merchandise.

A mark is a part of the brand which appears in the form of a symbol, design etc. It could be recognized only by sight but may not be pronounceable e.g. symbol of Maharaja of Air India, design of two arrows for Delhi Transport Corporation etc. When the brand mark is registered and legalized it becomes a Trade Mark. It is essentially a legal term protecting the manufacturers right to use the brand name.

In selecting a good brand name as a trade mark the various aspects require careful consideration.

1. It should identify the product, its characteristics easily and distinguish from other similar products.
2. As far as possible it should be most descriptive in nature e.g. Mysore Sandal Soap.
3. It should be unique.
4. It should be appropriate for the product concerned.
5. It should be registered so that any other firm might not take advantage of its popularity.

6. It should be helpful in advertisement.
7. It should be short and pointing (i.e. appealing and attractive)
8. It should be easy to print or embossed on packages.
9. As far as possible it should be heart touching so as to influence the mind of customer and catch his imagination (easy to visualize).

Patents, designs and copyrights can be commercially exploited in different ways. However, in case of trade mark the commercial exploitation is only possible by way of registration of the licenses as registered user. Hence, commercial exploitation of a registered trade mark by way of licensing it to others to use on a royalty basis is not permissible. In case of infringement of Registered trade mark, both civil and criminal remedies (imprisonment and heavy fines are available).

Procedure for Registration of Trade Mark:

1. Application for Registration: Any person claiming to be the proprietor of a trade mark used or proposed to be used by him, who is desirous of registering it, shall apply in writing to the Registrar in the prescribed manner for the registration of his trade mark. Subject to the provisions of the Act, the Registrar may refuse the application or may accept it absolutely or subject to such amendments, modifications, condition or limitations, if any, as he may think fit. In the case of refusal or conditional acceptance of an application, the Registrar shall record in writing the grounds for such refusal or conditional acceptance and the material used by him in arriving at his decision.

2. Advertisement of Application: When the application for registration of a trade mark has been accepted, the Registrar shall, advertise the application in the prescribed manner.

3. Opposition to Registration: Within three months from the date of the advertisement of an application, the Registrar on application made to him in the prescribed manner may allow any person to give notice of opposition to the registration.

The Registrar shall, after hearing the parties, if so required and considering the evidence, decide whether and subject to what conditions or limitations, if any, the registration is to be permitted.

4. Registration: Subject to the provisions of section 19, when an application for registration of a trade mark has been accepted and either

(a) The application has not been opposed and the time of notice of opposition has expired; or

(b) The application has been opposed and the opposition has been decided in favour of the applicant; the Registrar shall register the said trade mark.

On the registration of a trade mark, the Registrar shall issue to the applicant a certificate in the prescribed form of the registration thereof, sealed with the seal of the Trade Marks Registry.

For the purpose of this Act, a record called the Register of Trade Marks shall be kept at the head office of the Trade Marks Registry. In this register the following entries shall be made.

- All registered trade marks with the names,
- Addresses and description of the proprietors,
- Notifications of assignment and transmissions,
- The names, addresses and description of registered users,
- Conditions, limitations and such other matter related to registered trade marks etc.

Absolute Grounds for Refusal of Registration

The trade marks shall not be registered as a trade mark if -

i) It is not capable of distinguishing the goods or services of one person from those of another.
ii) It consist exclusively of marks or indications which have become customary in the current language or in established practices of the trade.
iii) It is of such nature as to deceive the public or cause confusion.
iv) It contains or comprises of any matter likely to hurt the religious feelings of any class or section of the citizens of India.
v) Its use is prohibited under the Emblems and names (Prevention of Improper Use Act, 1950).
vi) It consists exclusively of the shape of goods which results from the nature of the goods themselves.
vii) It comprises or contains scandalous or obscene matter.
viii) Its identity with an earlier trade mark and similarity of goods or services covered by the trade mark.
ix) Its use in India is liable to be prevented.
x) By virtue of law of copyright.

1.8.4 Copyrights

Copyrights are also products of intellectual effort and creative activity in the field of fine arts and applied arts or technology. The Copyrights Act has been founded in the enactment 'The Patents Act, 1970'. The Copyright Act confers a long lasting right in literary, dramatical, musical or artistic creation.

Copyrights is the right granted by statute to the author or originator of certain literary or artistic production, whereby he is authorized for a limited period, with the sole and exclusive privilege of multiplying copies of the same and publishing and selling them.

The object of the law is to facilitate, encourage and motivate artists, composers, software programmes etc. to create original works by a system of granting exclusive right for a limited period to re-produce the work for the benefit or consumption of the public. After the expiry of the specific period the work will belong to the public domain and one may reproduce these without permission.

Thus, the producer of an original work is enabled to prevent others from creating or reproducing his work and in this sense, the author gets the monopoly rights in favour. With the growth of science and technology as well as with the growth in inventive and creative flourish in various aspects of literary, artistic, musical and other arts, the need for copyright protection has become all the most important.

The importance of copyright was recognized only after the print media was invented about five centuries back which enabled reproduction of books and literatures in large numbers.

For the purpose of this Act, "copyright" means the exclusive right subject to the provisions of this Act, to do or authorize the doing of any of the following acts in respect of a work or any substantial part thereof, namely:

a) **In the case of a literary, dramatic or musical work, not being a computer programme:**
   i) To reproduce the work in any material from including the storing of it in any medium by electronic means.
   ii) To issue copies of the work to the public not being copies already in circulation.
   iii) To perform the work in public or communicate it to the public.
   iv) To make any cinematograph film or sound recording in respect of the work.
   v) To make any translation of the work.
   vi) To make any adaptation of the work.
   vii) To do, in relation to translation or an adaptation of the work, any of the acts specified in relation to the work in sub-clauses (i) to (iv).

b) **In the case of a computer programme:**
   i) To do any of the acts specified in clause (a).
   ii) To sell or give on commercial rental or offer for sale or for commercial rental any copy of the computer programme.

c) In the case of an artistic work:

i) To reproduce the work in any material form including depiction on three dimensions of a two dimensional work or in two dimensions of a three dimensional work.

ii) To communicate the work to the public.

iii) To issue copies of the work to the public not being copies already in circulation.

iv) To include the work in any cinematograph film.

v) To make any adaptation of the work.

vi) To do in relation to and adaptation of the work any of the acts specified in relation to work in sub-clauses (i) to (iv).

d) In the case of a cinematograph-film:

i) To make a copy of the film, including a photograph of any image forming part thereof.

ii) To sell or give on hire or offer for sale or hire, any copy of the film, regardless of whether such copy has been sold or given on hire on earlier occasions.

iii) To communicate the film to the public.

e) In the case of a sound recording:

i) To make any other sound recording embodying it.

ii) To sell or give on hire, or offer from sale or hire, any copy of the sound recording regardless of whether such copy has been sold or given on hire on earlier occasions.

iii) To communicate the sound recording to the public.

International copyright is the right of a subject of one country for protection against the republication in another country of a work which he originally published in his own country.

In order to adapt the rapidly changing global economical trade scenario, the 1957 Act was recently amended by the copyright (Amendment) Act, 1999. This Act (Amendment) extends the term protection of performers rights from 25 years to 50 years. The Amendment Act provides for powers to government to extend the provisions of the Act to broadcasts and performances made in other countries provided those countries give reciprocal protection to broadcasts and performances in India.

Offence of infringement of copyright or other rights conferred by this Act:- Any person who knowingly infringes or abets infringement of

(a) The copyright in a work, or

(b) Any other right conferred by this Act,

shall be punishable with imprisonment for a term which shall not be less than six months but which may extend to three years and with fine which shall not be less than fifty thousand rupees but which may extend to two lakh rupees.

Provided that [where the infringement has not been made for gain in the course of trade or business] the court may, for adequate and special reasons to be mentioned in the judgement, impose a sentence of imprisonment for a term of less than six months or a time of less than fifty thousand rupees.

1.8.5 The Designs Act

The Design Act, 2000 is intended to give protection to designs which are new and original i.e. novel designs. The Act deals more with appearance and looks. The Act aims at protecting the novel designs which are to be applied to particular goods which are the subject of manufacture and trade.

Lord Reid summed up the object of the law as to design as under.

"Those who wish to purchase an article for use are often influenced in their choice not only by practical efficiency but by appearance. Some look for artistic import, some are attracted by design which is strange. Many simply choose the article which catches their eye. Whatever the reason may be, one article with a particular design may sell abroad than one without it, then it is profitable to use the design. And much thought, time and expenses might have been incurred in finding a design which will increase sales".

The design Act gives monopoly protection in stronger sense than protection against copying is available under the copyright Act.

According to design Act, "Design" means only the features of shape, configuration, pattern, ornament or composition of lines or colours applied to any article whether in two dimensional or three dimensional or in both forms, by any industrial process or means, whether manual, mechanical or chemical separate or combined which in the finished article appeals to and are judged by the eye. But, it does not include any mode or principle of construction or anything which is in substance a mere mechanical device, and does not include any trade mark as defined in Trade mark Act.

When the design is accepted, the following entries are made in the register of designs:

- The names and addresses of proprietors of registered designs.
- Notification of assignments, and
- Of transmissions of registered designs, and
- Such other matter as may be prescribed.

Such a register may be maintained wholly or partly on computer floppies or diskettes, subject to such safeguards as may be prescribed.

The controller grants certificate and registration to the proprietor of the design when registered. When the design is registered, the registered proprietor will have a copyright in a design during the ten years from the date of registration. The registration can be extended for a second period of five years from the expiry of the original period of ten years.

The registered owner of industrial design gets an exclusive right to apply the design to the articles covered by the registration. A registered design can be commercially exploited either by assigning or by licensing the rights to others capable of exploiting it on a lump sum or on royalty basis.

1.8.6 Geographical Indications of Goods

"Geographical indication", in relation to goods, means an indication which identifies such goods as agricultural goods, natural goods or manufactured goods as originating or manufactured in the territory of a country, or region or locality in the territory. A given quality, reputation or other characteristics of such goods is essentially attributable to its geographical origin. In case where such goods are manufactured goods, one of the activities of either the production or of processing or preparation of the foods concerned takes place in such territory region or locality, as the case may be.

For the purpose of this clause, any name which is not the name of a country, region or locality of the country shall also be considered as the geographical indication if it relates to a specific geographical area and is used upon or in relation to particular goods originating from that country or locality, as the case may be.

Geographical Indication of Goods (Registration and Protection) Act, 1999, is an Act to provide for registration and better protection of geographical indication relating to goods. "Indication" includes any name, geographical, natural or figurative representation or any combination of them suggesting the geographical origin of goods to which it applies. "Goods" means any agricultural natural or manufactured goods or any goods of handicraft or of industry and includes food stuff.

For the purpose of this Act, a record called the Register of Geographical Indication is kept at the head office of the Geographical Indications Registry, wherein the following entries are usually made.

- all registered geographical indications with the names,
- addresses and descriptions of the proprietors,
- the names, addresses and description of authorized users and such other matters relating to geographical indications.

Such registers are maintained wholly or partly on computer.

The following geographical indications are not registered as geographical indications.

a) the use of which would be likely to deceive or cause confusion; or

b) the use of which would be contrary to any law for the time being in force, or

c) which contains scandalous or obscence matter; or

d) which contains any matter likely to hurt the religious susceptibilities of any class or section of the citizens of India, or

e) which would otherwise be disentitled to protection in court; or

f) which are determined to be generic names or indications of goods and are, therefore, not or ceased to be protected in their country of origin, or which have fallen into disuse in that country; or

g) which although literally true as to the territory region or locality which the goods originate, but falsely represent to the persons that the goods originate in another territory, region or locality, as the case may be.

QUESTIONS

1. What is business? State the characterisitcs of business.
2. Describe in brief the following types of business
   (i) Service
   (ii) Manufacturing
   (iii) Trade
3. Name the various industrial sectors and describe any two of them briefly.
4. What is process industry ? Name the various process industries.
5. Describe in brief Textile Industry with the strength of Indian textile industry.
6. Write short notes on any two of the following:
   (i) Chemical Industry
   (ii) Agro Industry
   (iii) Textile Industry
7. Define 'Globalization'. When a corporation can be said as 'Global' ?
8. What is Globalization? State the essential requirements for a firm to become a global unit.

9. State the advantages and limitations of globalization.
10. What do you understand by Intellectual Property Rights (IPR)? What are its contents? Describe the role played by IPR.
11. What is Patent? State the purpose of Patent Act, 1970.
12. State the meaning of Invention as per Patent Act, 1970.
13. Explain the term 'Trade Mark'. State the procedure for registration of Trade Mark.
14. What is 'Trade Mark' ? State the grounds for refusal of registration of Trade Mark.
15. What is copy right ? Explain. What is the object of Copyright Act, 1957.
16. Define the term 'Design' according to the Design Act. State the purpose of Design Act.
17. Describe 'Design Act' in brief.
18. What do you mean by "Geographical Indication of Goods".
19. Describe in brief Geographical Indication of Goods Act.
20. Write short notes on:
    i) IPR
    ii) Patent Act
    iii) Copy Right
    iv) Trade Mark

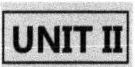

MANAGEMENT PROCESS

2.1 EVOLUTION OF MANAGEMENT THOUGHT

Handicraft System

As already stated, the history of management goes back to the dawn of human civilization, when human being started group activities for the attainment of some common objectives. From approximately the fourteenth century until well after the beginning of eighteenth century, the business units were under handicraft system. There were small privately owned shops which employed tradesman (workers skilled in different trades). The production was on a small scale and was carried out to fulfil the needs of the consumers. Consumer goods such as leather goods, furniture, metalware or other consumer commodities were produced in this manner. Specialization of tasks was not very common. Management was comparatively simple, and the tradesman were using their own initiative and judgment.

Factory System

During the beginning of eighteenth century there was industrial revolution because of the technological and economic development. To meet the increased demand of the products of better quality, a factory system was developed. The factory system made possible the rise of large scale manufacturing enterprises and created managerial problems of co-ordinating and controlling the factors of production (men, materials, machines and money) in order to attain the desired quality and quantity of goods economically. The managerial problems were the natural consequences of increased plant size, greater diversity and volume of manufactured products, intricacy of fabrication processes and specialization of labour. At this stage, the development of a formal theory of management both of work and workers became absolutely necessary. It was against this background that the foundation of modern management were laid.

2.1.1 Stages of Evolution of Management

The evolution of management theory may be divided into three stages:

1. **The Classical Theory of Management** consisting of three streams:

    (a) Bureaucracy

    (b) Scientific Management

    (c) Administrative Management

2. **The Neo-Classical Theory,** having two streams dealing with human factors *viz:*
   (a) Human Relations; and
   (b) Behavioural Science Approach
3. **The Modern Management Theories**
   (a) Technical and quantitative sciences offering quantitative decision-making through operation research and with the help of computer and information system.
   (b) System approach to organisation and management.
   (c) Contingency approach to organisation and management.

Bureaucracy: Max Webel, a German Sociologist offered bureaucratic model. He considered bureaucracy as the most efficient form for complex organisation. His model of bureaucracy included:

(i) hierarchy of authority, involving superior subordinate relationship and chain of command.

(ii) Clear cut division of work based upon competence and functional specialization.

(iii) A system of Rules, Regulations and procedures.

(iv) Impersonality of interpersonal or Mutual relations (based on positions)

(v) Selection and placement of employees based upon competence.

(vi) Legal authority and power: According to this the power does not belong to an individual; but it is due to position in the organisation.

In this, as the policies, rules and procedures are set and applicable to all, this leads to consistent employee behaviour. The jobs, duties and responsibilities are clearly defined. The overlapping or conflicting job duties are avoided.

Rigidity, impersonality, anxiety due to pressure of conformity to rules and procedures may create frustration, insecurity and dependence on the superior. Moreover, bureaucracy cannot offer satisfaction of higher level wants of employees. There is no human relations, employees are treated like machines and not like individuals.

Scientific Management

As a term scientific management was first used in U.S.A. in 1910 by Louis Brandies. As a process, it was first visualised in U.K. in 1832 by Charles Babbage. The utility of scientific methods to problems of management was first of all introduced by F.W. Taylor in America (1865-1915). He is regarded as a "father of scientific management".

We will study Scientific Management in detail in Article 2.4.

Administrative Management Theory (Henri Fayol and Others)

Administrative theory of management was initiated by H. Fayol. a French Engineer-cum-Manager in Europe. Sheldon, Mooney and Reiley, H. Simon, L. F. Urwick. L Gulic, C. Barnard were the followers of Fayol and they contributed a lot to the administrative theory of management. H. Fayol is called as a father of Modem Management He established the pattern of management and the pyramidal form of organisation. He pointed out that technical ability is more dominating on the lower level of management whereas managerial ability is more important on the higher level of management.

We will study Administrative Management in detail in Article 2.5.

Contribution of Frank Gilbreth

1. Frank Gilbreth and Lillian Gilbreth (1868-1924) did a lot of work in order to improve work methods and thus to discover best way of doing a job.
2. In 1917 Gilbreth defined motion study, "as the science of eliminating wastefulness resulting from unnecessary, ill-directed and inefficient motions". He is regarded as a father of motion study. He developed 'principles of motion economy'.
3. In 1921, he introduced process chart.
4. He also identified Therbligs - the fundamental motions involved in doing an activity.
5. He developed micromotion study, invented cycle graph, chrono-cyclegraph and flow diagrams.
6. Frank and Lillian Gilbreth carried out studies on fatigue caused to the industrial worker and its elimination. They concluded that fatigue can be reduced considerably by allowing rest periods, planning seating arrangement, improving working conditions and by using principles of motion economy.

Contribution of Gantt

1. Henry L. Gantt worked under Taylor and was his close associate.
2. He improved Taylor's differential piece rate wage system and introduced his task and bonus plan.
3. He developed a Gantt chart which is still used as a scheduling technique to have a immediate comparison between the planned work and the actual progress of the work. So as to enable the management to take corrective action if there is a significant deviation.

2.1.2 Neo-Classical Theory

Scientific management theory concentrated on physical resources rather than human resources. Prof. Elton Mayo and Fritz Roethlisberger of Hayward University conducted certain experiments at the Hawthrone plant of the Western Electric Company near Chicago. They concentrated on individuals and groups (human element) to study their impact on output level in the organisation. They found that work and productivity were influenced not only by economic needs but also by social needs and sentiments of people working within an organisation. This was the beginning of new era in the field of management which came to be known initially as 'human relations movement' and later as 'behavioural science movement'. It is called as Neo-classical theory which is based on human relations and behavioural science approach. It gave greater emphasis to man behind the machine and stressed the importance of individual as well as group behaviour in an organisation. It showed the importance of human values in business.

Mayo has stated that an organisation is essentially a social system and not merely technoeconomic system. Knowledge of human nature can solve many problems of management. He stressed that successful human relations approach can easily create harmony in an organisation, higher employee satisfaction and therefore higher operational efficiency and productivity.

A. H. Maslow developed a need hierarchy to explain human behaviour within an organisation. The knowledge of individual and group behaviour enables to develop suitable work atmosphere or situations which can increase productivity as well as employee satisfaction.

The areas of managerial application of behavioural science methods are:

1. Organisation is basically a social system and not just techno-economical system.
2. The employee can also be motivated by many social and psychological wants and not solely by economic incentives because his behaviour is also influenced by feelings, emotions and attitudes.
3. Democratic rather than authoritarian leadership is essential to honour psycho-social demands.
4. Effective two way communication network is essential to establish common flow of understanding in any organisation which will enable it to attain its goals.
5. Management must take greater interest in employee development and workers satisfaction as there is a very close connection between morale and productivity.
6. Informal group and informal organisation must be recognised.
7. Management must develop social skills in addition to technical skills. Man to man relationship, team spirit, group harmony should be given top preference by management.

Elements of Behavioural (Neo-classical Theory)

There are *three* elements of Neo-classical theory:

1. The Individual
2. Work Groups or Informal Organisations
3. Participative Management.

1. The individual: The Neo-classical theory stressed that individual difference must be recognised. Each individual has feelings, emotions, perception and attitudes; and ever changing psychology. Each is bringing to the job situation certain attitudes, beliefs and ways of life as well as skills, technical, social and logical. Each person is unique. The inter personal relations at work determine the rise or fall in productivity.

2. Work group: Workers are not isolated, unrelated individuals; they are social beings and should be treated as such by management. An individual in a group develops social wants, e.g. desire to belong, to be accepted by others in the work group. The existence of informal organisation is natural. The management must recognise its importance and it must be integrated intelligently with formal organisation. The informal communication is often very speedy and accurate. The Neo-classical theory recognises the vital effect of group psychology and behaviour on motivation and productivity.

3. Participative management: Classical theory was job-oriented and it focussed its attention on the scientific job analysis. Neo-classical theory focuses its attention on the worker and it is employee-oriented. It shifts the managerial style from product centred approach to employee and group centred approach. Neo-classical theory advocated worker participation in management. It allows labour to participate in decision making and problem solving primarily to increase productivity.

Behavioural approaches have clearly pointed out that job conditions and the job itself are the motivators that can satisfy the needs of both employees and the organisation. These motivators are recognition, sense of belonging, challenging job, independence, participation achievement, enlargement and enrichment of job itself.

2.1.3 Modern Management Theories

Modern management theories started after 1950. There are four streams under the modern management theory:

1. Quantitative Approach to Management
2. System Approach to Management
3. Contingency Approach to Management; and
4. Operational Approach to Management.

1. Quantitative Approach:

The scientific approach of Taylor could be classified as an early form of quantitative approach to management. The prominent contributors to management approach are Taylor, Gilbreth, Gantt, Joel Dean, Newman, Ackoff and Hicks. It believes that if management is a logical process, it can be expressed in terms of mathematical symbols. and relationships. Effective solution to problems of management can be achieved through application of suitable simulation and the use of analytic and synthetic mathematical techniques. The basic approach is the construction of a quantitative model. The construction of the model expresses the effectiveness of the system under study as a function of a set of variables at least one of which is subject to control.

The essential features of quantitative approach are:

1. Management is concerned with problem solving and it must make use of mathematical tools and techniques for the purpose.
2. The different factors involved in management can be quantified and expressed in the form of models i.e. in the form of equations which can be solved with the help of mathematical techniques.
3. Management problems can be described in mathematical models.
4. Operations Research, Mathematical tools, simulation and model building are the basic methodologies developed by this approach. It has helped the management in systematizing thinking.

However, the development of models requires the skills of many disciplines such as engineering, mathematics, economics, statistics, physical sciences and cost accountancy.

The mathematical models cannot be considered as a substitute for sound judgement.

There are certain phases of the management process which cannot be expressed in mathematical symbols and formulae.

2. System Approach:

The system approach is the recent contribution to management thought developed in the late 1960's. The prominent contributors to this approach are Kenneth, Boulding, Johnson, Rosen Zweig and Churchman.

What is a system?

The word system is derived from the Greek word, it means to bring together or to combine. A system is a set of inter-connected and inter-related elements or component parts to achieve certain goals.

In relation to organisation, system is defined as, "an established arrangement of components which leads to accomplishment of particular objectives as per plan".

This definition has three significant parts:

(i) Every system is goal oriented and it must have a purpose or objective to be attained.

(ii) In designing the system we must establish the necessary arrangement of components. This is nothing but organising function of management.

(iii) Inputs of information, material and energy are allocated for processing as per plan so that the outputs can achieve the objective of the system, *viz* productivity and satisfaction.

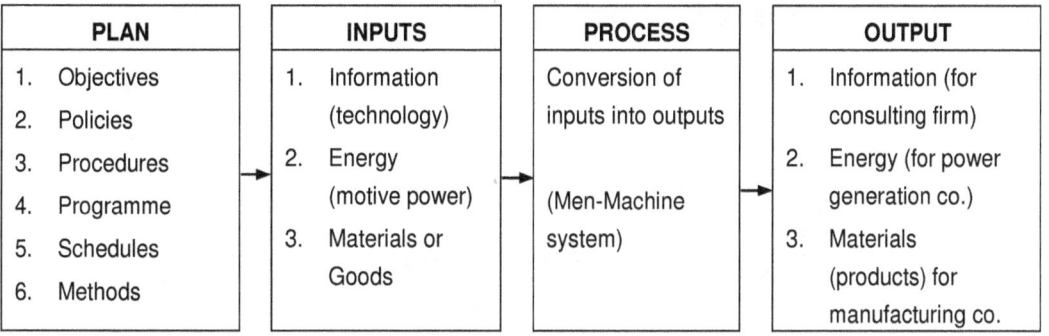

Fig. 2.1: The design of basic system

System Approach Applied to an Organisation

When system approach is applied to organisation, the following are the features of an organisation as an open adoptive system:

(i) It is a sub-system of its broader environment.

(ii) It is goal oriented - people with purpose.

(iii) It is a technical sub-system - using knowledge, techniques, equipments and facilities.

(iv) It is a structural sub-system - people working together on inter-related activities.

(v) It is a psycho-social system - people in social relationship.

(vi) It is co-ordinated by a managerial sub-system, creating, planning, organising, motivating, Communicating and controlling the overall efforts directed towards set goals.

Figure 2.2 shows an organisation as an open adaptive system.

Environment: Elements of environment include persons, physical resources, climate, economic and market conditions, attitudes, competition and laws etc. An organisation and its environment are interdependent. An environment of an organisation provides inputs, i.e. resources and opportunities and limits which determine the nature of success of an organisation.

The output is goods and services desired by its environment. The activities of an organisation must be acceptable to the environment. An organisation has also a feedback. The environment reacts to the output of an organisation. On this reaction, the environment determines the future inputs into the organisation.

System approach is important to management because it provides a world-view more consistent with the reality of organisational life. As it is oriented towards the accomplishment of objectives, system theory helps to generate co-ordinated efforts towards accomplishment of goals. It also stresses the inter-dependence of the elements within organisations and the interaction of organisations themselves as a part of a larger socio-economic system.

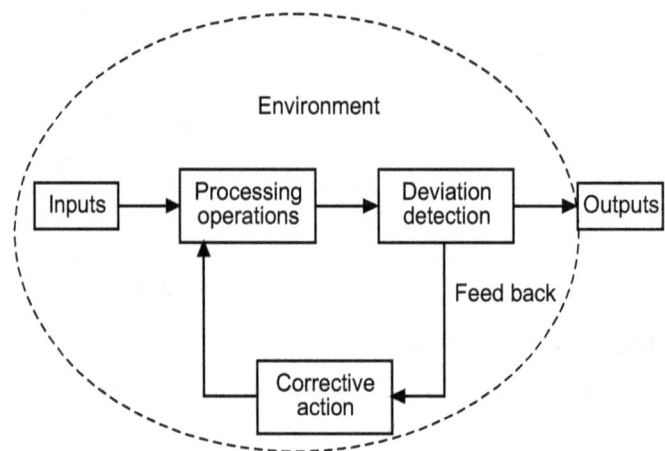

Fig. 2.2: Organisation as an open adaptive system

3. Contingency Approach to Management:

The major contributors to contingency thought are Joan Woodward, Fiedler, Lorsch and Lawrence.

The contingency approach to management is based upon the fact that there is no one best way to handle any of the managerial problems. The application of management principles and practices should be appropriate to specific situations (existing circumstances) in order to achieve best possible result. Process, behavioural, quantitative and systems tools of management should be applied situationally.

There are three major parts of the overall conceptual framework for contingency management

(i) Environment

(ii) Management concepts, principles and techniques.

(iii) Contingent relationship between (i) and (ii) above.

The environment variables are independent and management variables i.e. process, quantitative, behavioural and system tools are dependent. Every manager has to apply the various approaches to management according to the demands of the situation.

It is the basic function of managers to analyse and understand environments in which they function, before adopting any techniques, processes and practices. The choice of approaches and also their effectiveness is contingent on the behaviour and dynamics of situational variables. There is no universally valid one best way of doing things. Contingency thinking helps managers in several ways in performing their functions of planning, organising, direction and control. It enlarges the area of freedom of operation of managers. They are not handicapped by having to apply the same approach to diverse situations. They can even think of a blend of known approaches as demanded by the existing situations. The contingency approach seems to hold a great deal of promise for the future development of management theory and practice. The other approaches to management can all be incorporated into the contingency framework.

4. **Operational Approach to Management:**

Koontz O'Donnell and Weinrich, eminent writers of management have adopted the operational approach o management. They have attempted to draw together the pertinent knowledge of management by relating it to the managerial job i.e. what managers do and what job can be assigned to them.

The operational approach regards management as a universally applicable body of knowledge that can be brought to bear at all levels of managing and in all types of enterprises. Further, Koontz and O'Donnell attempted to set up the boundaries of management, just as system's theorists establish boundaries in order to understand and analyse a system. The environment which lies outside the boundaries will interact with the system.

The approach further recognises that the actual problems which managers face and the environment in which they operate may vary between different enterprises and levels and it also recognises that the application of science by a perspective practitioner must take this into account in drawing and designing practical problem solutions.

2.1.4 Characteristics of Modern Management Thought

1. **The System Approach:** An organisation as a system has *five* basic parts:

    (i) Input, (ii) Process, (iii) Output, (iv) Environment and (v) Feedback as already explained. The environment provides the inputs or resources. Management allocates and combines these resources to produce certain desirable outputs. The success of these outputs can be judged by means of feed back. If necessary, we need to modify our mix of inputs to produce outputs as per changing demands.

2. **Dynamic nature:** A dynamic process of interaction occurs within the structure of an organisation. The equilibrium of an organisation and its structure is itself dynamic or changing.

3. **Multi-disciplinary:** Management freely draws concepts and techniques from many fields of study such as, psychology, social psychology, sociology, ecology, economics, mathematics, operation research, system analysis etc.

4. **Multivariable in Thought:** Intelligent planning and control are necessary to face multivariable factors. These factors are inter-related and inter-dependent. Some factors are controllable, some uncontrollable.

5. **Multi-motivated in Action:** System approach recognises that there may be several motivations behind our actions and behaviour. Management has to compromise these multiple objectives, e.g. economic objectives and social objectives, i.e. productivity and satisfaction (shareholders, employees, customers, community and society).

6. **Multi-level and multi-dimensional:** System approach points out wheels with wheels or complex multi-level and multi-dimensional character. It has both a micro and a macro approach. A company is micro (little world) within a business system. It is a macro (the great world) with respect to its own internal units. Therefore, in a company as a system we have

   (i) Production sub-system

   (ii) Finance sub-system

   (iii) Marketing sub-system.

   (iv) Personnel sub-system.

   All parts or sub-systems are inter-related and all are equally important.

7. **Adaptive:** Organisation is an adaptive system which can continuously adjust to changing conditions. A viable organisation and its environment are in dynamic equilibrium. An organisation is an open system adopting itself through the process of feedback.

8. **It is probabilistic in approach:** Management principles indicates only the probability and never the certainty of its performance and the consequent results. There are so many variables which the business has to face one after the other. The events are subjected to lot of uncertainty. But intelligent forecasting and planning can reduce the degree of uncertainty to a large extent.

2.2 CONCEPT OF MANAGEMENT

Management is the organizational process that includes:

- Strategic planning
- Setting objecting
- Managing resources
- Deploying the human and financial assets needed to achieve the objectives, and
- Measuring results
- Recording and storing facts for later use

The concept of management planning involves direction, planning, adjustment, control and co-operation. It draws up specialized knowledge and skill in the mathematical, physical and social science together with the principles and methods of engineering analysis design.

Figure 2.3 illustrates the management process.

Management refers to the systematic management of all aspects of the industry. The techniques include productivity, organisation structure, administration and human/labour problems.

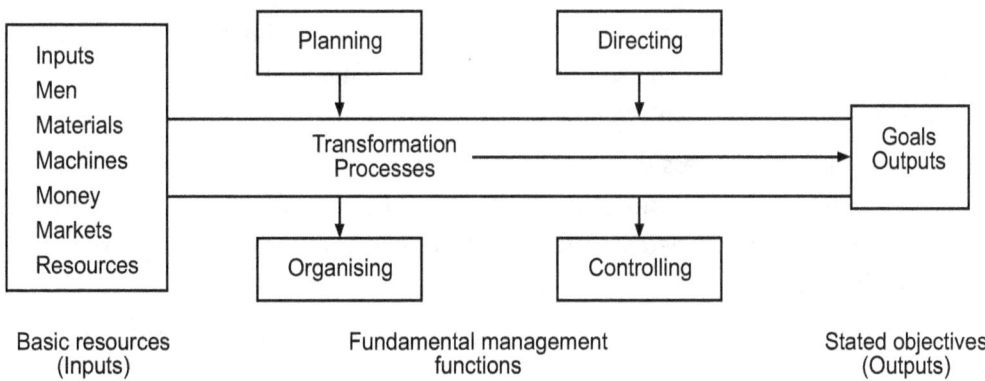

Fig. 2.3: Process of management

Essentially, the industrial management is concerned with the design of system and its primary function is management. It provides expert information. The facts are gathered problems are subjected to analysis, tentative conclusions are made-compared-tested for various alternatives and finally the findings are presented with recommendations to the top management. For doing all this various tools and techniques of management are used.

We have already seen definitions of Management by different thinkers in Article 1.1.

2.3 ADMINISTRATION, MANAGEMENT AND ORGANISATION

In the study of the management literature the use of the terms of Management and Administration has been a controversial issue and some of the writers do not find any difference between the two terms. While there are writers who maintain that Administration and Management has got two different functions.

According to *Oliver Sheldon*

"Management is a lower level function and is concerned with the execution of policies laid down by administration. But English authors like Brech and others have written that Management is a wider term which includes administration ".

At the outset it should be made clear that in practice the three words Administration, Management and Organisation are neither synonymous nor interchangeable. They have their own field of operation. Administration determines the objectives and policies of the enterprise. Management carries out these policies to achieve objectives of the enterprise. For Administration and Management to function effectively, there must be proper structuring of the enterprise and this is known as organisation (structure). Organisation can be termed as a keystone on which any enterprise is based.

Administration gives proper direction. Management properly executes, it is an execution function. And, organisation is an effective machinery for accomplishing company objectives in a team spirit. In brief, it can be said that, "Management carries out the policies of Administration through the framework of the organisation".

Organisation is the process of dividing work into convenient tasks and duties and then grouping such duties in the form of departments and posts, deligating authority to each post and of appointing qualified staff to be responsible to ensure that the work is carried out as planned.

The following table illustrates a clear distinction between Administration, Management and Organisation:

Table 2.1

No.	Administration	Management	Organisation
1.	It is the process of determining the objectives to be achieved.	It is the process of planning the work as per the objectives laid down by the administration.	It is the process of dividing the work into different tasks and duties as planned.

Contd...

2.	It lays down the policies and principles.	It executes the policies and programmes.	It organises the work.
3.	It prepares the framework under which one is asked to work and execute.	It supervises and controls the execution of assigned work.	It draws out the line of authority and determines the line of action.
4.	It provides: (i) direction (ii) guidance, and (iii) leadership	It co-ordinates activities.	It delegates the authority and fixes responsibility.
5.	It is the first and provides guidelines to the management and organisation.	It comes second, follows the administration and derives strength from administration.	It occupies the third place and solely responsible for what the management has planned and administration has set.

2.4 SCIENTIFIC MANAGEMENT BY F.W. TAYLOR

Scientific management is an attempt to determine and apply the facts and laws that are essential for efficient running of an enterprise.

The utility of scientific methods to problems of management was first of all introduced by F. W. Taylor in America (1865-1915). He is regarded as a "father of scientific management".

Scientific management may be defined as the

"Art of knowing exactly what is to be done and the best way of doing it".

Scientific management is the result of applying scientific knowledge and the scientific methods to the various aspects of management and the problems that arise from them.

The Aims of Scientific Management:

- It tries to make the best use of production resources (men, materials, machines, capital etc.)
- It discovers the economical and efficient methods of production so as to reduce effort and eliminate wastage of time and motions.
- It provides right man for right job through scientific selection and training of workers, shop supervisors etc.
- It results in improvement in the quality and rate of the output by research, quality control and inspection devices.

The Scientific Management involves:

(i) Scientific study and analysis of work

(ii) Scientific selection and training of employees, and

(iii) Standardization of raw materials, working conditions and equipment.

Principles of Management by F.W. Taylor

Taylor through his principles of management initiated a system in which there would be an effective and fruitful co-ordination and co-operation between the management and the workers.

1. Development of science for each element of work: Analyse the work scientifically, rather than using thumb rule. It means that an attempt is made to find out what is to be done by a particular worker, how he is to do it, what equipment will be necessary to do it. This information is provided to the worker so as to reduce wastage of time, material etc. and improve the quality of work.

2. Scientific selection, placement and training of workers: This principle states that select the workers best suited to perform the specific tasks, and then train them within the industry in order to attain the objectives of the enterprise. This eliminates the possibility of misfits in the organisation and ensures better working. Workers should also be trained from time to time keep them informed of latest development in the techniques of production.

3. Division of labour (Separation of planning function from doing function): Division of work in smaller tasks and separation of thinking element of job from doing element of the job, this is the principle of specialisation. It is essential for efficiency in all spheres of activities as well as in supervision work. To be more effective and efficient, Taylor, the founder of scientific management introduced functional organisation, in which one foreman was made in charge for each function.

4. Standardization of methods, procedures, tools and equipment: Standardization helps in reducing time, labour and cost of production. The success of scientific management largely depends upon standardization of system, tools, equipments, and techniques of production.

5. Use of time and motion study: Taylor introduced time and motion study to determine standard work. Taylor undertook studies on fatigue incurred by the workers and the time necessary to complete the task.

Taylor suggested that for increasing production rate, the work of each person should be planned in advance and he shall be allotted a definite work to complete by a given time by using a predetermined method.

6. Differential wage system: Taylor's Differential Piece Rate Scheme provides an incentive for a worker to achieve high level of optimum output. It distinguishes the more productive workers from less productive workers and motivates them to produce more. Taylor believed that if labour is suitably rewarded and is satisfied with job, he will work whole heartedly to achieve the objectives of the enterprise.

7. Co-operation between labour and management: Management also strives to get the thinking of management changed so as to make the management feel that mutual respect and co-operation between the workers and the management helps in providing proper and efficient leadership. The labour starts thinking that, it is their work and they must put their heart and soul in the work assigned to them. In fact the main job of scientific management is to revolutionize the mind of the both workers and management for mutual benefit and also for the benefit of the enterprise.

8. Principle of Management by Exception: In order to make effective utilisation of time of top managers, Taylor suggested that only major or significant deviations between the actual performance and standard performance should be brought to the notice of top management. Top management should pay more attention to those areas of work where standards and procedures could not be established and where there is a significant variation between standard performance and actual performance.

2.5 PRINCIPLES OF MANAGEMENT (14 PRINCIPLES OF HENRY FAYOL)

Administrative theory of management was introduced by Henry Fayol. He established the pattern of management and the pyramidal form of organization. He pointed out that technical ability is more demanding on the lower level of management, whereas managerial ability is more important on the higher level of management.

Henri Fayol analysed the process of management and divided the activities of an industrial undertaking into six groups:

1. Technical activities (*production, manufacture, adaptation*)
2. Commercial activities (*purchasing, selling and exchange*)
3. Financial activities (*optimum use of capital*)
4. Security (*protection of property and persons*)
5. Accounting (*stock taking, balance sheet, costing, statistics*)
6. Managerial (*planning, organising, commanding, co-ordinating and controlling*)

Fayol's Principles of Management

In 1916, H. Fayol described a number of Management/Organisation principles in his book - General and Industrial Management. These principles constitute the theory of management or administration of business enterprises.

Based on his management experience, Fayol listed the following *fourteen* principles of management:

1. Division of work: This is the principle of specialization. Division of work should be according to work, department, job etc. Both technical and managerial activities can be performed in the best manner only through division of labour and specialization. It can ensure maximum productivity and efficiency in all spheres of activity.

2. Authority and responsibility: The right to give order, the right to command, is called authority. The obligation to accomplish objectives or expected results or performance is called responsibility. They are interrelated and exist together. In any management process, delegation of power, utilisation of authority and fixation of responsibility are key to success.

3. Discipline: No organisation can work smoothly without discipline, it is the very core of administration. The rules, regulations, policies and procedures must be honoured by all the members of organisation. Discipline is imposed by administration. It requires good superiors at all levels, clear and fair agreement on rules, regulations, procedures. There must be penalties (punishment) for non-obedience or indiscipline.

4. Unity of command: In order to avoid confusion and conflict, each individual should receive orders and instructions only from one superior and should be accountable to one superior only. Unity of command provides responsible leadership, better guidance and direction, good co-ordination and disciplined performance.

5. Unity of direction: All members of an organisation must work together to accomplish common or same objectives. Their efforts shall be directed towards one common super goal.

6. Emphasis on subordination of personal interest to general or common interest: It means that the common interest of the organisation must be given more importance than the interest of the individual. The organisation will collapse when personal interest become supreme than the general interest.

7. Adequate remuneration to personnel: The persons working in the organisation should be paid suitably and adequately. This will help to maintain their interest in the work and the enterprise. Exploitation of employees in any manner must be eliminated. A wage policy should be based on adequate financial and non-financial incentives.

8. Centralization: The decision for centralization would naturally vary from organisation to organisation. However, there must be a 'good balance between centralization and decentralization of authority and power. Extreme centralization and decentralization must be avoided.

9. Scaler chain or line of authority: An organisation chart should be prepared for better communication and effective co-ordination. It shows the flow of authority and responsibility from top to bottom.

10. Order: "A place for everything and everything in its place" is a best norm, for material management, which also holds goods for management of men also, that is, 'a place for everyone and everyone in his place'. This is essential for successful execution of orders received from the top. Order or system alone can create a sound organisation and efficient management.

11. Equity: An organisation consists of human beings, a group of people working together for some common objectives of the enterprise. Hence, there should be equity justice and kindness on the part of managers to create loyalty and devotion among subordinates. Unbiased, meaningful and equal treatment should be the motto of a management in its relations with employees.

12. Stability of workers: Security of income and employment is a pre-requisite of sound organisation and management. This will reduce unnecessary labour turnover, and increase efficiency by having stable working force.

13. Initiative: This principle allows subordinates to utilize their initiative. Initiative is a freedom to think plan and to execute. The employees should be allowed to take initiative, of course, under watchful eyes. Initiative brings self-confidence in a worker which is essential for improving efficiency of the organisation.

14. Esprit de Crops (Team spirit): According to this principle "Union is strength". Management should not adhere the principle of 'divide and rule' instead it should try to achieve co-operation and team spirit in the employees. Pride, loyalty and sense of belonging is essential for efficient working and the prosperity of the organisation.

2.6 LEVELS AND SKILLS OF MANAGEMENT

2.6.1 Levels of Management

In an organisation, all those who are responsible for the work of others are usually, known as managers. Though their primary task remains the same, getting the things done by other people, there is a wide variation in their authorities and responsibilities. These differences are largely due to the differences in the levels of management. In any organisation, the total management job requires many skills and talents. Obviously therefore, the job of manager is divided and sub-divided. Such an arrangement implies levels of management. Levels of management, in fact, refers to a line of separation between different positions drawn with a view to distinguish each other in respect of their duties, responsibilities, rights and authorities.

The three levels of management that are commonly found in an organisation are:

(a) Top Management

(b) Middle Order Management

(c) Lowest Level or Supervisory Management.

(a) Top Management:

Top Management constitutes the highest level in the management hierarchy. This is the policy-making level in any organisation. This level consists of small group of executives, Board of Directors, Chairman, Managing Director, Personnel Manager, Chief Executive etc. Top Management is responsible for the overall management of the organisation. They define the aim of the company, establish the primary objectives, policies and strategies to be pursued to achieve these objectives. They also formulate the plans of organisation and procedure, inaugurate the board programme, and approve specific major projects in the programme. They provide direction to the organisation by guiding the organisations interactions with its environment.

(b) Middle Order Management:

Middle order management occupies a central place in the hierarchy. It is concerned with execution of the detailed policies and plans determined by top management (Administration) through the framework of organisation. Middle order management is answerable to top management. Its main functions are: (i) to plan (ii) to guide (iii) to supervise (iv) to co-ordinate (v) to exercise control over the lower level management. It often functions as a link between top management and lower level management.

(c) Lowest Level or Supervisory Management:

This is the lowest level in the hierarchy of management. Managers at this level function under the control and direction of the middle order management. Their functions are also to plan, to guide, to supervise and to exercise control, but all these functions are performed to get work done from the operating staff. This level of management takes orders from the middle order and explains them to the workers at operating level. In fact, this level of management is accredited with the responsibility of getting the work done and is made accountable to those who occupy the middle order management. This level includes Foreman, Supervisor, Superintendent, Inspector etc.

The following graphical account makes the above hierarchy more clear:

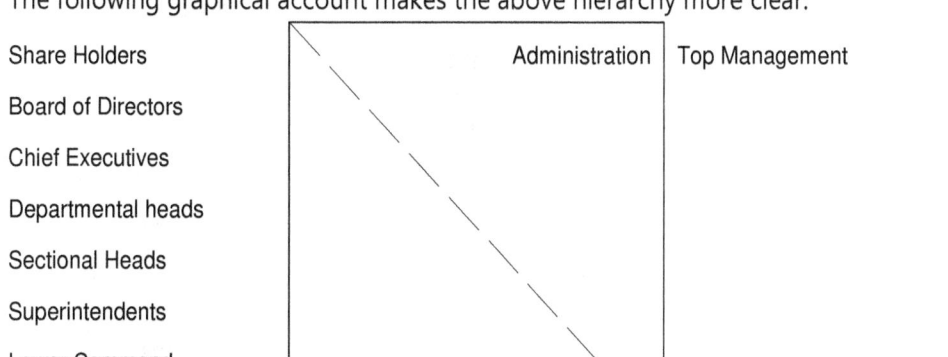

Fig. 2.4: Levels of Management

J. Beaty has divided the levels of management into five groups or activity levels as represented in the table:

Table 2.2

Level	Represented By	Function
1. Top Management	(a) Board of Directors (b) Managing Directors (c) Chief Executives (d) General Manager (e) Secretary	(a) Determine the objectives. (b) Establishing Policies. (c) Monitoring performance. (d) Judging the results.
2. Upper Middle Management	(a) Production or Works Manager (b) Finance Manager (c) Personnel Manager (d) Materials Manager (e) R & D Manager	(a) Establishment of organisation. (b) Selection training/placement of staff. (c) Assigning duties to subordinates. (d) Design operating policies and operating routines. (e) Exercise control over the sub-ordinates.

Contd...

3.	Middle Management	(a) Superintendents (b) Departmental heads	(a) To plan details of operation. (b) To co-operate with top management for the smooth functioning of organisation. (c) To active co-ordination between various departments. (d) Development of manpower for the organisation by imparting training.
4.	Lower Management	(a) Foreman (b) Supervisors	(a) To act as a link between management and the workers. (b) Direct supervision of the workers. (c) Arrangement of material, tools, facilities etc. for production.
5.	Working	(a) Workers (b) Service Staff (c) Security Staff	(a) Carry out the work assigned to them.

2.6.2 Managerial Skills (Skills of Management)

Managerial skills is the ability of a manager to make a smooth functioning team of people working under him. Management job is different from other jobs. It involves obligation to make effective utilization of human and material resources. It requires sound judgement to handle complex situations. Further, the nature of the job becomes increasingly complex at each higher level, because of the increase in the scope of authority and responsibility. Thus, the skills required in management are different in nature at different management levels. Each higher level requires increased knowledge, broader perspective and greater skills. Manager has to reconcile, co-ordinate and appraise the various viewpoints and talents of people working under him towards the organisation goals.

The skills required of a successful manager, whether he is working in a business organisation, an educational institute or a hospital, can be classified as under:

[I] Technical Skills

[II] Conceptual Skills

   (a) Decision-making skills

   (b) Organisational skills

[III] Human Relation Skills:

   (a) Communication skills

   (b) Motivating skills

   (c) Leadership skills

[I] TECHNICAL SKILLS

Technical skills refers to the ability to use methods, processes, tools, equipment, techniques and knowledge of a specialized field. It is primarily concerned with the ways of doing things. It refers to the proficiency in handling methods, techniques and related to a specific field of activity. Technical skills are most important for lower level managers, because by nature, their job involves supervision of the workers on the shop floor. Effective supervision, guidance, direction and co-ordination of the work performed by the subordinates, therefore depends on the technical skill possessed by the lower level managers. Any supervisor without a sound knowledge of the job cannot make an effective supervisor. Such supervisors are not respected by the workers at the shop floor. The relative importance of the technical skills, as compared to the other skills, diminish as one moves up to a higher levels of management. Fig. 2.5 illustrates the Managerial skills required at different levels of management.

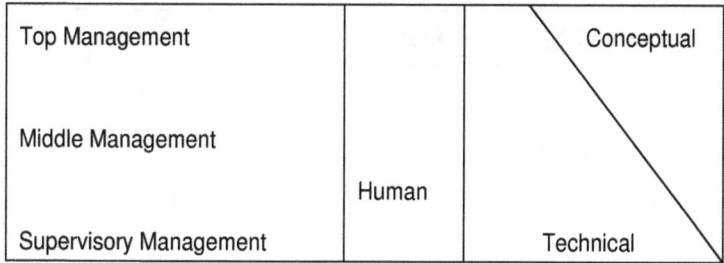

Fig. 2.5: Managerial skills

[II] CONCEPTUAL SKILLS

Conceptual skill is the ability to see the organisation as a whole, to recognize inter-relationships among different functions of the business and external forces and to guide effectively the organisational efforts. It is easier to learn technical skills than the conceptual skills. Conceptual skill extends to visualizing the relation of the organisation to industry, to the community and to the political, economic and social forces of the nation as a whole, and even to forces which operate beyond the national boundaries. It is the creative force within the organisation, which is concerned with design and problem solving. A high degree of conceptual skill helps in analysing the environment and in identifying the opportunities and threats.

- **(a) Decision making Skills:** Decision making skill is the ability of a person to take timely and accurate decisions. This requires mental ability, sound knowledge and presence of mind.
- **(b) Organisational Skills:** This helps in manpower planning i.e. for selecting people for different type of activities. It means placing right men for the right job.

[III] HUMAN RELATION SKILLS

Human skills are primarily concerned with persons as contrasted with 'things'. Human skill refers to the ability to work effectively with others and build co-operative group relations to achieve organisational objectives. It is the ability to work with, understand and motivate people. He understands why people behave as they do and is able to make his own behaviour understandable to them. He can foresee their reactions to possible courses of action and is able to take their attitudes into account.

- **(a) Communication Skills:** It is the ability to pass on information to others. Improper, insufficient and poorly expressed information, can create confusion and annoy the subordinates.
- **(b) Motivating Skills:** Motivating skill inspires people to do what the manager wants them to do.

2.7 FUNCTIONS OF MANAGEMENT

Management is an on-going activity consisting of number of functions.

The important functions of management are:

1. Planning
2. Organising
3. Co-ordinating
4. Directing
5. Controlling
6. Decision-making

2.7.1 Planning

Planning is the most basic of all management functions. Planning means thinking before doing. In other words, planning is the preparation for action. Every manager plans, no matter at what level he operates. It is a function to decide about what, where, when, who, why and how a particular activity should be done. It sets the objectives of the business, determines the different course of action to achieve these objectives, evaluates each course of action and decides about the best course of action under the given conditions. It thus provides direction to the enterprise.

Planning defines the goals, sets the policies, procedures, programmes, develops strategies so that the objectives of the enterprise can be attained most efficiently. It analyses all the difficulties that are likely to occur in running the business and decides in advance, how these difficulties can be overcome.

Planning is a rational, economic, systematic way of making decisions today, which will affect the future. Planning helps to have an optimum utilisation of the available resources. Without planning, the activities of an enterprise may become confused, haphazard and ineffective. For example, if a company making refrigerators, does not plan in advance as to how many refrigerators and of what capacity are to be made before summer starts and if it does not procure necessary materials, tools, supplies and personnel in time, it cannot approach the production target and hence may not run profitability.

Planning includes forecasting, formulation of objectives, policies, programmes, schedules, procedures and budgets. Generally, long range planning is undertaken by top management personnel.

Some of the definitions of planning given by different writers are as follows:

"Planning is deciding in advance what to do, how to do it, when to do it and who is to do it. Planning bridges the gap from where we are, to where we want to go. It makes it possible for things to occur which would not otherwise happen".   — *Koontz and O'Donnell*

"Planning is the thinking process, the organised foresight, the vision, based on facts and experience that is required for intelligent action".   — *Alfred and Beatty*

"Planning is deciding in advance, what is to be done. It involves the selection of objectives, policies, procedures and programmes from among alternatives".   — *M. E. Harley*

A careful analysis of these definitions reveals that:

(i) Planning involves visualising future course of action and putting it in a logical way.

(ii) It involves thinking and analysis of information.

(iii) It is concerned with determination of objectives and goals in the light of future.

(iv) It involves development of alternative courses of action to achieve such objectives.

(v) It involves decision-making i.e. selection of best course of action among these alternatives.

(vi) Its objective is to achieve better results.

(vii) It is a continuous and integrated process.

Objectives of Planning

The important objectives of planning are:

1. **Planning Helps in Effective Forecasting:** The first and the most important objective of planning is forecasting. Effective planning anticipates future and prepare themselves to meet the challenges of the future. A well thought out plan solves many of the problems associated with the uncertain future. Continuous planning by management, shows precisely, what the enterprise wants to achieve in a given period as well as how it intends to accomplish the objectives formulated in advance.

2. **Planning Provides Certainty in the Activities:** Planning decides the policies, defines the procedures and makes the rules for the activities of all the employees of the organisation. This helps in bringing certainty in the activities of the organisation.

3. **Planning Provides Performance Standards:** A good plan specifies clearly the targets to be accomplished. For example, five year plan of a company may prescribe that rate of return on shareholders' investment must double with five years from 15% to 30% per annum. The performance of the company is measured and controlled on the basis of such a specific standard. The specific objectives decided in advance, themselves become standards on the measuring tools.

4. **Planning gives a Specific Direction to the Organisation:** When you plan the events, you make them happen in a particular way. As a plan, a decision regarding a future course of action it specifies the sequence of events to be performed. It thus gives the specific direction to all the activities of an organisation by preparing the outlines of these activities well in advance.

5. **Helps the Organisation to tune with the Environment:** In general, organisations that plan, have been the winners against the non-planners. Planning helps the managers to control the events, rather than being controlled by them. A manager can establish through planning, a profitable relationship with the environment and minimize risk and insecurity.

6. **It Provides Economy in the Management:** Planning establishes the co-ordination among all the activities of the organisation. It guides the management and all the employees of the organisation in their activities. It helps in maintaining effective control and discipline. It checks all types of wastages and thus, brings an economy in management.

7. **It is very much Helpful in Preparing the Budgets:** Planning helps the management in accomplishing pre-determined budgets of the enterprise in a logical manner.

8. **The Need for Planning Arises from Constant Change:** A business enterprise lives in a dynamic and complex environment. Economic, social, political and technological trends must be noted and their influence must be taken into account in the plans and policies from time to time. An enterprise and its environment are mutually interdependent - interacting with each other continuously. Management through comprehensive business planning, can anticipate, meet and adopt creatively to everchanging environmental conditions and demands. It helps the management to assure the survival of the organisation under keen competition and changing environment.

9. **Planning is Directed towards Efficiency:** The main purpose of planning is to increase efficiency. The guiding principle of a good plan is the maximum output and profit at the minimum cost. *"Planning is the foundation of most successful action of the enterprise"*. It aims at efficiency. Planning is an intellectual activity, the main aim of which is (a) to suggest the best way of doing things; and (b) planning is linked to goals and objectives. Thus, planning is directed towards efficiency by achieving the objectives, through determination of best course of action.

It should be noted that

— "Failure to plan is planning to fail".

— "Planning is outlining a future course of action in order to acheive an objective".

— "Planning is looking ahead".

— "Planning is getting ready to do something tomorrow".

— "Planning is a trap laid down to capture the future".

Steps in Planning

The details of planning may differ, depending upon the specific requirements of a particular business. However, in all types of businesses, planning process involves certain necessary steps, summarised as follows:

1. Determination of Objectives:

Planning is not possible without definite objectives. If the objectives of the business are clearly defined, then only it is possible to plan for future. Planning in fact, begins with decision about what the organisation wants to achieve during a specified period. It is always desirable to express the objectives/goals in quantitative terms for all the key areas of the business like production, profit, productivity, market share etc. The time frame in which the objectives have to be achieved, must also be specified. Thus, what, how and with what resources, are a few important questions that should be answered at this stage. After determining the overall objectives of the business, it is necessary to fix up departmental objectives and the objectives for sub-departments and sections. These objectives are in harmony with overall objectives of the business.

Since goal/objective setting is the essential step in planning, managers who fail to set meaningful goals will be unable to make effective plans. If Telco is able to retain its prominence in the Heavy Commercial Vehicles Segment, it is because, all the employees of the organisation know that the primary objective is retaining the leadership in the industry.

2. **Forecasting to Assist Planning:**

Establish planning premises and constraints: Planning premises, in simple are the assumptions made about the various elements of the environment. Planning assumptions or premises provide the basic framework in which plans operate. Thus, it is a forecast of conditions - both internal and external to the organisation.

Internal premises: The important internal premises include sales forecasts, policies of the organisation, resources of the organisation, skills, attitudes and beliefs of the people. Each of these elements is a critical success factor. For instance, the accuracy of the sales-forecast, influences the procurement of resources, production, scheduling and the marketing strategies to be adopted to achieve the objectives.

External premises: Important external premises relate to all those factors in the environment outside the organisation. They include technological changes, general economic conditions, Government policies and attitudes towards business, socio-cultural changes in the society, political stability, degree of competition in the market, availability of labour, material, power etc.

It is evident that some of these factors are tangible, while others are intangible. Though accurate premising is difficult, anticipating future situations, problems and opportunities would definitely help the managers in reducing the risk; though not completely eliminating it.

3. **Decide the Planning Period:**

In some cases plans are made for a short period, varying from a few months to a year, while in some other cases, they are made to cover a longer period. The period may extend 5-10 years and even more. Companies normally plan for a period that can be reasonably achieved. The lead time involved in the development and commercialisation of a product and time required to recover the capital investment (pay-back period) influence the choice of the length of the plan. Again, in the same organisation, different plan periods may exist for different purposes. Operational plans focus on the short-term, strategic plans focus on the long term.

4. Collection, Classification and Processing of Information:

All relevant information pertaining to factors that affect planning is collected. Information must be classified, analysed and processed. It helps interpretation and the establishment of cause and effect relationship.

5. Deciding Alterative Courses of Action:

The objective can be fulfilled by more than one course of action. For example, if we want to increase the profit. We can increase the price, we can increase the sales keeping the price constant or we can reduce the cost of production by adopting improved techniques, reducing waste and by optimum utilisation of resources. We can raise capital by selling shares or by borrowing from financial institutions. All such possibilities must be explored during the planning of business.

6. Evaluation of Alternative:

The advantages and disadvantages of each alternative are then weighted against the other alternatives. Cost benefit analysis is made to evaluate each feasible alternative.

7. Selection of Best Plan:

After the evaluation of different alternative plans in terms of results; the best, feasible and economical plan is selected.

8. Subsidiary Plans to aid Master Plan:

After deciding the main plan, subsidiary plans are constructed to successfully implement the master plan. To implement the master plan each department head prepares a plan of his department.

9. Controlling Plans:

Plans and subsidiary plans are first tried on a pilot basis to test the possibility of their success. The plan is then implemented. It is constantly monitored and results are obtained as feedback from time to time. The drawbacks or shortcomings are removed as early as possible. Future plans are framed in the light of this experience.

Types of Planning

Planning can be classified as the basis of:

i) Coverage of organisational activities,
ii) Importance of contents in planning process,
iii) Time period of planning and
iv) Degree of formalisation in planning process.

Planning based on coverage of planning:

(a) Corporate planning

(b) Functional planning

(a) Corporate Planning: Corporate planning is the planning for the organisation as a whole. It is concerned with the planning activities at the top level, or corporate level. It covers the entire organisational activities. Corporate planning determines the long term objectives of the organisation as a whole, and then generates plans to achieve these objectives considering the probable changes in the environment.

(b) Functional Planning: Functional planning is the planning for different functions of the organisation. It is undertaken for each major function like production, marketing, finance, human resources etc. Corporate planning is integrative while functional planning is segmental.

At the second level, functional planning is undertaken for sub-functions within each major function. For example, planning may be undertaken for sub-functions of marketing such as sales, product promotion, marketing research etc. The functional planning is derived from the corporate planning.

Corporate planning may be divided into two types:

(1) Strategic planning (2) Operational planning

(1) Strategic Planning: Strategic planning sets the long term direction of the organisation. It is concerned with the planned allocation of its managerial, financial and physical resources over future specified period of time. Strategic planning is for long-term period, 3-5 years or even more. It takes into account the effect of changes in the environmental factors such as economic, political, technological and social factors of strategic planning. Strategic planning encomposes all the functional areas of the organisation. Strategic planning sets trend and direction for managerial actions. Strategic planning is formulated by top-level management and other specified planning staff in the organisation. Examples of strategic planning are planned growth rate in sales, human resource planning, diversification of business into new lines, capital expenditure etc.

(2) Operational Planning: Operational planning is also known as short-term or tactical planning. Operational planning is for one year or so. Operational planning is the process of deciding the most effective use of the resources already allocated. So as to achieve the organisational objectives. Operational planning is usually spread over a wide range within the organisation and is performed by operating managers with the help of subordinate staff. Operational planning tries to develop control mechanism to assure effective implementation of the actions to achieve the objectives.

It answers the questions about a particular function as follows:
1. Why is the action required?
2. What action is to be taken?
3. What will the action accomplish?
4. What are the results of the action required?
5. What objectives and conditions must be met?

The examples of operational planning are, planning the production to meet the demand for a particular periods, analyse the past performance for increasing efficiency of operating activities, budgeting future costs, planning the requirements of materials for a year or so etc.

Long-term Planning and Short-term Planning:

The planning period is divided generally into i) long term and ii) short term. The planning period depends on the interaction of many complex factors such as:
- the market demand
- industry peculiarities
- availability of resources
- the lead time involved in the product life cycle etc.

Thus, what might be a long period of planning for one organisation, might be a short period for others. The ideal planning period depends on commitment principle. A small manufacturer who completes his production cycle consisting of purchasing raw material, production, inventory, sales in six months or so requires a commitment period of six-months only which is the planning period.

Long-term planning is a strategic planning. The common long term planning period is 3 to 5 years. Short-term planning is also known as operational planning or tactical planning, usually covers one year or less.

Proactive Planning and Reactive Planning:

Planning is affected by environmental factors such as technological, political etc. which keep on changing continuously. However, organisations response to these changes differ. Based on these responses planning may be classified as i) Proactive or ii) Reactive planning.

(a) Proactive planning: Proactive planning involves designing suitable course of action in anticipation of likely changes in the relevant environment. Proactive planning requires broad planning approaches, broad environmental scanning, decentralized control and reserve sources to be utilized in future. The organisation adopting proactive planning do not wait for environment to change but take actions in advance of environmental change. Successful organisations, generally adopt proactive planning. In our country, Hindustan Lever, Reliance Industries etc. have adopted this approach and their growth rate has been much faster than others.

(b) Reactive planning: In reactive planning organisations starts planning after the environmental changes takes place. Rate of growth of such organisations is slower and they loose opportunities to those organisations which adopt proactive planning. By the time reactive planning is ready, the contextual variable of planning show further changes. Therefore, their planning do not remain valid in the changed circumstance. Reactive planning is suitable in an environment which is fairly stable over a long period of time.

Formal Planning and Informal Planning:

This classification is based on the degree of formalization used in undertaking planning activities.

(a) Formal planning: Formal planning is a well-structured process involving different steps. Formal planning is generally undertaken by large organisations. In formal planning, separate corporate planning cells are created at sufficiently high level in the orgnisation.

These cells are staffed by people with different backgrounds like engineers, staticians, MBAs, economists etc. depending on the nature of business. These cells monitor the external environment on continuous basis. Whenever any event in the environment shows some charge the cells carry out detailed study of the impact of the event on the activities of organisation and suggests suitable measures to take advantages of the changing environment. Formal planning process is rational, systematic, well-documented and regular.

(b) Informal planning: Informal planning is adopted by smaller organisations. The planning process is based on manager's memory of events, intuitions, and gut-feelings rather than based on systematic evaluation of environmental changes. Usually, planning affairs become the part of manager's regular activities, it is not assigned to any single cell. Informal planning is suitable to smaller organisations. Since, the environment for such organisations is not complex.

Features of Planning

On the basis of the definitions of planning the features of planning are:

1. Planning is a process which determines the future course of action. Effective planning anticipates future and prepares the organisation to meet the challanges of the future. Correct forecasting of future situation leads to correct decisions about future course of action.

2. Planning provides certainty in the activities. Planning decides the policies, defines the procedures and makes the rules for the activities of all the employees of the organsiation.
3. Planning involves selection of suitable course of action. This means that there are several alternatives for achieving a particular objective or set of objectives. However, all of them are not equally feasible and suitable for the organisation. Planning evaluates each alternative in terms of results and select the feasible, suitable and economical alternative.
4. Planning is undertaken at all levels of the organisation because all levels of management are concerned with the determination of future course of action. However, the roll of planning increases at successively higher levels of management.
5. Planning at different levels may be different. At the top management level, managers are concerned about the totality of the organisation and tries to relate it with the environment while at lower levels management may be involved in internal planning.
6. Planning is flexible as commitment is based on future conditions which are always dynamic. The environmental failures such as economic, political, technological, and social failures are subjected to change. As such, planning must be adjusted considering the changes in the environmental failures.
7. Planning is a pervasive and continuous managerial function involving complex processes of preception, analysis, conceptual thought, communication, decision and action.

2.7.2 Organising

Organising involves determining activities needed to fulfill the objectives, grouping these activities into manageable units of departments and assigning such groups of activities to managers. Oraganising provides a framework of management or a mechanism for positive, integrated and co-operative action by many people in a joint effort to implement plan. Planning decides what management wants to do, while organising provides an effective machine for achieving the plan or objectives.

Thus, organising involves identification and grouping the activities to be performed and dividing them among the individuals and creating authority and responsibility, relationship among them. Organisation, in fact, is a backbone of management, which establishes relationship between people, work and resources. It coordinates these factors in such a way, that maximum output is obtained effectively and efficiently with minimum total cost.

Steps in Organising

The Process of organisation involves the following steps:
(i) Determination of activities.
(ii) Division of activities.

(iii) Fitting individuals into jobs.

(iv) Developing relationships in terms of authorities and responsibilities.

For details of organising, refer chapter 3.

2.7.3 Directing

Directing is of great importance for the success and survival of the industry. This is an important managerial function, because the managerial decisions are put into action through effective direction. Actual activity starts only when manager issues directions to his subordinates, as to what is to be done and how it should be done.

Directing consists of guiding and supervising the subordinates in their activities. Only giving orders is not directing.

Directing involves motivating, guiding and supervising subordinates towards company objectives. Good planning may ensure the achievement of the predetermined objectives, only when human efforts, largely diverse are co-ordinated, guided and directed for the accomplishment of the objectives. This however, is a difficult task, since manpower resources are difficult to manage. In fact, the directing ability of the manager in the organisation determines its effectiveness. Therefore, the person who directs must have dynamic leadership. This work is done by the Director or General Manager or Managing Director.

The steps in directing function, are as follows:

1. Issue of orders and instructions.
2. Guidance and training of subordinates.
3. Supervision of subordinates' work.

Supervision is necessary in order to ensure that:

(a) the work is going on as per the plan established.

(b) the workers (or subordinates) are doing work as they were directed to do.

The position of the director (person who directs) in a factory is like a captain of a ship. Directions are not only to be given, but also to be obeyed. Hence they must be definite, clear cut, understandable, communicable and practicable. As far as possible, these must be in writing.

According to *Drucker* — Directing is that part of management process, which actuates the organisational members to work effectively and efficiently, for the attainment of organisational objectives.

A manager can plan and organise, but no tangible results can be achieved, until he implements the proposed course of action. This needs directing or actuating, which literally means moving into action.

2.7.4 Controlling

Introduction

In management literature, the word "Control" has a special meaning. It means setting standards, measuring actual performance, and taking corrective action. It is more than mere evaluation, appraisal or correction. It measures performance against goals and plans, indicates where deviations exist and helps accomplishment of objectives. It serves to determine personnel responsible for deviations to take necessary steps to improve performance. In short, control means setting standards, measuring performance and corrective action with a view to achieve best results.

Definitions

According to *Henry Fayol,* "Control consists in verifying whether everything occurs in conformity with the plan adopted, the instructions issued and the principles established".

According to *Koontz and O'Donell,* "Controlling implies measurements of accomplishment against the standard and the correction of deviations to ensure attainment of objectives according to plans".

Ernest Dale in his book 'Theory and Practice of Management' has stated that —

"The modern concept of managerial control envisages a system, that not only provides historical record of what has happened to the business as a whole, but also pin points the reasons, why it has happened and provides data that enable the chief executive or the departmental head to take corrective steps, if he finds, he is on the wrong track".

According to *E.F.L. Breach*, "Control is checking current performance, against predetermined standards, contained in the plans, with a view to ensuring adequate progress and satisfactory performance".

Necessity of Controlling

Controlling is essential in order to ensure that every activity is carried out according to the plan and directions. The orders may be mis-interpreted or delayed due to lack of control. Control enables a manager to keep a check and co-ordinate the activities of his subordinates, so as to meet the objectives of the company, economically and effectively. Any variation between actual performance and the laid down goals and objectives can be immediately detected and corrective action can be taken by the manager, so as to prevent such variations in future. Control is effected through organisation structure. Controlling is a continuous process of measuring actual results of the operations of an organisation, in comparison with the standards laid down as a guide.

The function of control is to match actual performance with the plans, and to point out defective works, to rectify them and prevent recurrence.

Controlling is therefore, necessary to ensure that orders are not misunderstood, rules are not violated and objectives have not been unknowingly shifted.

Control is thus an important function of management. Without control, a manager cannot do the complete job of managing. All other functions are preparatory steps for getting the work done and controlling is concerned with making sure that there is proper execution of these functions. It ensures work accomplishment, according to plans. It is essential feature of scientific and successful management.

Essential Steps in Controlling Procedure

There are three essential steps in the process of control:

1. Setting Standards: Standards are fixed against which, results can be measured. The standard established for the company as well as the individual departments may be stated in terms of output, quality, costs, production targets, time standards, sales quotas etc. These standards should be clear and meaningful. It is essential to identify responsibility for standards with definite individuals in the organisation.

2. Checking and Reporting on Performance: There are three methods of checking performance

(a) Prior approval by the executive to allow the work to proceed as planned.

(b) Personal observation by the executive to get realistic picture of the actual performance.

(c) Checking the unexpected.

Only when unexpected results occur, there is a need for reports and corrective action. In the absence of such reports, the management assumes that all activities are proceeding as planned.

3. Taking Corrective Action: The actual performance is compared with the plan. If there are any deviations, then the reasons for deviations are found out and analysed. Then necessary steps are taken to get back on plan.

Types of Control

Based upon the objectives, controls can be classified as:

1. Physical control, 2. Financial control, 3. Budgetary control

1. Physical control seeks to control quality and quantity, e.g. so many units of output must be produced during the course of a month etc.

2. Financial controls are expressed in monetary terms e.g. cost per unit of production, cost of material, labour, indirect expenses etc.

3. In budgetary control, physical and financial standards for future are determined and results are compared against these pre-determined standards.

Besides above classification, controls can be classified on the basis of activities of the organisation: Policy control, Quality control, Inventory control, Overall control etc.

Objectives of Controlling

The main objective of controlling is to ensure a high degree of efficiency of the business. This very objective helps the manager to attain the goals of the organisation in a systematic and effective way.

The following are the objectives of controlling:

(i) To ensure high efficiency of the business.

(ii) To understand what had happened or is happening, why and by whom is happening.

(iii) To ensure effective and proper communication between the management and workers at all levels - to achieve the objectives of the organisation.

(iv) To keep proper check and control over direct and indirect expenses.

(v) To reframe organisational, goals, policies and objectives.

(vi) To find out the various deviations from the planned and proposed targets and to take necessary corrective action.

(vii) To make sure that all the activities are performed according to the pre-determined plans.

2.7.5 Co-ordinating

Definition of Co-ordination

Co-ordination may be defined as "an on-going process, whereby, a manager develops an integrated, orderly and synchronized pattern of group effort among his subordinates and tries to attain unity of effort in the pursuit of a common purpose".

"Co-ordination is the orderly arrangement of group effort, to provide unity of action in the pursuit of common purpose". — *Alan C. Reiley and James D. Mooney*

George R. Terry, in his book 'Principles of Management' has said — "Co-ordination deals with the task of blending efforts in order to ensure successful attainment of an objective. It is accomplished by means of planning, organising, actuating and controlling".

According to *Ordway Tead*, "Co-ordination is the effort to ensure a smooth interplay of the functions and forces of all different component parts of an organisation, to the end, that its purposes will be realised with a minimum of friction and a maximum of collaborative effectiveness".

According to *E.F.L. Brech*, "Co-ordination is balancing and keeping the terms together, by ensuring a suitable allocation of working activities to the various members and seeing that these are performed with due harmony among the members themselves".

In simple terms —"Co-ordination is the orderly arrangement of group effort, to provide unity of action in the pursuit of common purpose".

Need for Co-ordination

Co-ordinating means achieving team spirit and unity of action amongst the subordinates for achieving the common objectives. In a business unit, work is performed by numerous individuals, in various work centres. The individuals are doing numerous different jobs; many of them are highly specialised in their own work. It is the function of management to see that the individuals in the organisation operate as a team.

Consider, for example, a cricket team having the best players known, may find it difficult to win, if there is a lack of co-ordinated effort. Similarly, the success for a commercial enterprise, is based on the collective efforts of individuals. If properly co-ordinated, these individuals supplement each other's efforts to the extent that the group can be more productive. If they are not co-ordinated, the individuals, in pursuing their particular duties, may undo or delete the effects of their colleagues.

The need for co-ordination by management, arises particularly because of the existence of:

(i) Several persons at work.
(ii) Subdivisions and complexity of work.
(iii) Delegation of authority and responsibility.
(iv) Chances of difference between executives and specialists.
(v) Human nature and their problems.
(vi) Growth in size of organisation.

Tools of Co-ordination

The usual tools of co-ordination are as follows:

(i) Clear cut objectives.
(ii) Clear cut authority and responsibility of every subordinate, so that he knows his specific duties and obligations.
(iii) Effective communication between the executive and his subordinates, supervisors and workers.
(iv) Good human relationship of the managers with their subordinates.
(v) Co-operation amongst the subordinates and between the executive and the subordinates.

Types of Co-ordination

1. **Internal Co-ordination:** Internal co-ordination means co-ordination among different departments, branches, sections and other parts of an enterprise. It also exists among employees of different departments, supervisory staff, managers, directors and other personnel.

2. **External Co-ordination:** It is mainly concerned with the co-ordination between customers, suppliers, society, government and other outside agencies with whom, the business concern has to deal with.

3. **Vertical Co-ordination:** Co-ordination from top level to the bottom or from bottom to top, for attaining common objective of the business, is called vertical co-ordination. .

4. **Horizontal Co-ordination:** Where activities of different departments such as purchase, sales, accounts, finance etc. are knit together is called horizontal co-ordination.

2.7.6 Decision Making

A decision can be defined as "a course of action consciously chosen from available alternatives for the purpose of a desired result".

Decision making means to decide the future course of action for the organisation, over short or long terms. It is necessary to take decisions throughout the business cycle, for achieving maximum returns on the assets of the business enterprise. Decision making is necessary to solve business problems; for example, Inventory control decisions, Marketing decisions, deciding volume of production, capital investment decisions, stock decisions etc. In other words - "The decision is the point at which plans, policies and objectives are translated into concrete actions". Planning leads to sound decision and implies decision-making i.e. selection from among alternatives of a course of action. Decision is at the core of planning.

Decision-making under certainty is comparatively easy. Decision-making under uncertainty requires that the person responsible for making decisions should use his judgement and experience about future events. He must make sure that, which outcomes are most likely than others and combine his knowledge with the consequences associated with the various decisions. While taking decision under uncertainty the management should be willing to take a calculated risk.

Stages in Effective Decision Making

(a) Define the Problem: Define the problem clearly and precisely. Before any attempt is made to take decision, it is important to identify the real problem. Correct diagnosis is the first phase of effective decision-making. It is also necessary to establish the objectives of the decision.

(b) Classify the Objectives and identify the Problem Environment: The objectives established are marked and listed as per their weightage and importance for the organisation. The real problem and the situation in which the problem exists are identified.

(c) Search for Alternative: Identify the feasible alternatives for consideration, as solution of the problem.

(d) Select Evaluation Criteria: To compare the various alternatives, it is necessary to select evaluation criteria, such as; cost effectiveness, performance, quality, output etc.

(e) Select the Best Alternative: The various alternatives are evaluated as per the criteria selected. From the results of evaluation, a suitable and economical course of action is selected under the existing conditions in the factory. It is necessary to ensure that the decision will accomplish the purpose and it will be acceptable to those who must implement it.

(f) Feedback: Decisions are made for the future. They are made by human beings and thus there is every possibility of their being wrong. The organisation must therefore, have a sound, fool-proof feedback system; such feedback would help in determining how the decisions are working out in action.

Characteristics of Decision Making

1. It is a continuous process. Decisions are necessary on numerous issues and problems in each area of business.
2. The question of decision-making comes into picture only when there are alternatives.
3. Decision-making is always purposive, in that decisions should aim at achieving some purposes.
4. It is an intellectual process, supported by sound reasoning and judgement. To make decision, means to make a judgement regarding what one ought to do in a certain situation after considering thoroughly the available alternative course of action.
5. Decision-making is all pervasive, in the sense, that all levels of managers take decisions, though the impact and scope of decisions vary.
6. It is always related to a situation in which a manager may take one decision in a particular set of circumstances and another in different set of circumstances.

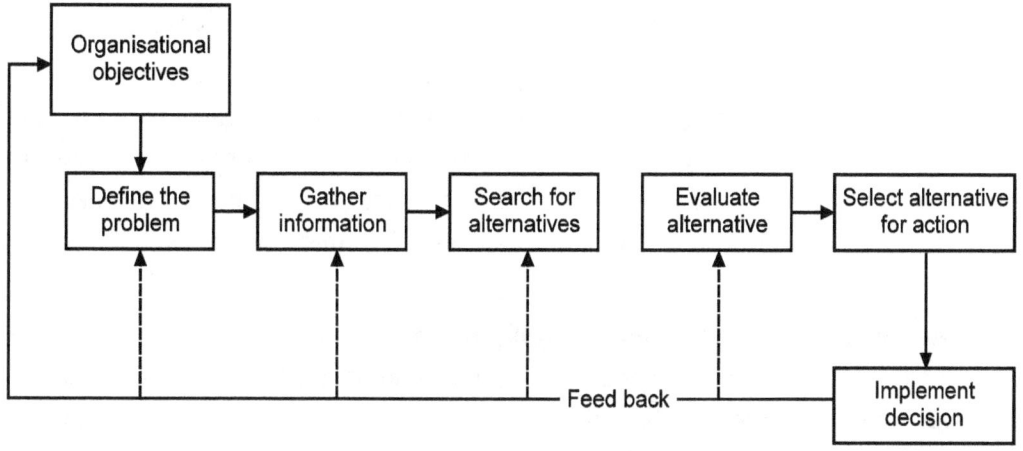

Fig. 2.6: Decision-making process

Types of Decisions

Decisions may be of different types. Some of the important types of managerial decisions are as follows:

1. Major and Minor decisions
2. Programmed and Non-programmed decisions
3. Strategic and Tactical (Routine) decisions
4. Policy and operation decisions
5. Long-term, departmental and Non-economic decisions
6. Individual and group decisions
7. Organisational and Personal decisions

1. Major and Minor Decisions: These can be categoriesed on the basis of their intensity. For example, purchase of a new automatic machine of worth 50 lakhs is categorised as major decision, while purchase of stationary (pencil, papers, pens etc.) for office use will be the minor decision.

2. Programmed and Non-programmed Decisions:

(a) Programmed decisions: These are classified on the basis of procedures adopted. Programmed decisions are routine and repetitive and are made within the framework of organisational policies and rules. These policies, procedures and rules are established well in advance to solve recurring problems in the organisation.

For example, the problem relating to promotion of employees is solved by promoting those employees who meet established promotion criteria. These criteria are established by promotion policy and the managers have only to decide which employees meet criteria for promotion and decision is made accordingly.

Programmed decision are easy to make and can be taken quickly because they are taken according to established policy already made. These type of decisions are subjected to quantitative assessment and can be easily programmed into a computer. Now-a-days the programmed decisions are made through management information systems (MIS) making use of computers.

(b) Non-programmed decisions: Non-programmed decisions are used for unstructured, unique ill-defined situations of non-recurring nature. In such decisions various alternatives cannot be decided in advance. A common feature of non-programmed decisions is that they are unique and non-recurring and therefore, readymade solutions are not available. Non-programmed decisions involve high risk, cannot be easily subjected to quantitative assessments involve greater expenditure of resources and cannot be programed into a computer. For example new product decisions acquisition and merger considerations allocation of organisations resources, decisions about a failing product line etc. represent non-programmed decisions.

The non-programmed decisions are made on the basis of judgement, intuition, insight and experience of the managers. The systematic approach to problem solving and decision making is useful for non-programmed decisions. Moreover these decisions are of high importance because of their long-term consequences. Hence, these are made by managers at higher levels in the organisation.

3. Strategic and Tactical (Routine) Decisions: Strategic decision relate to policy matter of the orgnaisations. It is one which is made during the current time period but whose primary effect will be felt during some future time period. Examples of strategic decisions are change in product mix, expansion of business, decision regarding plant location, issue of public equity shares or debentures, automation, introduction of new production line etc. These decisions are taken by higher level management.

In a strategic decision following characteristics are present.

1. Strategic decision is a major one which affects organisational structure, objectives, facilities and finances.

2. It contributes directly to the achievement of organsational objectives, and other decisions are derived from it.

3. A strategic decision may involve major departure from earlier one concerning some organisational practices; for example, change in product mix, use of automation etc.

4. The strategic decision has normally three elements.
   i) A course of action or plan which specifies the work to be done to achieve the result, known as action element.
   ii) The desired result or objective to be achieved through the implementation of the decision.
   iii) A commitment, which directs some part of the organisation to undertake the course of action, makes the personnel involved responsible for attaining the objectives and allocates resources to them i.e. commitment element.

5. The strategic decision is normally a non-programmaed decision, which is made under the condition of uncertainty. This is because strategic decision is to be taken in the context of environmental factors which are quite dynamic and uncertain.

Tactical or Routine Decisions or Operational Decisions: These decisions are made within the framework of strategic decisions and are designed to implement the well set policies and procedures.

Tactical decisions relates to day-to-day working of the organisation. The various features of tactical decision are as follows:

1) Tactical decision is a operational decision which relates to day-to-day operations of the organisation and has to be taken frequently. The decision is mostly repetitive in nature. For example, purchase of raw materials, assigning duties to employees etc.

2) It is programmed decision. The decision is programmed through the prescription of policies, rules, procedures etc. When the case for decision making comes, the decision maker simply applies those prescriptions and decides the things.

3) The outcome of tactical decision is of short-term nature and affects a narrow part of the organisation.

4) The authority for making these decisions can be delegated to lower-level management.

4. Policy and Operation Decisions: Policy-decisions are very important for the survival and growth of the organisation. Policy decisions are taken by the top management, they have a long-term impart on the business operations.

Operational decisions relate to day-to-day operations of the enterprise and are taken at lower or middle management level. For example, whether the piece rate system or time rate system is to be followed in the factory for calculating the wages to the workers is the policy decision and is required to be taken at higher level. While, the calculation of the actual wages to be paid to the workers is the example of operating decision.

5. Departmental and Non-economic Decisions: Departmental decisions are taken by the departmental heads and relates to the individual departments only.

Non-economic decisions are the decisions relating to non-economic factors such as technical values, moral behaviour, business ethics etc.

6. Individual and Group Decisions: Every manager makes decisions in the organisation either in his individual capacity or as a member of the group. In fact, organisational decisions are combination of individual and group decisions. Both types of decisions have their positive and negative aspects. Individual decisions are taken by a single individual in context of routine decisions where guidelines are already available. These decisions can be taken quickly.

The choice between individual decisions and group decisions depends upon

(i) Nature of problem, (ii) Time availability, (iii) Quality of decisions, (iv) Climate of decision making, (v) Legal requirements.

When a manager makes a decision as an individual he has to consider the steps involved in decision making and uses techniques decision making. However, when he has to make decision as a group member he has to consider a group behaviour also. Many specific techniques have been developed for improving group decision making such as brain storming, delphi technique, consensus mapping, nominal group technique etc.

7. Organisational and Personal Decisions: Decisions taken by the managers in their official capacity are called organisational decisions. These reflect the basic policy of the company.

Personal decisions relate to the manager as an individual and not as a member of organisation.

QUESTIONS

1. State the various stages of Evolution of Management.
2. Write short notes on:
    i) Factory system
    ii) Classical Theory of Management
    iii) Scientific Management.
3. Describe the principles of scientific management, in brief.
4. State and describe the Fayol's principles of management.
5. State the contribution of Frank Gilbreth and Gantt in the evolution of management.

6. Describe the 'Neo-classical Theory of Management'.
7. State and describe the elements of 'Neo-classical Theory of Management'.
8. Describe the following in relation to modern management theory:
   i) Quantitative Approach
   ii) System Approach
9. What is a system ? Describe the system approach applied to an organisation.
10. Describe the following in brief:
    i) Contingency approach to management
    ii) Operational approach to the management.
11. State and describe the characteristics of modern management thought.
12. Define Management. Explain the concept of management.
13. Enumerate the relationship between Administration, Management and Organisation.
14. Define:
    i) Administration
    ii) Management
    and differentiate clearly between them.
15. Name and describe the various levels of management with their functions.
16. Give a generalized as well as precise definition of management and comment on both.
17. Distinguish between Management, Organisation and Administration.
18. State and describe the "Managerial Skills" in brief.
19. Explain the importance of conceptual skills required of the successful manager.
20. Describe the importance of human relation skills to a manager.
21. Write short notes on any two of the following in connection with managerial skills:
    i) Technical skills
    ii) Conceptual skills
    iii) Human relation skills
22. Name the various functions of management, describe any one of them in brief.
23. Define planning – state its objectives.
24. Name the various types of planning and describe any three of them in brief.

25. Describe the various steps involved in planning.
26. Differentiate between "Formal Planning" and "Informal Planning".
27. State the various features of planning.
28. Describe following types of planning.
    i) Strategic planning
    ii) Operational planning
    iii) Proactive and reactive planning
29. Define Controlling. Describe its objectives and importance in managing the business organisation.
30. Describe Co-ordination as a function of management. State the various types of Co-ordination in business oganisation.
31. Describe the various stages involved in effective decision-making.
32. Name the various types of decisions and describe any three of them.
33. Write short notes on:
    i) Strategic decisions
    ii) Tactical decisions
    iii) Programmed and Non-programmed decisions.

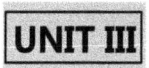

ORGANISATIONAL MANAGEMENT

3.1 INTRODUCTION

Every business needs to be organised for effective and efficient performance. Once the objectives, strategies and necessary plans to carry out are formulated, the next phase in management process is that of organisation. Organisation is thus a function of management which basically deals with the establishment of organisation structure. To start and run a business the essential requirements are men, materials, machines and money. Organisation is a co-ordination of these factors in such a way that maximum output is obtained efficiently and effectively with minimum total cost. Organisation in fact is a backbone of management, which establishes relationship between people, work and resources. A clear understanding of the objectives and strategies of an organisation enables structuring, functioning and performance of an organisation. Organisation involves division of work among people whose efforts must be co-ordinated to achieve specific objectives and to implement pre-determined strategies.

3.1.1 Necessity of Organisation

The increasing size of the manufacturing plant, introduction of most complex methods of production, tough competition between the enterprise and labour problems has necessitated every factory to be well organised, in order to produce required quantity of the products of the required quality, at the required time with minimum production cost.

A well designed organisation structure with qualified personnel in all key positions achieves execution, co-ordination and control of all policies and functions of the firm.

The importance of organisation can be judged from the following words of *A. Carngie*, an American industrialist.

"Take away all our money, great works, ore mines, and coke ovens but leave our organisation and in a few years, I shall have established myself. In fact the success or failure of any enterprise largely depends on the nature of organisation".

3.1.2 Advantages of Good Organisation

A good organisation offers the following advantages:
(i) It establishes responsibility for accomplishment of certain objectives.
(ii) It eliminates jurisdictional dispute between individuals.
(iii) It provides for easier communication and helps in developing executives.

(iv) It helps in equitable distribution of work and function.

(v) It assists in measuring a person's performance against his responsibilities.

(vi) It permits expansion and contraction without seriously disrupting the existing structure.

(vii) It prevents duplication of work.

(viii) It ensures good co-operation and higher morale.

(ix) It makes organisational growth possible with adequate control and without over-burdening the top executives.

(x) It ensures optimum utilization of resources at minimum possible cost.

3.2 Definitions

The following are some of the useful definitions of organisation

1. "Organisation is a process of (i) identifying and grouping the work to be performed, (ii) defining and delegating the responsibility and authority and (iii) establishing the relationships for the purpose of enabling people to work most efficiently together in accomplishing objectives". — *Louis A. Allin*

2. "Organisation is the form of every human association for the attainment of a common purpose". — *Mooney and Reily*

3. "Organisation is a system of co-operative activities of two or more persons". — *Chester Barnard*

4. "Organisation is a process of defining and grouping the activities of the enterprise and establishing the authority relationship among them". — *Haimann*

5. "Organisation involves the grouping of activities necessary to accomplish goals and plans, and assignment of these activities to appropriate departments and positions for authority delegation and co-ordination". — *Koontz and O' Donnel*

6. "Organisation is the process of combining the work which individuals or groups have to perform with facilities necessary for its execution, that the duties so performed provide the best channels for efficient, systematic, positive and co-ordinated application of available effort". — *O. Sheldon*

7. "An Organisation is the rational co-ordination of the activities or roles of a number of people for the achievement of some common explicit purpose or goal, through division and labour and function, and through a hierarchy of authority and responsibility". — *E. H. Schien*

8. "An Organisation consists of people who carry out differentiated tasks which are co-ordinated to contribute to the organisation's goals". — *G. Dessler*

3.3 STEPS IN FORMING ORGANISATION

The logical steps involved in the process of organisation are:

1. Determination of Objectives, Strategies, Plans and Policies: Organisation is a tool which is applied for the attainment of the objectives of the business. The objectives should be clear, precise, and complete because the entire organisation is to be built around the objectives of the enterprise. Objectives decide the purpose of organisation and the nature of work to be accomplished through the organisation.

2. Determination of Activities: The next step is to determine activities needed to execute these plans and policies and accomplish the objectives. From the objective of the company the principle activities are determined. The work load is broken down into component activities that are to be performed by all the employees. The activities are so split to determine the job which can be performed by an individual.

3. Separation and Grouping of Activities: It is necessary to classify and group the activities in the best possible way. To attain the benefits of specialization and division of labour, every company, will separate its activities on the basis of primary function — finance, engineering, purchasing, production, sales, and industrial relations. All the similar or directly related activities are grouped together in the form of departments. They can be further subdivided into sections. For example, the manufacturing function and the department handling it may be subdivided according to the products, processes, or type of equipment; and the selling department may be subdivided according to the territory, type of product or class of customers. The subdivision should be definite and avoid overlapping.

All groups must have approximately same workload. If there is expansion of certain activities in one group, sub-grouping or rearrangement of certain activities should be done. In small business unit, purchasing, storekeeping, machine operations, repairing, quality control are combined in one group, viz. production activities while in large scale industries there are separate purchase department, stores, maintenance, quality control department etc.

4. Delegation of Authority: The right given to superior for directing and guiding the actions of his subordinates to extract the work from them (smoothly and efficiently without any friction) is called "Authority".

Authority is necessary for the performance of the job and therefore authority is delegated to the subordinates for enabling them to carry out their work smoothly and efficiently.

Authority in other words is the right to command and exercise one's absolute power which compels others to behave in a desired way. The authority, always flows from superior to subordinates. For example, the works manager, by virtue of his authority, directs a foreman to arrange production of a job in this shop and the foreman in turn exercises his authority over his workers and directs them to produce the same.

5. Delegation of Responsibility: Responsibility must always be accompanied by the authority. Responsibility may be described as the obligation and accountability for the performance of delegated duties. A superior is always accountable for the acts of his subordinates. Therefore, responsibility always flows from subordinates to superior. A worker has the responsibility to perform a task as directed by foreman. The foreman, in turn is under obligation to manage to do as directed by his superior (the production superintendent). In any organisation, the superior is held responsible for the actions of his subordinates and the subordinates are accountable for the work to their superiors. Effective management necessitates a clear flow of formal authority and responsibility.

6. To Establish Interrelationships: The grouped activities are placed in the overall organisation structure at appropriate level. It is necessary to integrate or tie these groups of activities: (a) through authority relationship horizontally, vertically, and laterally and (b) through organised information or communication systems i.e., with the help of effective co-ordination and communication.

By integration of activities we have unity of objectives, team work and team spirit. It establishes harmony of efforts of different individuals and groups avoiding the conflicts arising out of it.

7. Providing Physical Facilities and Proper Environment: It is necessary to provide right type of physical facilities and create environment for the smooth running and prosperity of the organisation. Physical facilities may include machinery, tools, equipments, infrastructure etc. Right environment means proper lighting, ventilation, heating, cooling arrangements at the workplace, reasonable hours of work, rest pauses, safety devices, job security, job satisfaction and above all human approach by the management.

8. Preparation of Organisation Chart: An organisation chart is then prepared. Organisation chart is a graphic means or record which shows the formal organisation structure. It shows the formal superior subordinate relationships. A chart is a blueprint of company. It shows who supervises and controls whom and how the various units / departments or sections are interrelated. It gives visual ideas about formal relationships. By showing the main line of authority the main lines of communications, and the flow of authority (downwards) as well as the flow of accountability (upwards) throughout all the levels and management hierarchy.

3.3.1 Principles of Organisation

Efficiency of the enterprise depends on the organisational structure. Some of the important principles to be followed for developing sound and efficient organisation structure are:

1. **Consideration of Unity of Objectives:** The objectives of the enterprise influence the organisation. structure. The organisation is a mechanism to achieve the objectives of the business. In view of this the objectives must be clearly defined for the entire enterprise, for each department and even for each position in the organisation structure. There must be unity of objectives so that all efforts can be concentrated on achieving the set goals at minimum cost.

2. **Principle of Specialization:** Effective organisation must include specialization. Precise division of work facilitates specialization. The organisation structure should be formulated in such a way that the activities of the enterprise are divided according to functions. Work should be distributed among the persons very carefully on the basis of their skill, experience and ability to do that work.

3. **Principle of Authority:** Authority empowers the superior to make a subordinate to do the work. Everybody in the organisation, from top level downwards should be given some authority to secure co-operation from subordinates. Lines of authority should be clearly established in the structure of organisation in order to avoid overlapping actions, omission of acts etc.

4. **Principle of Co-ordination:** The organisational structure should be such that different departments co-ordinate with each other to achieve the common goals. Co-ordination is necessary for unity of action i.e., to facilitate integration of the basic managerial function.

5. **Principle of Unity of Command:** According to this principle, each sub-ordinate should have only one superior and dual sub-ordination should be avoided. For example, X is the boss of Y ; Y is accountable to X. Y is the boss of Z ; Z is accountable to Y. Thus, no one on the organisation should have more than one boss. This principle avoids the possibility of conflicts in instruction and develops a sense of personal responsibility for the work.

6. **Principle of Span of Control:** The number of persons who are directly responsible to the executive is called the span of control. No single executive should have more people looking to him for controlling and guidance than he can reasonably manage, because (a) The time at the disposal of the executive is limited (b) He has limited available energy/capacity. The number of persons which can be effectively supervised by a single executive should be limited to six in average firm. However, where the operations are routine or automatic, executive can direct a large number upto 20.

3.4 TYPES OF ORGANISATION

The organisation structure is a skeleton of a framework that divides the total activities into related groups, develops superior and subordinate relationship among the persons by prescribing the authorities.

Thus, it indicates the hierarchy (persons arranged according to rank), authority structure and reporting relationships (who should report to whom).

The organisational structure differs from industry to industry. It usually depends upon:

(i) Size of the organisation.

(ii) Nature of the product being manufactured.

(iii) Complexity of the problems being faced.

There are *four* main types of organisation structure:

- Line Organisation
- Line and Staff Organisation
- Functional Organisation
- Project Organisation

3.4.1 Line, Military or Scalar Organisation

This is the simplest and earliest type of organisation. It is also called as Military or Scalar Organisation (Fig. 3.1).

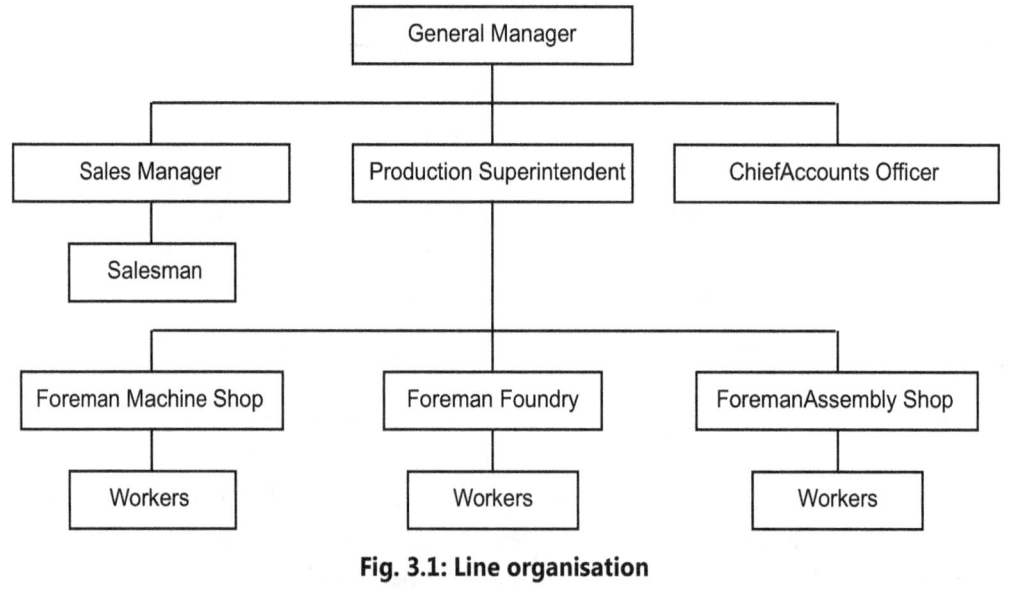

Fig. 3.1: Line organisation

In this type of organisation, the line of authority flows directly from top to bottom and the line of responsibility from bottom to top in opposite direction. In line organisation, the business activities are divided into *three* groups:

(i) Finance or Accounts, (ii) Production, (iii) Sales (Distribution).

Each of these departments is subdivided into certain self-contained departments or sections. Each departmental head has complete control over his section and he is fully authorized to select his labour, staff, purchases of raw materials, stores and to set the standards of output etc. The responsibility of each departmental head is clearly defined. Each department works as a self-supporting unit.

The following diagram shows the chart of the organisation. The General Manager is the overall in-charge. The whole work is divided into *three* sections *viz. Production, Distribution.* and *Finance* and given into the charge of each departmental head. The line of authority flows from G.M to three departmental heads, from there it moves down to the labour through lesser and lesser superior bosses. However, the line of responsibility flows in opposite direction i.e., labour is responsible to the foreman, each foreman is to the production superintendent and three executives independently are responsible to the General Manager. In this type all men of the same authority level are independent of all others similarly situated.

Advantages

1. **Simplicity:** It is easy to establish and simple to understand. The entire activities are broadly grouped into departments. The departmental head has the sole authority over his department. The different departmental heads are put at the same level of authority, each having a complete command over his department.

2. **Clear cut Authority and Responsibility:** The delegation of authorities and assignment of responsibilities are clear and precise. There are no chances of authority conflicts and shifting of responsibilities.

3. **Strong in Discipline:** Due to unity of command and unified control it is possible to maintain strict discipline. There is a clear cut authority and responsibility. The duties and responsibilities of each individual are clearly defined.

4. **Unity of Command:** It establishes clear cut superior subordinate relationships. Each subordinate is responsible to only one superior. This develops a sense of responsibility and loyalty.

5. **Quick Decisions:** The entire management is in the hands of one individual namely General Manager, quick decisions and speedy actions are therefore possible.

6. **Rapid Communication:** There is a clear channel of communication, which results in rapid communications of orders, suggestions and instructions.

7. **Co-ordination:** The complete responsibility is in the hands of the heads and therefore effective co-ordination within the department is obtained.

8. **Development of All-round Executive:** The departmental head has to look after all the activities of his department, therefore, it encourages the development of all round executive at the higher level of authority.

9. It is flexible to expand or contract and stable.

Disadvantages

1. **Undue Reliance:** The success of the enterprise depends upon the caliber and ability of few departmental heads. Loss of one or two capable men may put the organisation in difficulties.

2. **Personal Limitations (Lack of specialization):** In this type or organisation an individual executive is supposed to discharge different types of duties. He cannot do justice to all different activities, because he cannot be specialized in all trades.

3. **Overload of Work:** Departmental heads are overloaded with various routine jobs, hence they cannot spare time for important managerial functions like planning, development, budgeting etc.

4. **Dictatorial Way:** In line organisation too much authorities centre around line executives. Hence it encourages dictatorial way of working.

5. **Duplication of Work:** Conflicting policies of different departments result in duplication of work.

6. **Unsuitable for Large Concerns:** It is limited to small concerns.

7. **General Interest of Enterprise may be Over-looked:** Departments may work for their self-interest and may sacrifice the general interest of the enterprise.

8. **Scope of Favouritism:** As the departmental head has the supreme authority, there are chances of favouritism.

9. **Wastage of Materials and Man hours:** Because of lack of specialization perhaps there may be more wastage of materials and man hours.

Applications

Line organisation can work satisfactorily under following conditions:

(i) Small enterprises free from complexities.

(ii) Automatic and continuous process industries such as paper, sugar, textile etc.

(iii) Where few activities are to be performed.

(iv) Less number of workers are employed.

(v) Where the work is routine e.g., Government department.

3.4.2 Line and Staff Organisation

Line and staff organisation is that in which the line heads are assisted by specialist staff.

If the firm is of large size, managers cannot give careful attention to every aspect of management. They are busy with ordinary task of production and selling. Hence staff is deputed to do the work of investigation, research, recording and advising to managers. Thus the staff brings specialization by assisting the line officers. The line maintains discipline and stability, staff provides experts information and helps to improve overall efficiency. Thus the staff are thinkers while the line are doers.

Usually the staff has an administrative authority. They serve only in advisory capacity in their field of specialization.

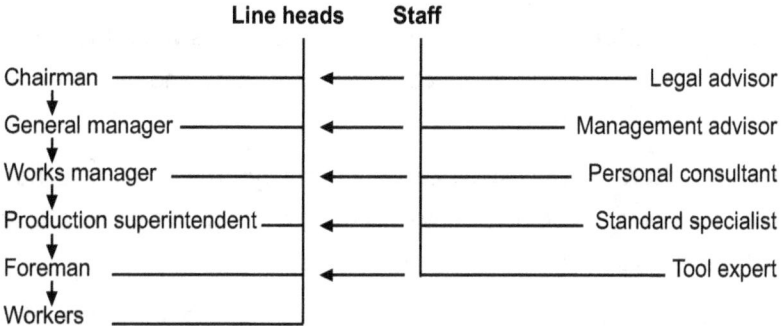

Fig. 3.2: Line and Staff organisation

Advantages

1. **Planned Specialization:** The line and staff is a duplex organisation, dividing the whole work into creative plan and action plan. The creative plan is concerned with original thinking and the action plan takes care of the execution of work. Line executives therefore, have enough time to organize, control and supervise the production effectively.

2. **Well-defined Authority and Responsibility:** The line officers have definite responsibility and authority. The subordinates receive order only from one superior. Therefore, it is possible to maintain strict discipline.

3. **Availability of Specialized Knowledge:** The staff with expert knowledge provides opportunities to the line officers for adopting a rational multidimensional views towards a problem. Therefore it helps to lake sound decisions.

4. **Adaptability to Progressive Business:** This type of organisation contains good features of both line as well as functional organisation. Specialized staff can devote their time for planning, method study research, collection of data etc. Therefore, line and staff organisation is most suitable for progressive and flourishing business Most of the industries in India today are using this plan after slightly modifying it to meet their specific needs.
5. **Less Wastage:** There will be less wastage of material.
6. **Improved Quality:** Quality of the product will be better.

Disadvantages

1. **Chances of Mis-interpretation:** Although the expert's advice is available, yet it reaches the workers through line supervisors. The line officers may fail to understand the meaning of advice and there is always a risk of misunderstanding and misinter-pretation.
2. **Chances of Friction:** There are bound to be occasions when the line and staff may differ in opinion may result in conflict of interests and prevents a harmonious relationship between the two.
3. **Ineffective Staff in the Absence of Authority:** The staff have no authority to execute their own advice. Their advice is not a binding on the line officers. Therefore, the advice given by specialists may be ignored by line heads.
4. **Expensive:** The overhead cost of the product increases because of high salaried specialized staff.
5. **Lithargic Staff Officer in the Absence of Accountability:** The line officer is accountable for the success or failure of his action, not the staff officer. This may make the staff officer indifferent. He may not stretch his talents to give the right advice.
6. **Loss of Initiative by Line Executive:** If they start depending too much on staff it may loose their initiative drive and ingenuity.

Application

Line and staff organisation is generally followed by all Government and Private concerns involving complicated processes or operations i.e., big steel plants, heavy electricals electricity boards, large manufacturing plants etc.

3.4.3 Functional Organisation

F.W. Taylor suggested functional organisation, because it was difficult to find all-round persons qualified to work at-middle management levels in the line organisation.

Functional organisation divides managerial activities, so that each head from the works manager down has few functions to perform as possible and is able to become specialist in these. Authority from top to down is delegated according to the function. In this type of organisation, specialists like production enginner, design engineer, maintenance engineer, purchase officer etc. are employed.

Each specialist is supposed to give his functional advice to all other foremen and workers. Taylor divided the responsibility of shop supervision among several foreman, each specially qualified and in charge of certain aspect of work. Each specialist is authorised to give orders to workers, but only in regard of his field of specialization.

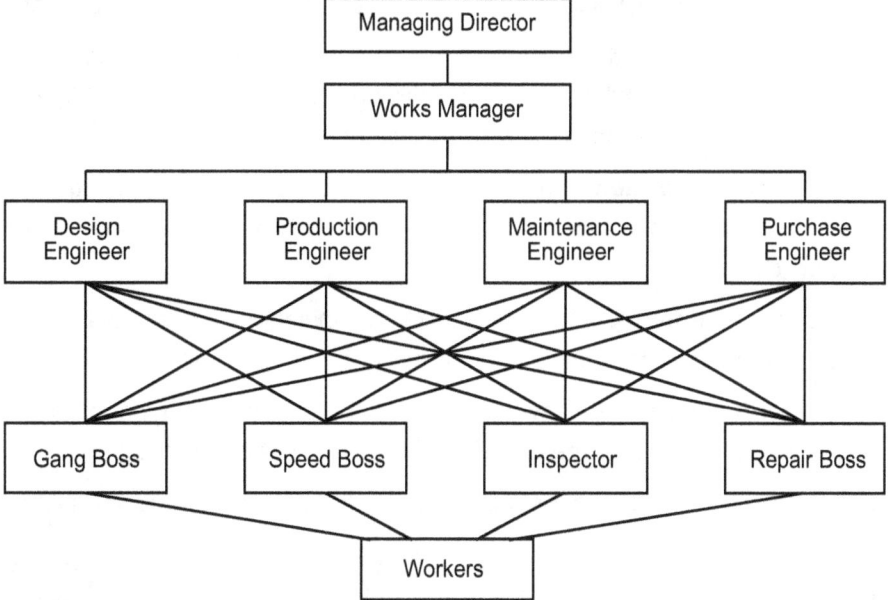

Fig. 3.3: Functional organisation

Fig. 3.3 illustrates a typical organisation chart of functional organisation. The Specialists, Design Engineer, Production Engineer, Maintenance Engineer, Purchase officer gives functional advice to all foreman (supervisors) and guide them in their respective field of specialization only. The shop supervisors (e.g., gang boss, speed boss, inspector and repair boss) supervise and help the workers, each foreman assisting only in his particular function. The gang foreman directs the setting up of tools into machine and the efficient movement from machine to machine. The speed foreman instructs workers in proper use of cutting tools and machine operations so that they may reach a specified rate of output. The inspection foreman regulates the quality of the work. The repair foreman supervises upkeep and maintenance, and guides the workers regarding routine lubrication, cleaning and upkeep of machines.

Advantages

1. **Separation of Work:** In functional organisation, mental work has been separated from routine work. The specialist has been given the authority and responsibility for supervision and administration pertaining to their field of specialization unnecessary over-loading of responsibilities is thus avoided.

2. **Specialization:** Specialization and skilled supervisory attention is given to workers. The result is increased in rate of production and improves quality of work.

3. **Narrow range with high depth:** The narrow range of activities enables the functional expert to develop in-depth understanding in his particular area of activity.

4. **Ease in Selection and Training:** Functional organisation is based upon expert knowledge. The availability of guidance through experts make it possible to train the workers properly in comparatively short span of time.

5. **Standardised Operations:** The work of subordinates is divided into standard parts. Expert knowledge is available for each part. The job requirements of each part are definite, clear and few.

6. **Reduction in Prime Cost:** Since for every operation expert guidance is there, wastage of material, is reduced and this helps to reduce prime cost.

7. **Scope for Growth and Development of Business:** This type of organisation presents ample scope for the growth and development of business.

8. **Standardization:** It helps mass production by standardization and specialization.

Disadvantages

1. **Indiscipline:** Since the workers receive instructions from number of specialists (which may be conflicting) it leads to confusion to whom they should follow. Therefore, it is difficult to maintain discipline.

2. **Shifting of Responsibility:** It is difficult for the top management to locate responsibility for the unsatisfactory work. Everybody tries to shift responsibilities on others for the faults and failures.

3. **Kills the Initiative of Workers:** As the specialized guidance is available to the workers, the workers will not be using their talents and skill, therefore their initiative cannot be utilized.

4. **Overlapping of Authority:** The spheres of authority tends to overlap and gives rise to friction between the persons of equal rank.

5. **Lack of Co-ordination between Functions:** Except the function in which he is specialized he is absolutely indifferent to other functions. Therefore, there is a lack of co-ordination of function and efforts.

6. **Increase in Cost:** High salary is paid to the experts employed. This increases the total cost of the job.

3.4.4 Project Type Organisation

Depending on the authority that is given to the person responsible for the project, the project organisation may take one of the following forms:

- Line and staff organisation. (project manager as a staff assistant to chief executive).
- Project manager as a specialized staff function.
- Matrix organisation.

1. Project Manager as a Staff Assistant Chief to the Executive

Fig. 3.4 shows an arrangement in which the project manager serves as a staff assistant to the chief executive. The project manager, in this position, has no authority. He does not make any decision for the project, nor does he provide any staff service to the functional departments. The project manager merely collects information and communicates the same to the chief executive. He may influence some decisions taken by the chief executive or by functional departments, but he cannot himself make any decisions which can become binding for others. This arrangement may be chosen by a chief executive who wants to directly control the project but cannot devote much time to keep track of details.

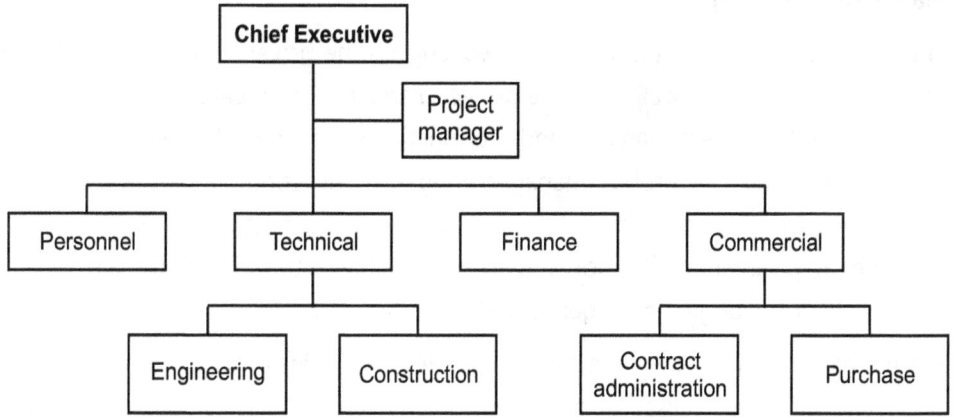

Fig. 3.4: Project manager as a staff assistant to the chief executive

2. Project Manager as a Specialized Staff Function

The project manager, in this case, will be a specialist in project management tools and techniques, and in view of his superior knowledge relating to scheduling, budgeting and information systems, he is in the best position to advise other functions. He can carry out service activities like collection, and transmission of data, follow-up of one functional group to service another group, maintain records, measure progress, analyse progress and prepare progress reports. He may advise the functional groups but a final decision would rest with the functional groups. He does not have any authority which can shape the destiny of the project.

Most companies tend to use this arrangement when project management is used for the first time in the company as this does not require much change in the working of the organisation.

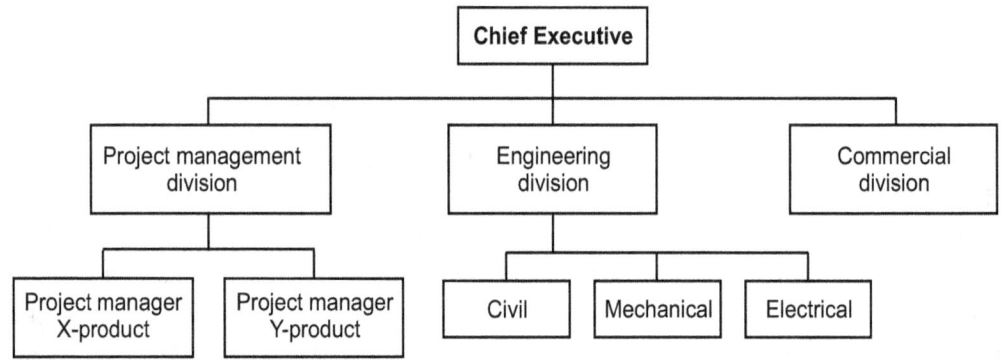

Fig. 3.5: Project Management as a specialized staff function

3. Matrix Organisation

In a matrix organisation, the personnel working on the project have a responsibility to their functional superior as well as to the project manager. This means that the authority is shared between the project manager and the functional managers. Fig. 3.6 shows a matrix form of organisation. The project manager integrates the contributions of personnel in various functional departments toward the realisation of project activity. While the personnel maintain their departmental affiliation and are responsible to their functional superiors, they are responsible to the project manager as well.

The matrix form of organisation, seeks to achieve the twin objectives of efficient use of resources and effective realisation of project objectives of course, at the cost of greater organisational complexity.

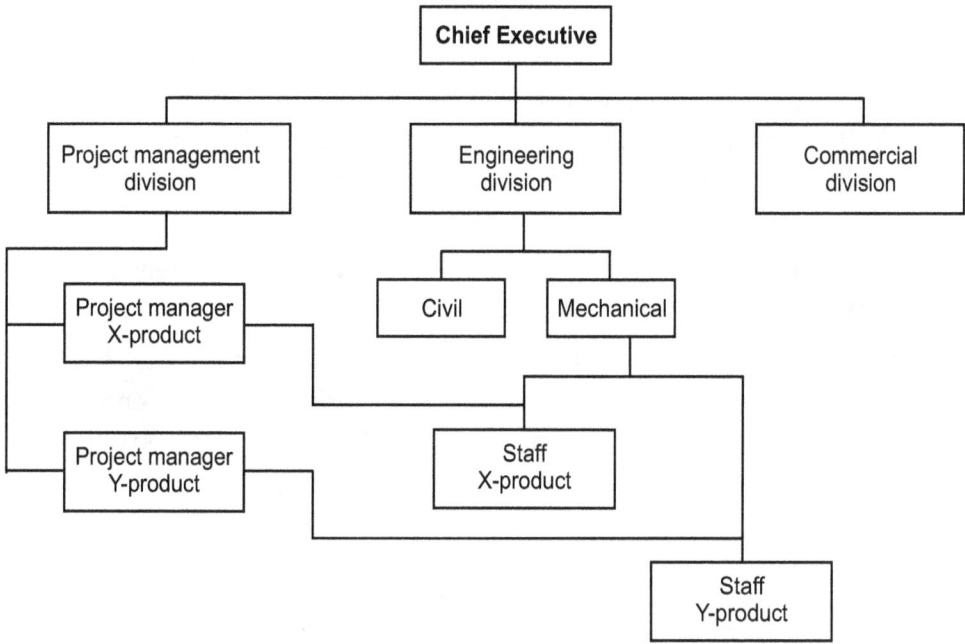

Fig. 3.6: Matrix organisation

Advantages of Matrix Organisation

1. It enables efficient utilization of manpower resources working in different departments.
2. Allows flexibility in coordination.
3. Increases awareness of interdependencies.
4. Enhances job enrichment.
5. Allows more innovative and creative use of key personnel.
6. Allows individual to have multiple roles and assignments.

Disadvantages

1. It creates dual overlapping authority.
2. The multiple leadership may confuse group members.
3. It highlights problems of communication between technical specialists.
4. Coordination and control becomes difficult.

3.5 DEPARTMENTATION

Industrialization has created problems which are complex in nature. It created a necessity of large scale industries to meet the increased demand. In large scale industries, there are large number of employees. For the sake of efficient supervision and control, the factory/enterprise is divided into different departments. Each department is entrusted with a particular function for carrying out particular activity. Each departmental head is expected to control and supervise the work in his department. He has the authority over the worker in his department and he is responsible for the smooth and efficient working of his department. This is what is generally meant by departmentation. Departmentation leads to grouping of both functions and personals who are assigned to carry out the allocated activity.

Departmentation refers to division of the whole enterprise into different groups with a view to facilitate the administration of the enterprise.

Departmentation is the process of breaking down of enterprise into various departments. In other words, identifying and grouping of similar activities on some logical basis so that the operators may be organised in order to attain the objectives of the enterprise is called departmentation.

Departmentation is also defined as,

"The process of dividing the work and then grouping them into units and subunits or departments for the purpose of administration.

Departmentation is one of the primary tasks in designing organisation structure. More precisely,

"Departmentation is a process where tasks are grouped into jobs, jobs into effective workgroups and workgroups into identifiable segments or departments. It leads to grouping of both activities and personnel".

A department may be called division, branch, bureau, section and in military it is called as regiment, battalian group or company.

Aims or Objectives of Departmentation

1. Smooth and Efficient Administration: The process of departmentation is to administer the enterprise efficiently and effectively. It aims at scientific distribution of work of the enterprise among different sections and their personnel in a manner in which their work can be (a) supervised (b) guided (c) controlled and (d) co-ordinated to the maximum advantage of the organisation and to the benefit of the personnel working in the organisation.

2. To Attain Goals: Departmentation seeks diffusion of authority and responsibility aiming at the attainment of the goal of the enterprise effectively.

3. Division of Work in Groups and Sub-groups: It divides the work and then groups them into units and subunits which can be managed effectively.

4. Specialization: Departmentation brings specialization in the performance of various activities.

Benefits of Departmentation

Departmentation is an important process in designing the organisation structure. The following are some of the advantages for benefits of departmentation:

1. **It Increases Efficiency:** Well-defined duties and responsibilities help in motivating the employees to put better performance which increases the efficiency of the organisation.

2. **Specialization:** *It leads* to benefits of specialization various activities are grouped according to their specific function. It thus divides the whole of the enterprise into separate departments according to their function. For example, sales, purchase, production, finance, stores, maintenance etc.

3. **Effective Administrative Control:** It limits the number of persons to be supervised, secondly, the standard of performance for each department can be laid down precisely. Therefore, effective administrative control is possible.

4. **Fixation of Responsibility:** The jobs are well defined and responsibilities are well clarified, this helps in getting the work completed in time with satisfaction.

5. **Development of Managerial Talents:** Assignment of work according to skill, knowledge, training, experience and aptitude brings specialization. It also brings standardisation to both job and the product. This may result in the best utilization of available human talent in the field of management or in actual operation.

6. **Helps in Independent Decision and Initiative:** It provides opportunity to departmental managers to take independent decisions, initiative and learn new managerial skills.

7. **Easy Evaluation of Work:** It helps in evaluating the work carried out by an individual or group of individuals or the department as a whole.

8. **Effective Economy and Proper Budgeting:** Budgeting according to departments helps in controlling the finance effectively.

9. **Basis for Co-ordination:** Departmentation provides a basis on which top management can co-ordinate the activities of different departments.

Methods of Departmentation

There are various methods of creating departments in an enterprise. Some of them are as described below:

- By product
- By process
- By function

3.5.1 Departmentation by Products or Services

In this method, departments are created on the basis of products. All activities related to a particular product line may be grouped together. This basis of departmentation has become increasingly important, especially for large, complex organisations producing different types of products or offering different types or services. In this, the product lines are segregated and each product line has its own manager. Each department is responsible for manufacturing, selling and further developing of one distinct product line. A product department may further be divided on functional basis.

An automobile industry, for example, may departmentalize its activities as follows:

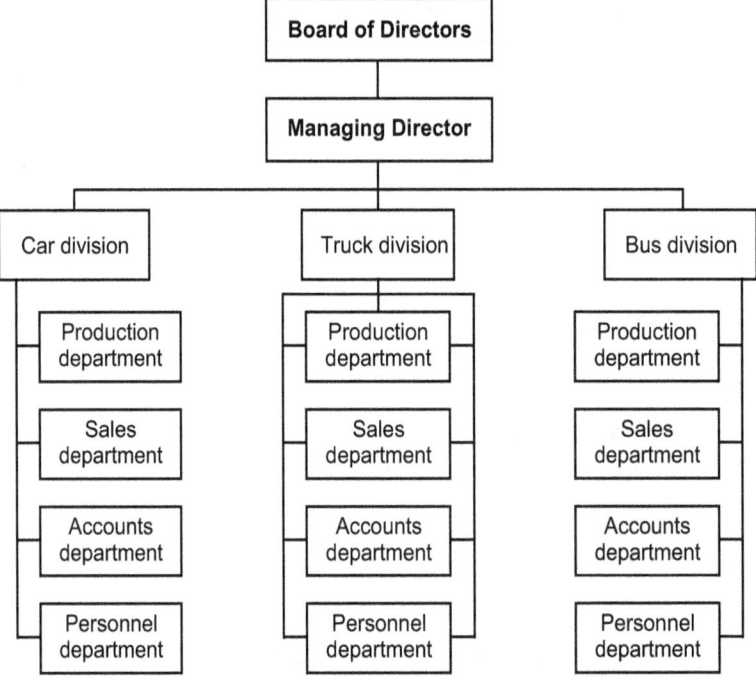

Fig. 3.7: Product departmentation of an automobile unit

Advantages of Departmentalization by Product

1. It is easier to evaluate the performance of each product line. Unprofitable lines may be dropped. Moreover, proper attention can be given to each product.
2. The problem of co-ordination present in functional departmentation is removed.
3. It enjoys the advantage of specialized product knowledge.
4. It is suitable in organisations where product lines are complex and diverse and requires specialized knowledge for selling, marketing and manufacturing.
5. It provides flexibility. A new product line can be added without dislocating the existing lines of product or unprofitable product lines may be dropped.

Disadvantages

1. There is a duplication of physical facilities and many functions. Each product line maintains its separate facilities and functional personnel.
2. Advantages of centralization of certain activities like accounting, selling, purchasing, stores etc. cannot be achieved which increases management cost.
3. It is not suitable for small enterprises.
4. There may be under-utilization of plant capacity if the demand of a particular product is not sufficient.

3.5.2 Departmentation by Process

In this method, the manufacturing activities are sub-divided on the basis of their process of production. Similar machines such as all lathes, drilling machines, grinding machines, milling machines etc., are grouped into separate sections, such as lathe department, drilling department, grinding department, milling department, welding department etc.

Advantages

1. It has the advantages of functioning, maintenance of equipment and manpower utilization.
2. Duplication of physical facilities is avoided and equipment utilization is better.

Disadvantages

1. The volume of production must be large enough to have a separate department.
2. It may be difficult to achieve co-ordination of departments based on different processes.

3.5.3 Departmentation by Function

In this method, the activities of the organisation are divided into primary functions to be performed such as – production, marketing, finance, personnel etc. Each function is allotted in a separate department. These functions can further be subdivided into various sub-functions as the size of the business increases and the number of departments may be increased for these sub-functions. This may be called divisions or sub departments. Such as there may be market-research department, advertising department, sales department under the marketing department. This process of functional sub-divisions may be continued through several successive levels in the hierarchy as shown in Fig. 3.8.

It is the most common and popular method of departmentation and is found not only in business enterprises but in hospitals, Government agencies and almost in every enterprise at one level or the other.

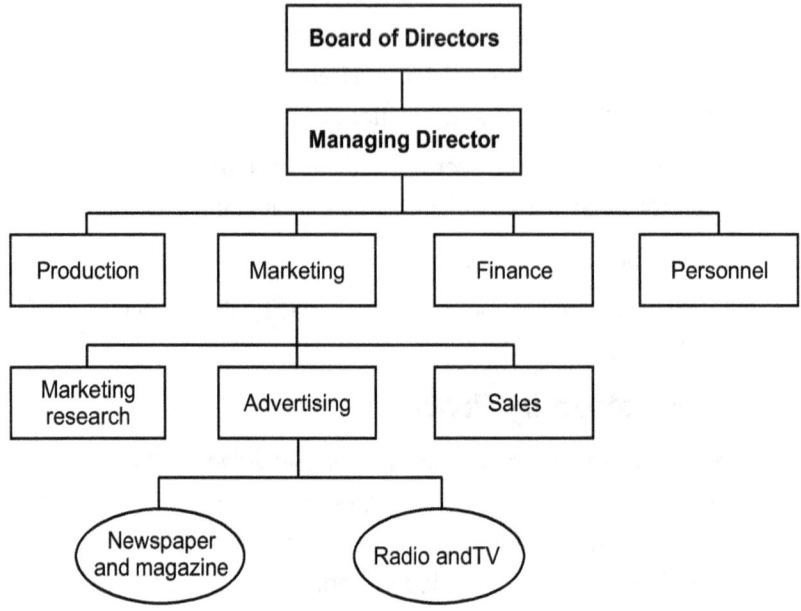

Fig. 3.8: Departmentation by function

Advantages of Departmentation by Function

1. This arrangement has the advantage of specialization and concentration of similar activities with a departmental unit. This enables efficient utilization of man power.
2. It represents a sound and logical way of grouping activities of enterprise.
3. It facilitates control and co-ordination of activities within the department and at the inter-departmental level.
4. Functional experts are employed in various functional areas to perform activities requiring specialized knowledge.
5. This method is flexible. There is much scope for expansion, as the size of the organisation increases, more departments may be established by sub-dividing the basic function.
6. It facilitates delegation of authority and thus reduces the burden of the chief executive.

Disadvantages

1. The major problem associated with this form is the co-ordination of the specialized activities.
2. The departmental head thinks only in terms of his own department and not the business as a work.
3. There is too much emphasis on specialization, this may hamper the broadening of outlook of various people.

3.6 CENTRALIZATION AND DECENTRALIZATION

These terms are used in connection with administrative processes, physical and geometrical location, various functions being performed or degree of delegation of authority.

Centralization refers to concentration of authority and decentralisation dispersion of authority.

Generally, there can be i) geographical decentralization or ii) functional decentralization. Geographical decentralization refers to dispersion of an organisation's operations throughout the country. Centralization refers to the reservation of authority at the top management level of the organisation and decentratlization refers to systematic delegation of authority in the organisation. However, there can neither be absolute centralization nor there can be absolute decentralization.

Factors Determining Degree of Decentralization:

1. Size of organisation: Decentralization depends on the size of the organisation. The larger the size of the organisation, the more is the need of decentralization. In large organisations more decisions are to be made at more places. Therefore, if authority is concentrated only at top management level, quick decisions are not possible, this may involve delay in the process or functions of organisation.

2. History of the Organisation: Decentralization of authority depends on the way the organisation has been built up over the period of time. Normally, those organisations which starts and expands under the direction of the owner founder show a market tendency to keep the authority centralized. On the other hand, organisations that represent amalgamations and consolidations are likely to show a definite tendency to retain decentralised authority.

3. Management Philosophy: The management philosophy of top level managers has considerable influence on the extent to which authority is decentralised. In many cases top managers may see decentralization as a way of organisational life. It takes the advantage of internal desire of the people to create to be free to take decisions to have status. With decentralization the managers at the top level keep themselves free to devote for some more important functions.

4. Availability of Managers: Availability of managers of required caliber directly affects the degree of decentralization. If better quality managers are available, there is more chance for decentralization.

5. Pattern of planning: Assigning the various activities and delegation of authority to managers at various levels depends on how planning duties have been allocated and the extent to which planning activities have been undertaken.

6. Control Techniques: Higher the degree of development and use of control techniques, better is the prospect for decentralization. In fact decentralization helps improvement in statistical devices, accounting control and other techniques.

7. Decentralized Activities: Decentralization is necessary to take advantage of division of labour, opportunities for using physical facilities at various locations and nature of work. For example, the activities of banking, insurance and transport organisations have been decentralised. It may be based on geographical nature.

8. Expansion of the Organisation: If the business organisation is developing and is under expansion, there is more change that the authority will be decentralized, this is necessary to avoid overburden of the top managers, and making them free to concentrate on more important functions. The problem of overburden can be overcome by delegating authority at the lower level.

9. Environmental Influence: The environmental influences also determine the degree of decentralization. Among the more important environmental forces are the government regulations over the private business in determining price structure and sometimes even distribution pattern.

Advantages of Centralization

1. It helps to reduce the number of undesirable decisions by less experienced executives.
2. It reduces the need of experienced sub-ordinate managers because, the decisions are taken at the top management level.
3. It reduces the cost of staffing, because fewer competent managers can handle the jobs.
4. It makes communication and control easier in the organisation.
5. Quick decisions are possible, hence emergencies can be handled easily.
6. It helps to eliminate duplication of efforts.
7. There is uniformity of action throughout the organisation and thus co-ordination can be achieved easily.

Advantages of Decentralization

1. It helps ensure that the decisions are made by those managers who have the best experience of local conditions which are important for such decisions.
2. It reduces the burden of the top management. So they can pay more attention on strategic management functions.
3. It facilitates growth and diversification in the organisation.

4. It emphasizes horizontal growth of the organisation thereby reducing the number of management levels and increasing the span of management.
5. It helps to make the overall organisation stronger by facilitating the personal development of individuals.
6. It helps stimulate initiative and creates better feeling of satisfaction among competent individuals.
7. Quick decisions at departmental level are possible.

3.7 AUTHORITY AND RESPONSIBILITY

Authority

Authority empowers the superior to make a subordinate to do the work. A person at higher position in the organisation exercises authority or power over his subordinates for getting the work done. Every body in the organisation from top level downwards should be given some authority to secure co-operation from subordinates. Lines of authority should be clearly established in the structure of organisation to avoid overlapping actions, omission of acts etc. Authority is delegated through the lines of authority established in the structure of the organisation. The authority always flows from the superior to subordinates. For example, the works manager by virtue of his authority, directs a foreman to arrange production of a job in his shop, and the foreman in turn exercises his authority over his workers and directs them to produce the same. A major task of a top executive, therefore, is delegating authority to proper individuals in order to secure appropriate action. Authority is always associated with responsibility to get things done when an employee is authorised to take up a job, he is held responsible for its performance also.

Responsibility

Responsibility is the obligation of the subordinate towards the (boss) superior for completing the assigned work. It means accountability. The authority and responsibility should go hand in hand. It would not be just to hold a person responsible for performing a task without first giving him the authority necessary to do the job. For example, a supervisor cannot be held responsible for the output of his department unless he has been given the authority to direct the actions of the workers working under him.

3.8 SPAN OF CONTROL

The number of persons who are directly responsible to the executive is called the span of control. No single executive should be more people looking to him for controlling and guidance than he can reasonably manage, because, (a) The time at the disposal of the executive is limited, (b) He has limited available energy / capacity. The number of persons which can be effectively supervised by a single executive or departmental head should be limited to six in an average firm, however when the activities are routine or closely related the executive can direct and supervise a large number upto 20.

If the span is small, an executive may tend to over supervise and may even do spoon feeding to his subordinates. On the other hand if the span is large, the executive may not be able to supervise his subordinates effectively and they may become careless or they may feel neglected.

Factors determining the span of control are

(a) Capacity, experience and skill of the subordinate.

(b) Capacity and skill of the executive.

(c) For specialized and routine work, span of control can be large.

(d) Complex nature of work demands a small span of control.

(e) A small span of control is also ideal when a number of workers are working in isolated areas, doing different types of works and requires close supervision and control.

(f) A wider span of control can be employed if the objectives, plans and policies are clear and definite with no confusion in the minds of employees, and if each employee knows about his job, duties, responsibilities and motivated to work whole heartedly.

3.9 FORMS OF OWNERSHIP

The forms of ownership selected depend upon the following factors:

1. Size and nature of the business to be started.
2. Technical difficulties.
3. Market competition and scope of the articles in the market.
4. Capital required to start the business and means to collect funds.
5. Limitations and restrictions put forth by the Government in connection with grant of loans, foreign exchange and such other things.

Forms of Ownership

Modern business is carried out by the following types of ownership organisations (form of business organisation):

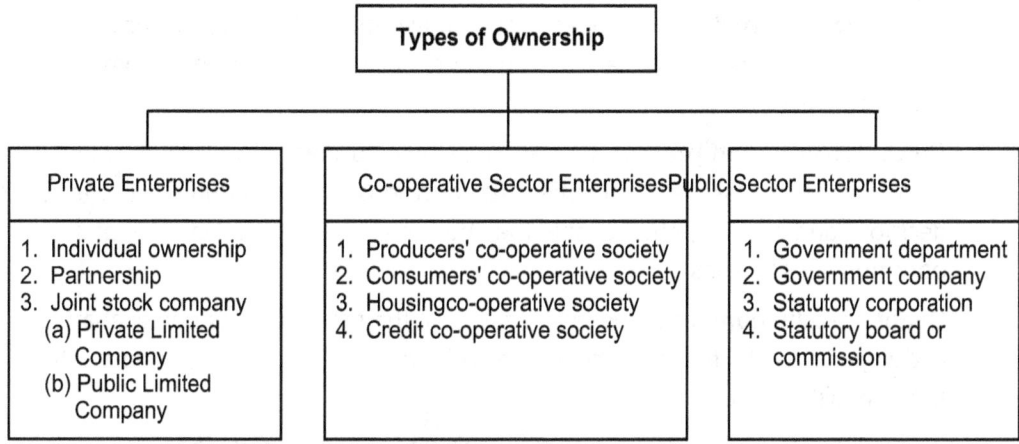

Fig. 3.9: Types of Ownership Organisation

3.9.1 Proprietorship (Individual Ownership)

This is the simplest and oldest form of business organisation.

In this type of enterprise the individual entrepreneur supplies the entire capital (even if he has to borrow). He organizes and manages the business himself, and takes the entire risk. The entire authority and responsibility in the matter of decision-making, policy making and working belongs to him and all profits and losses are of his own. If necessary he can employ some persons to assist him. This type of business can be started by any one having initiative, tact, selling aptitude and little capital to enter into business. It is owned, managed and controlled by only one man, hence it is also called as one man business.

Legal Liability: His legal liability covers all his possessions. The creditor can collect his personal property.

Applications

This form of ownership is most satisfactory in the following cases:

1. For small scale business requiring small capital which can be spared by one man, for example, agriculture, small scale industries, cottage industries, retail trade, handicrafts, professional services, commercial shops etc.
2. Where the risk covered is not too heavy.
3. Where management by one man is possible.
4. Where local market is available.

Advantages

1. **Simple and easy:** This type of ownership is simple in nature and easy to manage. The labour knows for whom they are working and to whom they are accountable.

2. **Least legal formalities:** It does not involve much legal formalities or other complicated procedure to start the business. Only a formal licence from the local authority is necessary.

3. **Quick decisions and prompt actions:** The whole business is controlled by one man, therefore, he can take and implement the decisions quickly and in right time. Quick decisions and prompt action enable the entrepreneur to take advantage of business opportunities for gains.

4. **Quality production:** Since the owner takes all the risks, he gives personal attention and supervision to the products made. This may result in reduction in waste and better quality products.

5. **Better labour relationship:** Since the business is small, the number of workers are less and the owner comes in close contact with the workers. This helps to maintain good employer-employee relationship.

6. **Personal attention to customers:** Since the business is small it is possible to pay personal attention to customers and their requirements and to give them entire satisfactions by overcoming their complaints about the product.

7. **Small capital:** Since capital required is small, talented men of small means can start independent business of their own and earn living.

8. **Maintenance of secrecy:** The individual entrepreneur can easily maintain the secrets of the business as he only know everything of his enterprise.

9. **Incentive:** The direct relationship between efforts and rewards acts as an incentive to the owner to put his best efforts to manage the business efficiently and increase his earning. Self-interest can be a driving force to secure economy and efficiency.

10. **Flexibility:** The individual ownership is highly flexible as it is capable of adjustment to the requirements of changing business conditions.

Disadvantages

1. **Limited capital:** Due to limited capital it is not possible to expand the business even if it is much profitable.

2. **Unlimited liability:** In case the owner is not able to pay the debts, the same can be recovered out of the sale of his business assets and personal property. The individual owner will have to think twice before adopting new and risky ventures, latest and new methods etc. as his private property is constantly in danger of meeting the debts and obligations of his business.

3. **Personal limitations:** The individual owner has to control all the aspects of his business alone. He cannot be expert in all techniques like management, sales,

engineering, processes etc. Further growth and expansion of business may not be possible due to want of proper and adequate organising power.

4. **Small income:** Inspite of all efforts, such a business can yield only a small income. The resources are limited. Many profitable ventures are ruled out.

5. **Cannot compete with a big business:** Since the business is small it cannot compete with a big business producing the same articles.

6. **Short life:** If the owner dies the business may collapse. Because, his successors may be incapable or not interested in this type of business. Disability, prolonged illness or death of owner may result in the business coming to standstill or its closure unless his successors take the interest and ability to run the business.

7. **Division of labour is not possible:** The owner as well as the worker has to perform variety of activities, therefore they cannot be specialized in a particular activity.

8. **No economies of large scale:** Economies of large scale manufacturing, buying and selling cannot be obtained on account of small size organisation.

3.9.2 Partnership Organisation

Sometimes the one man business reaches such a stage of development that it becomes impossible for one man to control the business and to contribute the necessary capital. The original entrepreneur may become too old for work. It would seem essential to take a younger person into a partnership to prevent the firm from decaying. Partnership may also be formed to start a new business altogether. Partnership is usually formed to combine capital, labour and varied specialized skills or abilities.

Partnership business is owned by two or more persons (upto 20) who share the powers, responsibilities and profits according to an agreement reached amongst themselves.

A person may possess exceptional business ability, experience, talent but no capital, he can have a financing partner. A financier may need a managerial expert as well as a technical expert and all of them may combine to set up a business with common ownership and management by mutual agreement to form a partnership business.

According to Indian Partnership Act 1932, Partnership is defined as,

"the relation between two or more persons who have agreed to share profit of a business, carried on by all or any of them acting for all".

Formation

Partnership can be formed either verbally or by written agreement but to avoid the possibility of conflict at a later stage, it is advisable to enter into written agreement. The written agreement is known as "Partnership Deed". The partnership deed contains the terms and condition relating to partnership and the regulations governing its internal management. It also lays down the rights and duties of the partners. The deed is a duly stamped and sealed document containing the terms of contract is also registered in a Court of Law. Thus, a partnership deed enjoys legal status and it serves as legal evidence in future to settle any dispute or differences.

The partnership deed should have the following details:

1. Name of the firm.
2. Nature of business.
3. Date of starting partnership.
4. Duration of partnership.
5. Rate of interest on capital invested, if any
6. Money contributed by each partner.
7. Allotment of managerial functions among the partners.
8. Share of profit and losses.
9. Salary if any allowed to managing partners.
10. The basis for the inclusion of any new partners.
11. The amount which can be withdrawn by each partner.
12. The aim of partnership as well as the manner in which it can be dissolved.
13. Accounts of the firm and authority for signing cheques, bills of exchange, etc.
14. Provision of Arbitration for settling the disputes that may arise in future. In absence of any agreement, profits and losses are shared equally as per the provisions of the Indian Partnership Act, 1932.

The partners have to prepare a statement which will have the following particulars:

1. Name of the firm.
2. Place of business — principal place and branches, if any.
3. Name and addresses of all partners.
4. Date of joining the firm in case of every partner.
5. Duration, if any.

The statement should be duly dated and signed by all partners. It is required to be submitted to the Registrar of Firms along with necessary registration fees. All subsequent changes in the constitution of the partnership incoming and outgoing partners etc. will have to be communicated to the Registrar within 14 days of such alterations.

Types of Partners

1. **General partners:** All the partners who participate in the working of the firm and are responsible jointly with other partner, for all liabilities, obligations and defects of the firm are the general partners.

2. **Limited partners:** The liability for debts of the limited partners is limited to the extent of their contributed capital. They are not entitled to interfere in the administration of the firm.

3. **Active or managing partners:** Active partners are those who take active part in the management and formulation of policies. Sometimes they get salaries in addition to the normal profits as partners.

4. **Sleeping and silent partners:** *They* do not take any active part in the business. They simply contribute their capital in the business and get their share in the profit of the firm. They are liable for all liabilities of the firm as partners.

5. **Nominal partners:** They lend their reputed name for the company's reputation. They do not invest money and do not take any active part in the management.

6. **Minor partners:** Minor partners are those whose age is below 18 years and associated with the business. Such partners can be allowed only with the consent of other partners. Their liability is limited to their investment only. Within six months of attaining the age of majority, they have to give public notice about their desire to serve or continue their connection with the firm. In such a case they will be regarded as full-fledged partner with unlimited liability.

Advantages

1. **Easy formations:** The formation of partnership is easier as compared to joint stock companies. Voluntary mutual agreement is enough to start the partnership. Procedure for registration is simple and also registration is not compulsory.

2. **More capital:** *Two* or more partners combine their resources in partnership, therefore, the amount of capital is larger as compared with individual ownership.

3. **Diverse talent:** In this type of organisation persons possessing different abilities and skills may come together. Persons having good ideas and experience of business make partnership with rich people. Thus money and knowledge both are combined to earn profit.

4. **Less possibility of error of judgement:** A problem is examined from more than one point of view, therefore the decision arrived at is likely to be sounder than in one man business.

5. **Prompt decisions:** There are limited number of partners who are in continuous and intimate touch with each other. Therefore prompt decisions can be taken. It can decide on a suitable course of action before it is too late.

6. **Large economics:** As compared to individual ownership, the advantage of division of labour, specialization, standardization and economics of large purchasing are more.

7. **Personal factor:** Partnership can maintain personal relationship with employees and the customers.

8. **Divisions of labour:** The partners can divide the work among themselves on the basis of their personal capabilities. Therefore they can run the business more efficiently.

9. **Simple dissolution:** The partnership business can be dissolved easily. The partnership is purely voluntary association.

    It can be dissolved by giving 14 days notice to other partners.

10. **Cautious and sound approach:** As the private property of every partner is constantly in danger of meeting all business obligations of the firm, partners will have to think twice before undertaking any highly speculative/risky business.

The unlimited liability can also act as the best security for raising loans or advances because private property of all partners can be used as additional security in addition to the property and assets of partnership organisation.

Disadvantages

1. **Unlimited liability:** Because of unlimited liability any one partner can be held liable for the whole debt of the firm. This frightens away-the moneyed people. They are reluctant to join those who have ability, skill but no capital.

2. **Short life:** After the death or retirement of any one partner, the partnership may come to an end.

3. **Insufficient capital:** It can raise much less capital as compared to joint stock company. This prevents the expansion of the business to take advantage of increased demand.

4. **Disagreement:** Sometimes due to misunderstanding friction may arise between the partners which adversely affects the efficiency and expansion of the business.

5. **Less secrecy:** A partner may withdraw from the firm and establish his own enterprise with the knowledge of the secrets of the business.

6. **Non-transfer of partnership:** No partner can transfer his interest in the firm to any body without the unanimous consent of other partners.
7. **No direct relation between efforts and rewards:** The profits are shared by the partners. So, there is no incentive for hard working. Sometimes it encourages lavish expenditure.
8. **Lack of public confidence:** As the financial matters are strictly confined to partners only, and in absence of any strict legal control over the affairs of partnership, there is much less public confidence in partnership. It creates suspension in the mind of the outsiders who are dealing with firm.

Suitability of Partnership

Partnership is an ideal form of organisation for small scale and medium size business where there is a limited market, limited risk of loss and limited capital and limited specialization in management is needed. Examples are: wholesale trade, retail trade, commercial forming, small scale industries, local enterprises, warehousing, transport services, professional services, marketing services etc.

Distinction between Individual Ownership and Partnership

No.	Parameter	Individual Ownership	Partnership
1.	Membership (One Man Business)	Individual Owner.	Minimum 2, maximum 50.
2.	Requirement for its formation	No agreement is required for its formation.	An agreement (Partnership Deed)
3.	Capital only by the owner	Limited capital contributed by number of partners.	Comparatively large capital.
4.	Registration	Not necessary.	Registration is necessary under the Partnership Act 1932.
5.	Risk/Profit	Individual owner has to bear the risk and enjoys the entire profit.	Risk spread out amongst the partners. Profit is shared according to the agreement between themselves.
6.	Management	Individual owner has to manage the entire business.	The management of the business is shared by the partners.

Contd...

7.	Secrecy	The individual entrepreneur can easily maintain the secrets of the business.	A partner may withdraw from the firm and establish his own enterprise with the knowledge and secrets of business.
8.	Soundness of decisions	An individual owner may not be expert in all aspects of business, hence sometimes his decisions may go wrong.	The problem is examined from more than one point of view, hence decisions arrived are likely to be sounder.
9.	Suitability	Suitable for small scale business.	Suitable for small as well as medium scale business.
10.	Division of labour	Not possible.	The partners divide the work among themselves. Division of labour is thus possible to some extent.

3.9.3 Joint Stock Company

The industrial revolution brought about a radical change in the system of production and commerce. With the introduction of factory system, large-scale organisation and mass scale production came into being. With the change in the scale of production from small scale to large scale and with the widening of the market from local to national and international, the individual ownership and partnership firms with their limited capital, short life span, limited managerial skill and unlimited liability failed to meet needs of the time. This resulted in the evolution of joint stock company. The companies are formed and registered under the Indian Companies Act, 1956.

In this type, capital is contributed by large number of persons, in the form of shares of different values. Persons who purchase the shares are called shareholders and the managing body known as "Board of Directors" is elected by the shareholders. The shares are transferable.

A simple but comprehensive definition of the company can be given as under:

"A company is an artificial person having an independent legal entity and a perpetual succession with a distinctive name and a common seal having a common capital divided into shares of fixed value which are transferable and carry limited liability".

Characteristics of Joint Stock Company

The following are some of the characteristics of joint stock company:

1. A company is created by registering or incorporating an association of persons under the Company Act.
2. It has a separate legal existence as distinct from its members.
3. Artificial personality enabling it to exercise certain legal powers.
4. Perpetual life and a very stable existence.
5. It has a common seal on which its name is engraved and this common seal acts as its signature. It is affixed on all important legal documents and contracts.
6. There is a complete separation of ownership from management.
7. Liability of shareholders is limited.
8. Lower tax liability.
9. Easy transferability of shares.
10. There is a wide distribution of risk of loss.
11. Large membership.
12. Statutory regulations as provided in the Indian Companys' Act, 1956.

Joint Stock Company (Definition)

The joint stock company is legal business owned by the shareholders having limited liability, and managed by an elected "Board of Directors". The most important type of business organisation today is the joint stock company. Infact, a business on respectable scale can be organised only in this manner.

Formation of Joint Stock Company

An entrepreneur (promoter) prepares a scheme of business, he secures the co-operation of at least six more persons, because the minimum number of persons to form a company is seven. The promoters of the company prepare the following document:

(a) Memorandum of Association.
(b) Articles of Association.
(c) A list of persons who have consented to be the Directors of the Company along with the consent in writing of such persons.
(d) A declaration by an advocate to the effect that all the requirements of the Act have been fulfilled.
(e) Name and address of promoters.

The memorandum of association contains
1. The name of the company.
2. Its aims and objectives.
3. The location of head office.
4. The amount of share capital.
5. The kind and value of each share.
6. A declaration that the liability is limited.

Articles of association contains: Rules and regulations governing the internal management of the company. The rights of the shareholders, Duties, Powers of Directors, Regulations regarding rights to vote and issue of capital etc.

These documents are then submitted to the Registrar of joint company. If the Registrar is satisfied that the requirements of the law have been fulfilled, he issues a certificate of incorporation. The company then comes into existence.

Raising Finance: Funds can be taken from banks and finance corporations etc. in the form of loans, or by selling shares and debentures.

Managing the Business: The shareholders elect the directors to manage the business on their behalf. The board of directors only lays down the general policy and discusses major issues. The day-to-day business is carried on by the salaried manager or the Managing Director.

Organisation Structure

The organisation structure of the joint stock company is as follow:

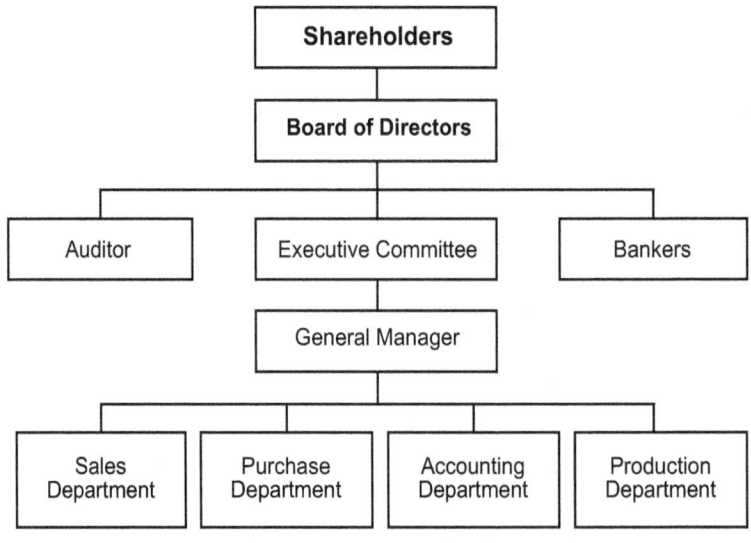

Fig. 3.10: Organisation structure of Joint Stock Company

Types of Joint Stock Company

There are *two* types of Joint Stock company:

1) Private Limited Company, and   2) Public Limited Company.

1) Private Limited Company: This type of company can be formed by two or more members. The maximum number of members is limited to 50 (excluding the employees). The company is registered under the Indian Companys' Act, 1956. In this the transfer of share is limited to members only and general public cannot be invited to purchase shares.

Normally, the members of such company are friends or relatives. In this system persons who want to take the advantage of limited liability and at the same time keep the business as private, forms the private limited company. Most of the middle sized industries are run in this manner.

The company need not circulate the Balance Sheet, Profit and Loss Account etc. among its members; but it should hold its annual general meeting and place such financial statements in the meeting. A private Ltd. Company enjoys a separate legal status, continuity of life, benefit of limited liability, larger capital raising power, business secrecy to certain extent and above all the number of privileges and exemptions (not possible for public company) as per Companies' Act.

2) Public Limited Company: As its name indicates, the membership of public limited company is open to general public. The minimum number of persons required to form a public limited company is seven, but there is no upper limit. Such companies can advertise, to offer its shares to general public. Public limited companies are subjected to greater control and supervision of the Government. This control is necessary to protect the interest of the shareholders and the member of the public. Shares are transferable without any prior approval. The affairs of the company are managed by "Board of Directors".

Advantages *of* Joint Stock Company

1. **Economies of large scale:** Joint stock company can take advantage of internal and external economies in buying and selling, lower overhead charges relating to distribution, publicity and administration, research and experiments etc.
2. **Limited liability:** The shareholders have a limited liability. It is limited only to the value of their shares. In case the company fails the personal property of the shareholders cannot be attached by the creditors.
3. **Huge capital:** The capital of the company is raised by the sale of shares. The value of each share is low, this attracts all sorts of people, rich and poor to invest their capital. Therefore, large amount of capital can be raised.

4. **Share transferable:** When the shareholder needs money he can get it by selling his shares.
5. **Economical administration:** The directors have not to be paid salaries but just a fee for attending the Board meeting. Thus, the company can get advice of persons of mature wisdom and good experience at a small cost.
6. **Democratic:** The directors are elected by shareholders in case the shareholders feel that the directors are not working properly they can be removed and new directors chosen in their places.
7. **Permanent existence:** Any number of shareholders may leave it, but the company continues.
8. **Legal control:** The Government exercises control over working of the company. The object is to prevent fraud and to protect the interest of shareholders and the public at large.
9. **Risk spread out:** There are large number of investors and secondly, an individual investor can buy shares of different companies and thus widely distribute his risk of loss.
10. **Mobilization of scarce saving:** Limited liability, transferability of shares and unlimited membership makes the joint stock company a very effective instrument for mobilization of scarce saving of the society towards industrialization.
11. Accelerated economic growth of the country is possible through industrialization.
12. It creates huge employment possibilities.

Disadvantages of Joint Stock Company
1. **Dishonest directors may exploit the shareholders:** The transferability of shares kills the interest of the shareholders, therefore the directors are all in all, they can deceive the shareholders.
2. **Legal complexities:** Its formation, functioning involves very large legal procedures.
3. **It is democratic in theory only:** Due to small capital of each shareholders, transferability of shares and since the shareholders are from different parts of the country, they do not take active interest in the affairs of the company. Therefore, the real power to run and manage the business is in the hands of the directors. The directors, self elected at first manage to get themselves re-elected.
4. **Delay in decisions:** The Board of Directors manages over affairs of a joint stock company and hence quick decisions are not possible. Moreover, there may be disagreement among directors which may hamper the business.

5. **Favourisms:** The directors may show favourism by selecting their own persons for high posts.
6. **Difficult labour relations:** The owners of company have no personal touch with the employees. There are often labour troubles. Inspite of these disadvantages, business on a large scale can only be started and run successfully in this manner.
7. **Lack of initiative and personal interest:** Lack of personal interest on the part of salaried managers may lead to inefficiency and waste (because there is no direct relation between effort and income for them).
8. Concentration of economic power and wealth in a few hands.
9. **Misuse of internal information:** Misuse of internal information by the managing group in bringing wide fluctuations in the market price of equity shares is possible.

Considering both merits and demerits of the company form of organisation, it can be concluded that in the present day world, this form of business organisation is very essential for the industrial development of a country. In the absence of joint stock principle, the exploration of a country's natural resources and its economic and industrial development would not have been possible.

Liquidation

It becomes difficult to run joint stock company if liability becomes much more than assets and when creditors press for payment of loans. In such circumstances the company has to dissolve of wind up. This is known s liquidation.

Liquidation may be compulsory or voluntary or under the supervision of court. If the resources are not adequate to make the payment, then the assets of the company have to be sold. The amount thus collected is paid to the creditors in proportion of the credit. If some amount is left after payment it is distributed among the shareholders.

Comparison between Private and Public Limited Joint Stock Companies

No.	Particulars	Private Limited Joint Stock Company	Public Limited Joint Stock Company
1.	Membership	The membership is confined to the close friends and relatives of the promoters; they contribute their capital. They cannot invite public to share the capital.	The membership is open to the General Public. Any person interested can contribute and become shareholder.

Contd...

2.	Limits to Membership	The minimum number of member required is two, while the maximum number is limited to 50.	A minimum of 7 members are required to form the company. There is no limit to the maximum number of members.
3.	Election of Directors	There is no need of holding a statutory meeting to elect the director.	The statutory meeting has to be held and the shareholders elect the directors.
4.	Resale of Shares	The shares cannot be resold or transferred without the consent of the company.	The shares cannot be resold or transferred without the consent of the company.
5.	Audit of Accounts	There is no legal provision of the audit of company's account.	The accounts have to be audited legally and circulated among the members of the company.
6.	Minimum Capital	Cart be started with any amount without any legal binding.	Minimum lay-down capital is legally required before starting the business.
7.	Name	It has to use words "Private Limited" at the end of its name.	It has to use only the word 'Limited' at the end of its name.
8.	Number of Directors	It has to have minimum 2 directors.	It has to have minimum 3 directors.
9.	Legal Control	There are less legal controls.	Regulations are more strict.
10.	Remuneration of Directors	Restrictions are less for Directors' Remuneration.	Remuneration of Directors is restricted to 11% of the net profits.

Distinction between Partnership and Joint Stock Company

No.	Partnership	Joint Stock Company
1.	In a partnership firm, the liability of the members is unlimited.	Liability is limited to the value of their share.
2.	Minimum number of partners is 2 and maximum number is 20.	In private limited company, minimum number of shareholders is 2 and maximum number is 50. In public limited company, minimum number of members is 7 and there is no maximum limit.

Contd...

3.	A partnership firm has no separate legal entity.	A joint stock company has a legal existence.
4.	Limited capital.	Large amount of capital can be collected.
5.	It is managed by the partners.	It is managed by the elected board of directors.
6.	The partners cannot transfer his share without the consent of all other partners.	In public limited company the shares are transferable ; but not in private limited company.
7.	It has short life. The partnership may come to an end due to death or retirement of any partner.	It has permanent/perpetual existence.
8.	It can be started very easily. Procedure for registration is simple and moreover registration is not compulsory.	Its formation, functioning involves very large legal procedures.
9.	Selfish attitude among partners may create difficulties in business.	Smooth and efficient management is possible as it works on the democratic principles.
10.	There are no restrictions of keeping detailed accounts and they are not required to be submitted to Government.	It has obligation to keep detailed accounts of business and present the balance sheet and audit report (by some authorized Chartered Accountant) to the Government.
11.	It is governed by the Partnership Act, 1932.	It is governed by the Indian Companies Act of 1956.

3.9.4 Co-operative Organisations (Societies)

Small scale and cottage industries were gradually replaced by large scale industries as a result of Industrial Revolution. The wealth began to concentrate in few hands. It divided the society into two classes – the capitalists and the poor. The capitalists tried to exploit the poor through long working hours, poor wages, bad working conditions etc. Similarly, with the expansion of market from the local to national and international boundaries, there appeared very long chain of middlemen and intermediaters in the channel of distribution, trying to link the primary producer and the ultimate consumer. This created extraordinary differences in the two prices, producers' price and the price at which ultimate customers get the product. The hardship suffered by exploited class compelled it to unite for their economic uplift through self and mutual help. The co-operative movement was evolved. The industrial co-operative and consumers co-operative societies were developed in Germany. Later on it spread all over the other countries of the world.

Definition of Co-operative Organisation

Co-operation is a form of organisation, wherein persons, irrespective of caste, creed and religion, voluntarily associate together, as human beings, on the basis of equality for the fulfilment of their common economic interests.

The International Labour Organisation gave a comprehensive definition of a co-operative organisation as follow:

"A Co-operative organisation is an association of persons, usually of limited means, who have voluntarily joined together to achieve a common economic end through the formation of a democratically controlled organisation, making equitable contributions to the capital required, and accepting a fair share of risks and benefits of the undertaking".

Mr. N. Barrow defined co-operative society as:

"A voluntary organisation of persons with unrestricted membership and collectively own funds. Consisting of wage earners and small producers, united on democratic basis for the establishment of enterprises under joint management for the purpose of improving their household or business economy".

A simple definition can be stated as,

"A co-operative society is a voluntary association of economically weak persons who work for achievement of their common economic objectives on the basis of equality and mutual service.

The definitions given above clearly illustrate the distinctive characteristics of the principles of co-operative organisation.

Thus, if we have (i) Common need, (ii) Its full realization by all, and (iii) Willingness to seek the common objective by joint action, the only method is co-operation. Co-operative spirit is the heart of a co-operative society. "Each shall work for all and all for each" is the motto of co-operation.

The members supply the capital, manage the business and share all profits and losses. The main object of co-operative society is to promote self help and mutual assistance among men of moderate means and income, having needs and interest in common. Such men are industrial workers, small artisans, agriculturists and members of middle class.

Mutual trust, mutual supervision, self-reliance, spontaneity and equality are the five pillars of a co-operative organisation and co-operative spirit is the backbone.

Distinctive Features/Characteristics of Co-operative Organisation

Main characteristics of co-operative organisation are as follows

1. **Voluntary organisations:** Co-operative society is a voluntary organisation. A member can continue his membership as long as he desires and can withdraw his capital and discontinue his membership by giving a notice.

2. **Open membership:** There is no limit to its members. Membership is open to all adults, whether man or woman, rich or poor without any distinction of caste, creed and religion. Value of each share is quite less which a poor can also afford.

3. **Economic and democratic management:** The management is based on democratic lines of equality. Every member can cast only one vote irrespective of the number of shares he may hold. A man having only one share can become the president of the cooperative organisation. Generally, the management is honorary.

4. **Profit is not important:** The objective of co-operative society is to promote self-help and mutual assistance and thus to serve the members and not to earn profit.

5. **Spirit of co-operation:** Under co-operative service is of primary importance and self-interest is of secondary importance. "Each for all and all for each" is the moto of co-operative organisation.

6. **Unity:** Unity of joint action is the basis of co-operation.

7. **Common interest:** The members come together to fulfil their common interest. It may be a social or economic activity such as agriculture trade, finance, manufacturing etc.

8. **Co-operative status:** A co-operative society has to be registered under separate legislation. It gives a separate legal status and certain exemptions and privileges under the act.

Aims and Objectives of Industrial Co-operatives

As already described the main objective of co-operative society is to promote self-help and mutual assistance and fulfil their common economic interest. However, some of the objectives of industrial co-operatives may be as follow

1. To purchase and supply raw-materials, tools and equipment to members.
2. To secure contracts and execute them with the help of members.
3. To market the finished goods of members.
4. To purchase machinery for giving on hire to members.
5. To borrow funds from members and non-members.

6. To grant loans and advances to members on the security of raw-materials and finished goods belonging to them.

7. To undertake all such activities as are conductive or incidental to the accomplishment of the aforesaid objectives and secure material and social progress of all members.

8. From the social point of view, the industrial co-operatives are expected to safeguard the interest of the poorer sections of community against exploitation by the capitalists and lead to equitable distribution of wealth and income.

Formation of Co-operative Societies

In our country there is a special legislation governing the registration, working and management of co-operative organisations. To start a co-operative society an application is submitted to the Registrar of Co-operative Societies. The application for registration should provide all essential information e.g., name and address of the society, its aims and objectives, particulars of share capital etc. The application should be signed by at least 10 members. The application should accompany duplicate copies of By laws, i.e., rules and regulations governing the internal organisation and management of the society. The Registrar after the scrutiny of the application, if satisfied with the soundness will issue a certificate of registration and the society will be formed. Once the society is duly registered, it can admit new members and also issue it shares.

The various types of Co-operative Societies are

- Consumers' Co-operative Society
- Producers' Co-operative Society
- Housing Co-operative Society
- Credit Co-operative Society, etc.

1. Producers' Co-operative Society: In this form of co-operative, the workers wish to be their own masters the business is owned by them. They elect their own managers. They are their own employees. The profit instead of enriching the few individuals, goes to the actual workers. The workers are supposed to put in very hard work. There are no strikes and lock-outs. It prevents the workers from being exploited; and teaches them how to work in team spirit.

This type of ownership is suitable where large capital and much technical and expert knowledge is not needed.

Examples: Agricultural and cottage industries.

Shortcomings

(i) Inadequate capital.

(ii) Inefficient management.

(iii) Lack of discipline.

2. Consumers' Co-operative Society: The consumers living in a particular area combine together. Each contributes a small capital. A store is opened in which articles of common use are stocked and sold at reasonable prices. Such co-operative stores are found in many colleges and schools in India.

Advantages

1. Much capital is not needed.
2. The management is simple and honorary.
3. There is legal control and inspection.

Disadvantages

1. They offer very little selection for customers.
2. The honorary office bearers do not take much pains, they are sometimes dishonest.

3. Housing Co-operative Society: Housing Co-operative Societies are formed for the purpose of getting plots or constructing houses for the needy persons, Government provides great facilities (providing loans at low rate of interest etc.) for this purpose.

4. Co-operative Credit Society: Its object is to finance the poor cultivators by providing loans at low rate of interest for the development of land, purchase of agricultural machinery, fertilizers etc.

A credit co-operative society may be formed by persons working in the same organisation to provide loans to the members in case of financial difficulties or for purchasing necessities of their life such as cloth, wheat etc.

In general, the advantages and disadvantages of the co-operative organisation are as follows:

Advantages of Co-operative Societies

1. Co-operative societies protect the interest of the weaker section of the community as under: (a) Provide better methods and tools of production to small manufacturers and craftsmen. (b) Help the farmers in farming and marketing their products efficiently. (c) Provide financial assistance at moderate rate of interest. (d) Opening super bazaar types of stores gives relief to the weaker section of the society and helps in establishing price level.

2. **Elimination of middleman:** The commodities are purchased directly from the manufacturers and supplied to the members. It thus eliminates the profit of middleman; and the goods can be sold at cheaper rates.

3. **Services motive:** The co-operative sector is based on service motive and therefore, there is no question of profit making, black marketing etc.

4. **Democratic nature:** Its management is democratic, elected by shareholders.

5. **Sense of co-operation:** It promotes a sense of co-operation among the members and also among the people of the locality. Thus it serves the social purpose also.

6. **Socially neglected class:** Provides occupation and means of earning to socially neglected class like widows, physically handicapped or poor section of the community.

Disadvantages of Co-operative Societies

1. **Lack of co-ordination:** It may suffer due to lack of co-ordination between various members. Conflict may arise in sharing of duties and responsibilities and also in sharing produce and profit.

2. **Chances of undue advantages:** Some of the forceful members sometimes try to take undue advantages and succeed in it.

3. **Favourism:** The executive committee and the employees favour their friends and relatives at the cost of other members.

4. **Limited capital:** Co-operatives are generally association of low income group people. They cannot finance expanding business.

5. **Inefficient management:** The lack of educated and trained persons practically in villages badly affect the successful working of the Co-operative Organisation.

6. **Political influence:** Many a time co-operatives are exploited by the politicians for their selfish gains.

Distinction between Co-operative and Joint Stock Company

No.	Parameters	Co-operative	Joint Stock Company
1.	Formation	Under Co-operative Society Act. Minimum member 10.	Under companies Act. Minimum members 2 for Private Ltd. and 7 for Public Ltd.

Contd...

2.	Fundamental Principles	Spirit of co-operation. Promote self help and mutual assistance among members. Unity of purpose. Community interest. Socialist bias.	Spirit of competition. No need for unity of purpose capitalistic bias. Large number of shareholders.
3.	Membership	Generally local or regional territory (from limited area).	Wide spread membership.
4.	Capital	Limited	Large capital.
5.	Transfer of shares	A member can withdraw his share capital, shares are not transferable.	Shares are transferable.
6.	Liability	Limited	Limited
7.	Distribution of Profit	Maximum dividends of shares 12 p.c. Its main purpose is to serve members profit is not important.	No limit on dividend. Profit motive.
8.	Privileges	Govt. gives special privileges to encourage co-operative movement.	No such special privileges on the other hand Govt. exercises strict legal control.
9.	Management	Democratic with equal voting rights ("One Man One Vote").	Democratic unequal voting right ("One Share One Vote").
10.	Contact	Members are generally known to each other they come together to fulfil their common need.	Shareholders have no contact with each other they invest money to earn profit.
11.	Life	Short. It may be dissolved if the common need is fulfilled, members lost their interest.	Perpetual or permanent existence.

Distinction between Private Sector and Public Sector

No.	Private Sector	Public Sector
1.	The main objective of private sector is to earn more and more profit. It benefits only the owners.	Social benefit is of primary importance while profit motive is given secondary importance.
2.	The enterprise is owned and managed by individual or a group of individual.	It is owned and managed by the Central or State Government.
3.	There is a limit to the capital which can be raised by private sector.	Govt. has ample funds and can borrow more if needed, in the money market at lower rate. Hence large amount of capital be collected.
4.	It causes concentration of wealth in the hands of few capitalists.	It leads to equitable distribution of wealth and income. Profit is utilized for the welfare of the notion.
5.	Private sector has to face competition in the market.	There is absence of competition generally the projects undertaken needs huge capital and private sector is not attracted to them.
6.	Private Sector dominates in the production of consumer goods.	It generally dominates in the production of producer goods.
7.	There are chances of exploitation of general] public (workers and consumers).	Public sector enterprises are subjected to greater control and it helps to protect the people from exploitation.
8.	Private sector does not undertake risky ventures or those having low profit margin.	It helps in the growth of industries which require huge capital but useful for the welfare of the nation even though profit margin is less.
9.	Private sector leads to.unbalanced growth of industries.	Public sector encourages industrial growth of under-developed regions in the country.
10.	Wastage of material and labour is minimum.	Public sector can rarely attain the efficiency of private sector; wastage and inefficiency can seldom be reduced to minimum.

3.9.5 Public Sector Organisations

Faster and planned economic development cannot be fulfilled by private sector alone. Hence, the public sector has to play a key role to accomplish quick industrialization and rising standard of lining of the people through developing key and basic industries, e.g., Iron and steel industries, aircraft, defence industries, fertilizer industries etc. In our country, the expansion of the public sector was in accordance with Industrial Policy Resolution, 1948 and 1956 and as per the directives of our Five-Year Economic Plans.

The objectives of public sector enterprises can be stated as

1. Equitable distribution of wealth and income.
2. Balanced economic development through dispersal of industrial location.
3. Adequate employment opportunities.
4. Speedy agricultural and industrial development without the growth of monopolies.
5. Self-sufficiency of the nation modern technology and managerial skills so that in due course our country need not depend on foreign collaboration in capital technology, skill etc.

Public sector includes:

(i) State Enterprise (Government Sector) and

(ii) Public Corporations.

Government Undertaking (State Ownership)

Private ownership causes accumulation of wealth in the hands of few capitalists. These dominate motive to earn more and more profit has led to economic unbalance and neglect of the well being of workers and welfare of community as a whole. The exploitation by the capitalists increased the gap between richer and poorer. The monopolistic tendencies of the Private ownership necessitated the State's participation in trade and industrial fields.

The State ownership are the business organisations which are owned, managed and run by the Government or local bodies like municipality, district board etc. This is generally done in the case of public utility services like gas, electricity, water supply, bus, railways navigation etc. The railways, post and telegraph are completely owned by Central Government. Some other industries such as ship building, steel industry, electricity generation, railway engine manufacture etc. are owned the Government and also by joint stock companies.

The Government either starts or nationalizes certain industries to prevent economic imbalance in the nation. The social benefit is of primary importance while profit motive is given a secondary consideration.

Advantages

1. Profits go to the Government, and are utilized for the benefit of the society at large. Nation building departments can be liberally financed from the increased resources.
2. Purity of supply is guaranteed. There is no incentive for adulteration for a Government undertaking as there is for private business.
3. Government has ample funds and can borrow more, if needed, in the money market at low rates. This would lower the cost of production.
4. The best talent is attached towards Government service. The Government can, therefore, engage superior staff. The business, therefore, will run better.
5. Government can afford to wait long for an enterprise to yield profit. Big business ventures like iron and steel works, heavy electricals, defence projects can be started.
6. Consumer's interests are properly safeguarded.
7. Government enterprise is subjected to greater control. Public cannot be exploited for long.

Disadvantages

1. Government Officer behaves like a big boss, and a respectable citizen receives no courtesy.
2. The Government servant has not the same incentive to do the best as a man in private service. In government service promotion is by seniority, and not by merit. Therefore Government servants do not work hard.
3. Frequent transfers of Government servants are harmful to the success of the enterprise. There is no continuity of policy.
4. The Government business is all routine and there is little initiative. Economic progress is therefore slow.
5. There is little check on extravagance and inefficiency. There are no shareholders to question the directors in the annual meeting.

In under-developed countries, the public sector (i.e., State enterprise) has to play an increasingly expanding role. It has a special role to play in creating an infra-structure of social overhead capital like means of transport, communications etc. These projects need huge capital, but since they are not productive in the narrow sense private sector is not attracted to them. But they are of vital importance to the development of the economy hence they have to be undertaken by the State. Therefore state enterprise assumes special importance in an under-developed or developing economy.

Event in the sphere reserved for the private sector, the state can step in, if the private sector is not showing sufficient progress as required by the countries needs. There is also a wide field in which both private and public sector can start enterprise. This policy is being given effect to by the Indian Five Years Plans.

Public Corporation

A public corporation is a body created by a Law of Parliament with its powers, duties and liabilities defined in the written law. Public corporations try to combine the public interest of the Government body and the autonomous management of the public sector. These corporations have no profit motive and work for the sake of social welfare.

The main characteristics of the public corporation are

(i) It is created, by the separate act passed by the Parliament or State Legislative Assembly.

(ii) It is owned by the Government – either Central, State and or local bodies.

(iii) It is managed by the board of directors nominated by the Government.

(iv) It enjoys complete internal autonomy and is free from parliamentary or political control in the internal and routine management.

(v) It enjoys financial freedom and can raise financial resources independently. It has not to depend on budget appropriations. It has borrowing power. Its bond issue is guaranteed by Government.

(vi) The employees of the public corporation are not treated as the Civil servants of the Government. The corporation is empowered to follow its own personal polices for recruitment, training, transfer and promotion.

(vii) Its primary objective is to serve the public interest an hence it is accountable to the Parliament for its policy decisions and the resultant functioning.

Public corporation is the best mechanism through which large public enterprise can be administered. Based on the principle of maximum autonomy, consistent with public accountability, eliminating bureaucracy it has introduced public service into community ownership.

Limitations/Disadvantages of Public Corporations

1. It is suitable only for the management of very big enterprises.
2. It needs special legislation and hence its formation is elaborate an time consuming.
3. It is a rigid form of organisation as any change in its constitution will require amendment of the special act.
4. The autonomy of the corporations are only on paper. In reality the Ministers, Government Officers and Politicians interfere in the working of such corporations.
5. Public corporations possess monopoly and in the absence of competition, these are not interested in adopting new techniques and making improvements in their working.

At present, Insurance, Finance, Industry, Mining, Transport and Trade in many countries are carried on through public corporation.

Examples of Public Corporation are: Air India, Food Corporation of India, Oil and Natural gas Corporation, Road Transport Corporation, Financial Corporation, Industrial Development Corporation, Electricity Board, Damodar Valley Corporation etc.

Developing countries welcome and encourage formation of joint venture to import capital, skill and technology in order to achieve quick industrialization and economic development.

To prevent exploitation by multinational partner the terms and conditions of collaboration agreements are subjected to Government scrutiny and approval. Foreign Exchange Regulation Act 1973, exercises rigid control over joint ventures of all, multinational companies. Joint venture helps to remove technological gaps and deficiencies.

At the end of 1985 there were 208 Indian Joint Ventures abroad of which 156 were in operation and 52 at different stages of implementation.

QUESTIONS

1. Define organisation. Explain the importance of organisation in an industry.
2. Name and describe the various principles of organisation.
3. Describe the various steps in organisation.
4. Define organisation. Describe the principles of organisation.
5. State the advantages of good organisation.

6. Name the various types of organisation structure. Describe any one of them in brief.
7. Describe functional organisation with its advantages and limitations.
8. Describe Line any Staff organisation with its merits and demerits.
9. Describe matrix organisation with its merits and demerits.
10. Differentiate between "Line organisation" and "Functional organisation".
11. Define 'Departmentation'. Explain its need in industries.
12. State the benefits of departmentation.
13. Name the various methods of departmentation. State the advantages of departmentation by Function.
14. Differentiate between "Centralization" and "Decentralization" and state the benefits of Centralization.
15. Describe the principles of effective delegation.
16. Describe the following principles of organisation.
    (i) Balance
    (ii) Stability
    (iii) Flexibility
    (iv) Span of control.
17. Define communication. State the essentials of communications.
18. Differentiate between Authority and Responsibility.
19. Name the various forms of ownership organisation. State the factors to be considered before deciding the form of ownership to be started.
20. Describe 'Individual Ownership' with its advantages and limitations.
21. Compare Proprietorship with Partnership Organisation.
22. Describe Partnership organisation with its merits and demerits.
23. Define 'Partnership deed'. State its contents.
24. Describe the procedure to be adopted for starting Partnership.
25. State the characteristics of 'Joint Stock Company' responsible for making it the most important type of ownership of industrial organisation.
26. What is meant by 'Joint Stock Company' ? Describe briefly the procedure for forming 'Joint Stock Company'.

27. Differentiate between 'Private Limited Company' and 'Public Limited Company'. Explain the following with reference to Joint Stock Company.

   (i) Formation of Joint Stock Company.

   (ii) Liquidation.

   (iii) Characteristics of Joint Stock Company.

28. Distinguish between 'Partnership' and 'Joint Stock Company'.

29. Define Partnership, describe the different types of partners.

UNIT IV

HUMAN RESOURCE MANAGEMENT

4.1 Personal Management

Introduction

In all business organisations, there is one common element i.e. human resources. People working in the organisation is one of the most important inputs. However technically sophisticated and automated an industry may be, it cannot be denied that it is the human brain which designs, creates and maintains it. It is the human being only who can extract work from other resources (machines, equipments etc.), create perfect environment for the human minds to function effectively. The efficiency and effectiveness of any organisation is determined by the performance of the people working at all levels in the organisation. Performance is determined by several factors, most important of them are ability to perform and willingness to perform.

Because of unique importance of human resources and its complexity due to everchanging psychology, behaviour and attitudes of men and women at work, personnel management has acquired a new dimension in to day's business organisations.

Personnel management is one of the specialized functions necessary for the effective utilization of human resources. It is an extension of general management, that of promoting and stimulating every employee to make his fullest contribution to achieve the objectives of the business. It is also called as Personnel Administration or manpower management.

Definitions

The important definitions of personnel management are given below

It is that part of the total management of an organisation which specifically deals with human resources in respect of:

(i) their procurement (ii) their development in terms of skills, knowledge and attitude (iii) their motivation towards the attainment of organisational objectives by creating and maintaining an organisational climate conducive to such development.

According to Professor *Michael Jucius* "Personnel management is that field of management which has to do with planning, organising and controlling various operative functions of procuring, developing, maintaining and utilising a labour force in such a way that:

(a) The objectives for which the company is established are attained economically and effectively.

(b) Objectives of all levels of personnel are served to the highest possible degree.

(c) Objectives of the community are duly considered and served."

According to *Edwin B. Flippo* "Personnel management is the planning, organising, directing and controlling of the procurement, development, compensation, integration and maintenance of personnel of an organisation for the purpose of contributing towards the accomplishment of the organisational, individual and social goals.

In a sense, management is personnel administration. It is the development of people and not merely direction of material resources. If we define the term MANAGEMENT as to MANAGE-MEN-T-ACTFULLY, the importance of the management of human resource becomes quite clear.

Personnel management is the direction and co-ordination of human relations in the business organisation, thereby obtaining maximum production with minimum of physical and mental effort, stress and strain on the individual workers and groups of workers and without sacrificing the genuine well-being of the employees.

4.1.1 Aims or Objectives of Personnel Management

(i) Personnel management aims at getting the best out of the people by winning and maintaining their whole-hearted collaboration.

(ii) Its objective is to attain maximum individual development, desirable work atmosphere and inter-personnel relations and effective moulding of human resources as contrasted with physical resources.

(iii) The essence of personnel management is the understanding of people at work (human factor in industry) and on the basis of this knowledge, formulating policies of the enterprise.

(iv) It also aims at improving the service rendered by the enterprise to society through building better employee morale and motivation, that leads to more efficient individual and group performance.

(v) To establish in the minds of those connected with the enterprise employees, shareholders, creditors, customers and the public at large, the fact that the enterprise is rendering the best service of which it is capable and distributing the benefits derived there from fairly in the light of the relative contributions of each to the success of the enterprise.

4.1.2 Functions/Scope of Personnel Management

The subject-matter of personnel management is human being. The more profit could be obtained by controlling the men in industries. Pointing out to this fact a famous American industrialist has stated that, "We do not manufacture automobiles, aeroplanes, refrigerators, radios or shoes but we manufacture men and they in turn manufacture the goods".

The scope of personnel management involves obtaining and maintaining an efficient work-force as a means of achieving profitable production of goods and services. "Obtaining" means such activities as selection, recruitment and employment of personnel, and testing their aptitudes and capabilities.

"Maintaining" implies employee's satisfaction with respect to wages, hours, working conditions, employee's benefits, health and safety, and day-to day relations and, the term "Efficient"denotes the necessity for proper placement and training and high job performance as well as job satisfaction for the individual employee.

Personnel Management (Human Resource Management) is thus a managerial activity involving advisory, executive, and administrative responsibilities and functions as given below:

1. **Development of a personnel policy:** The personal policies serve as a guide to the executives, managers to discharge their duties and responsibilities related to personnel administration. The personal manager has specialized education and training in managing human relations. He advises the top management in formulation and evaluation of personnel programmes, policies and procedures. He also gives advice to the departmental heads for achieving and maintaining good human relations and high employee moral.

2. **Manpower planning:** Ascertaining the requirements of human resources in the light of organisational goals.

3. **Organising:** Once the personal manager has established objectives and developed plans and programmes to reach them, he must design and develop organisational structure to carry out the various operations.

4. Recruitment and selection of manpower, attracting, selecting and employing suitable individuals.

5. Carry out job analysis, description and valuation of the work.

6. **Keeping personnel records:** Personnel department maintains the records of the employees working in an enterprise. It keeps full record of their training, achievements, transfer, promotion, labour turnover etc.

7. **Motivation:** The personnel manager helps the various departmental managers to design a system of financial and non-financial records to motivate the employees.

    Designing schemes of appraisal of the work and informing the employees about their accomplishments and failures to facilitate their development.

8. Maintenance of working conditions and welfare of the employees. Working conditions certainly influence the motivation and morale of employees.

9. Maintenance of safety programmes.

10. Training and development of manpower.

11. Wages and salary administration.

12. Collective bargaining i.e. negotiations with trade unions and maintaining and industrial relations.

13. Employee grievance handling i.e. labour relations.

14. Promotion, transfers and retirement of employees etc.

4.2 STAFFING

Staffing is the process of acquiring, developing, employing, appraising, remunerating and retaining people so that right type of people are available at right positions and at right time in the organisation.

Within each function there are various sub-functions. For example, acquiring personnel involves human resources planning, job analysis, recruitment and selection.

Thus, staffing covers wide range of activities through which organisational positions created through organising process are kept filled.

4.2.1 Importance of Staffing

Human resources of an organisation are considered as the most vital assets because it is the people who make other resources moving. They perform various activities in the organisation in different functional areas like production, marketing, finance, R & D etc.

A growing number of managers in India and abroad have begun to recognize that fundamental basis of competition has began to change. The scare resource, and primary source of competitive advantage is no longer physical or financial capital, but human capital.

Human resource plays an important role in organisational effectiveness and development in the competitive age. Hence, it is necessary for the companies to strengthen their staffing function.

The importance of staffing can be realised in the following context.

1. Filling Organisational Positions: A basic problem being faced by organisations throughout the world is the acute shortage for good quality human resources with increasing competition for human resources, the cost of acquiring them has increased. In our country, there is abundant supply of unskilled labour but acute shortage of good quality managerial and technical personnel. In such a situation, there is a need for systematic staffing so that organisation can fill its various resources with personnel of good quality.

2. Developing competencies: It is not sufficient that various organisational positions are filled but there should be development of competencies among personnel becasue of changing job profile due to technological developments. Therefore, there is a need for developing competencies among personnel on continuous basis. In addition to develop specific skills, it is also necessary to develop differential competencies and multiskill to make the employees competent to face the growing challanges in the business world. Newer training and development techniques are employed for this purpose.

3. Retaining Personnel: Apart from acquiring and developing personnel, retaining them in the organisation is equally important. Employee turnover particularly at the managerial level is a big problem. Particularly, IT industry has one of the highest turnover, with employees constantly looking for more money and opportunities abroad.

In order to retain their employees, organisations are adopting many methods having long-term implications besides persuading their employees and remain with them.

4.2.2 Factors Affecting Staffing

Staffing is basically a dynamic process and is affected by a variety of factors, both external and internal.

External factors:
1. Nature of competition for human resources
2. Legal factors
3. Socio-cultural factors
4. External influences etc.

Internal factors:
1. Organisational business plan
2. Size of organisation
3. Organisational image
4. Past practices etc.

(A) External Factors:

1. Nature of competition for human resources: It determines the organisational approach towards its staffing policies to a great extent. increased competition for management talent and skilled persons has forced many companies to amend their policies for attracting, developing and retaining these talents.

2. Legal factors: The various legal provisions affect the staffing policy. For example, restrictions to free recruitment of child labour (Prohibition and Regulation) Act, 1980, Employment Exchange (Compulsory Notification of Vacancies) Act, 1959, the Apprentices Act, 1961, the Factories Act. etc.

In addition to this, provisions regarding mandatory employment of certain categories of personnel such as scheduled caste/tribes, OBC, etc. affect staffing policy of an organisation more particularly public sector.

3. Socio-cultural factors: For example, our socio-cultural factors almost prevent the employment of women in certain manufacturing operations such as those involving physical exertion.

4. External influences: There are various forces which exerts pressure on employing organisations. For example, political pressure, pressure from the community to which the promoters of the organisation belong, pressure from business contacts, trade unions etc.

(B) Internal Factors:

1. Organisational business plan, future expansions: Organisational business plan directly affects staffing function because, it determines the type of personnel that may be required in future.

A growing organisation undertakes various new projects either in the same line of business or different business. Such an organisation requires more personnel in future in addition to maintaining its existing personnel. Such organisations attract personnel by offering higher remuneration and financial incentives.

A stagnating organisation focuses more on retaining its present personnel by offering them suitable rewards and financial incentices.

An declining organisation offers voluntary retirement scheme and pays below average financial incentives in order to control cost.

2. Size of organisation: A small organisation may not be able to attract highly talented personnel. They try to retain existing personnel by offering rewards and other facilities.

3. Organisational image: It is an important factor for attracting personnel for selection. Organisational image depends upon the facilities for training and development chanches of promotion, compensation and incentives and work culture.

4. Past practices: Post practices relating to staffing adopted by an organisation have their impact on the future practices. Therefore, there is consistency in these practices over the period of time.

4.3 INTRODUCTION TO HUMAN RESOURCES PLANNING (MANPOWER PLANNING)

Manpower planning is a very important part of the overall planning of a business organisation. It is obvious that a business cannot prosper, unless the right number of employees, having required skills, talents and qualifications is available at right time. Manpower planning is done to fulfill the two main objectives, namely:

(i) To utilize the present employees fully, and

(ii) To fill up future manpower requirements.

The fulfillment of these two objectives is absolutely necessary for the success and survival of any business organisation. Manpower planning is a continuous, dynamic process and manpower assessment should be done every year and revised periodically at fixed interval, keeping in view the yearly manufacturing programme. For effective manpower planning, it is necessary to carry out job analysis.

4.4 HUMAN RESOURCES PLANNING PROCESS

Human resources planning is a process and it proceeds through various interrelated activities as follows:

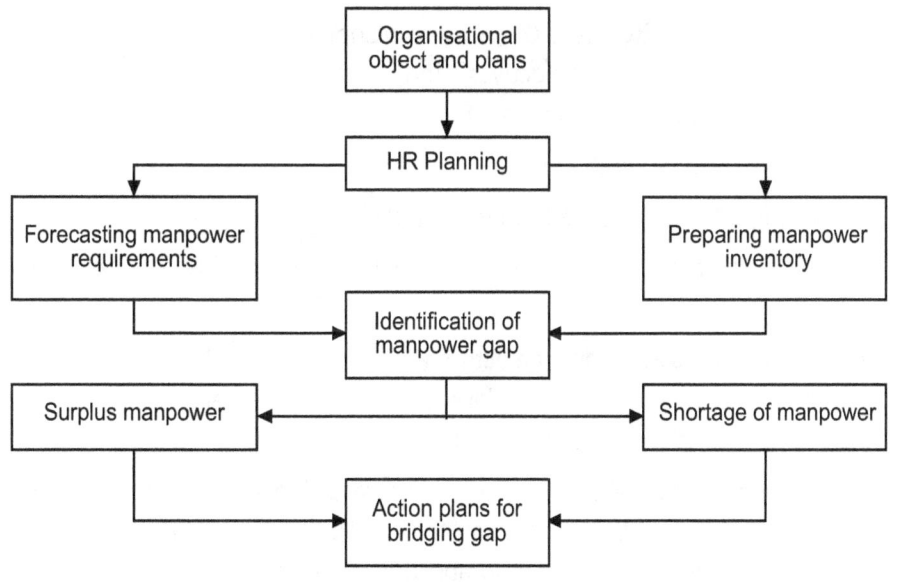

Fig. 4.1: HR planning process

Thus, HR planning involves forecasting manpower requirement, preparing manpower inventory to assess the internal supply of manpower, identification of manpower gap which may be in the form of either surplus manpower or shortage of manpower, and designing action plans for bridging this gap.

Definitions:

Manpower planning may be defined as, the scientific process of allocating the right number of right men to be required in future, at right time on the right job.

According to *E.B. Geisler*, "Manpower planning is the process including forecasting, developing and controlling, by which, a firm ensures that it has the right number of people and right kind of people at the right places, at the right time, doing work for which they are economically most useful".

According to *James J. Lynch*, "Manpower planning is the integration of manpower policies, practices and procedures, so as to achieve the right number of the right people in the right jobs at the right time".

According to *Dale S. Beach*, "Human resource planning is a process of determining and assuring, that the organisation will have an adequate number of qualified persons, available at the proper times, performing jobs which meet the needs of enterprise and which provide satisfaction for the individuals involved".

4.3.1 Steps in Manpower Planning

Manpower planning involves the following steps:

1. **Understanding the Business Objectives:** Manpower planning should start with the study of the basic company objectives and strategies, such as, growth through diversification/expansion/merger/takeover etc. This would indicate:

   (i) The new activities required to be undertaken.

   (ii) The existing activities required to be deleted.

   (iii) Changes/modifications in the existing activities in view of technological and other changes.

2. **Identification of Tasks:** Once the activities are ascertained, the specific tasks required to be performed at each organisational level should be identified. Identification of tasks would indicate the type of knowledge and skills required.

3. **Manpower Forecast:** Manpower demand forecasting at micro-level, could be done in either of the two ways, i.e. by ascertaining the total number and kind of people needed for the entire enterprise for a given period and then estimating requirements of each unit,

division or department, or alternatively, first determine the manpower requirement of each department and subsequently make a total projection. While estimating manpower requirements, it is necessary to consider the vacancies on account of retirements, resignations, deaths, dismissal etc.

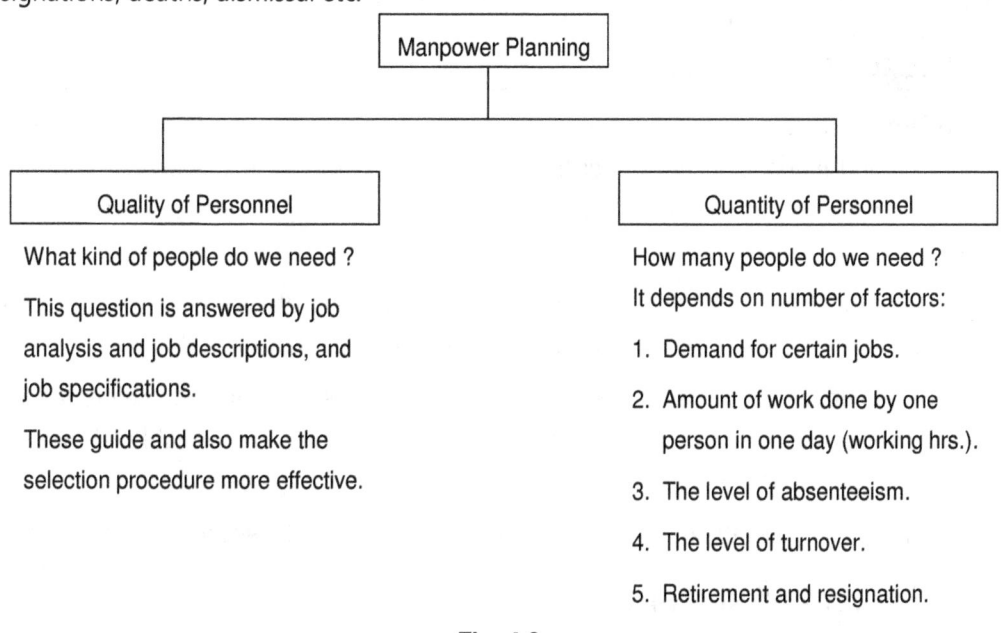

Fig. 4.2

4. **Job Analysis:** To decide the quality (kind of personnel needed it is necessary to carry out detailed analysis of various skills required to do the jobs and to spell out the duties and responsibilities associated with job i.e. job description and job specification). This will enable to determine the education, professional qualifications and the work experience required on the part of the personnel for specific jobs.

5. **Reviewing the Existing Manpower (Manpower Inventory):** A catalogue of present manpower incorporating their educational and professional qualifications, work experience, personal background, assignment handled, training received etc. should be maintained by the personnel department. The purpose of such manpower inventory is to know the number and quality of personnel available from within the organisation to fill up vacancies in various positions. The vacancies which cannot be filled through internal sources, indicate the shortfall.

6. **Anticipating the Availability of Manpower from External Sources:** The vacancies may be filled, partly by promotion from within, (internal sources) and partly by recruiting from outside sources. Assessment of labour market situation tells us the availability of the required manpower to be employed, through advertisement, recruitment and selection.

6. Manpower Management: Planning scientific recruitment, selection, training, development, utilisation, transfer, promotion, motivation, compensation etc. to ensure that future manpower needs are met. Thus, manpower planning covers forecasting future manpower needs and developing manpower plans for implementation.

4.5 RECRUITMENT PROCEDURE

Modern industries are in greater need of skilled workers, administrative, technical, supervisory and managerial personnel than in the past. Once the manpower requirements are estimated, the next step is to attract interested, competent applicants and then choosing the best of these for the available jobs.

According to *Edwin B. Flippo*, "Recruitment is the process of searching for prospective employees and stimulating them to apply for jobs in the organisation".

According to *Dales S. Beach*, "Recruitment is the development and maintenance of adequate manpower resources. It involves the creation of a pool of available labour upon whom the organisation can depend, when it needs additional employees".

Recruitment enables the management to select suitable employees for different jobs.

4.5.1 Sources of Recruitment

The sources of manpower supply for different categories of workers (unskilled, semi-skilled and highly skilled) can be broadly classified as:

(i) Internal i.e. recruitment from within the industry.

(ii) External i.e. recruitment from outside.

(i) Internal Sources of Recruitment

Many a time, just the right kind of employees are available in the organisation itself, either by promotion or from company's training schemes. Usually, announcements are made within the organisation about a vacancy and applications are invited for recruitment.

The employees may be transferred from one job to another. At the time of transfer, it should be ensured that the employee to be transferred to the new job, is capable of performing it. In fact, transfer does not involve any drastic change in the responsibilities and status of the employee.

The employees may be promoted to higher position carrying higher responsibilities, status and pay. This method is very much favourable with workers, because it provides them chance to develop financially and socially.

Advantages of Recruitment from Internal Sources:

1. This method creates a goodwill of the employees towards the industry. This helps to built up loyalty among employees to the organisation.
2. The employees promoted are fully aware of existing environments and can rapidly adjust themselves in their new positions as compared to those employed from outside. This reduces the period of induction training.
3. This method is less time-consuming.
4. Reliable information on the candidate's past work experience and background.
5. Reduces labour turnover and creates a sense of security amongst the workers.

Disadvantages of Recruitment from Internal Sources:

1. Pre-conceived ideas and prejudices may hinder the performance on the job.
2. Some of the employees who are not promoted are likely to be unhappy and employees at large may consider recruitment decision as unfair.
3. Inflow of new blood for new ideas may not be possible.
4. There is a limited choice for promotion to higher posts.
5. It may not be possible to find required talent, skill from within the organisation.

(ii) External Sources of Recruitment

1. Former Employees: Sometimes, certain persons leave the industry on their own accord or are retrenched. These persons, if ready to return, may be employed on the basis of the former record of their service.

2 Recommendations: Applicants introduced by friends and relatives may prove to be a good source of recruitment. Many employers prefer to take such persons because when the present employer recommends a person, a type of preliminary screening takes place. (Something about their background is known). But, in case the recommended applicants are rejected it may hurt the employee's feeling. Secondly, this method may lead to favourtism, whereby the advantage is largely offset.

3. Employment Exchange: Employment exchanges run by the government are regarded as a good source of recruitment for skilled, semi-skilled and unskilled employees. In this source, the prospective applicants for employment get themselves registered with the employment exchanges. The demand regarding the number, skill, educational qualification, experience etc. required for employment is sent by the employer to these agencies. In some cases, compulsory notification of vacancies to the employment exchange is required by law.

4. Advertisement: Advertisement in newspapers, employment news, trade and professional journals, radios, television etc. usually help to get prospective employees having suitable skills and qualifications. A well thought and nicely prepared advertisement reduces the possibility of receiving applications from those persons who do not possess the qualification, experience etc. necessary for the job. Most of the senior positions in industry and commerce are filled by this method. Advertisement also gives a wider choice.

5. Applications at the Gate: Even if vacancies do not exist in the organisation, the candidates who come to the factory gate for employment are allowed to fill up applications. These applications are kept in a file for future use. These are scruitinized whenever vacancies arise.

6. Educational and Academic Institutions: This method is being used by many industries. These companies send their selected teams in Industrial Training Institutions, Polytechnics, Engineering Colleges, Management and other professional institutions etc., to interview the candidates, who are nearing the completion of their studies and make selection. In fact these professional institutions have provided an excellent recruitment source to the firms, who are capable of offering an attractive salary and future to these talents.

7. Labour Unions: The labour unions also supply the workers to the factory for employment. This source is not reliable and sometimes not sufficiently fit for the specific job. Now-a-days this system of recruitment is losing popularity.

4.5.2 Scientific Selection

Selection process is a tool in the hands of management to differentiate the qualified and unqualified applicants by applying various techniques, such as, interviews, tests etc. It is a decision-making process, where the management decides certain norms and principles to adhere to standards, on the basis of which, a discrimination between qualified and unqualified candidates may be made. A scientific selection procedure ensures the selection of suitable candidate for a particular job. The object of scientific selection is to place on each job, a worker who can maintain a given output with minimum expenditure of energy and who will be best fitted to the job, "right person for the right job".

The major factors in individual fitness for a job are:

1. **Physical Characteristics:** Sound body, limbs, height, weight, eye sight etc.
2. **Personal Characteristics:** Age, sex, marital status, previous experience, place of birth, number of children etc.
3. **Proficiency or Skill and Ability:** This is the basic characteristic in fitting worker to a job.
4. **Competency:** Potentiality of an individual for learning and becoming proficient in a job. It points out the capacity to acquire knowledge and skill for success on the job.

5. **Temperament and Character:** Emotional, moral and social qualities, honesty, loyalty, etc. It is important to know about individual's character, his habits, his way of reacting in particular situation, his driving forces in determining his fitness for the job.

6. **Interest in Vocational Fitness:** Interest makes the work meaningful and worthwhile to the individual and with interest, abilities are developed as well as accomplishments are realised. Even if a person has skill, competency, efficiency, but he has no interest in the job, he may not be able to carry out the work effectively and may be found misfit for the job.

4.5.3 Selection Procedure (Method of Selection)

It is essential to devise a suitable selection procedure because, if the right type of persons are not selected, it will lead to huge loss to the organisation in terms of time, effort and money. Each step in action process should provide more and more information about the applicant to facilitate decision making in proper selection. However, the steps in recruitment and selection may vary from organisation to organisation.

The important steps followed by the modern organisations to select right type of persons, are as on the next page.

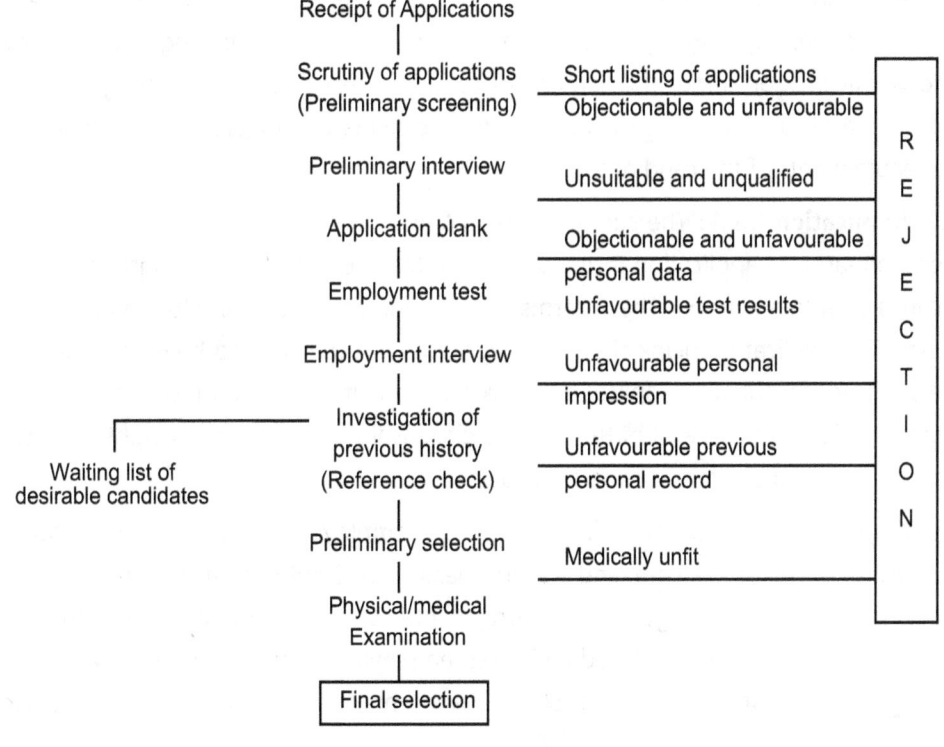

Fig. 4.3: Selection procedure

1. Receipt of Applications: The job has to be carefully studied and analysed to determine the kind of requirements of knowledge, experience and skill necessary to do it effectively. The applications received, gives details of family background, education, age, training experience, interest in extra curricular activities, hobbies, previous employment, salaries drawn, salary expected etc. The detailed information contained in the application gives a fair idea about the applicant.

2. Scrutiny of Applications (Preliminary Screening): In order to ensure that no time, money and energy is wasted in interviewing unsuitable candidates, the applications received are scrutinised and manageable number of suitable candidates are called for preliminary interview. The applications received could be classified under the following categories:

(i) Must be interviewed

(ii) Should be interviewed

(iii) Need not be interviewed.

If there are adequate candidates in 'must be interviewed' category then candidates in the 'should be interviewed' are deleted at this stage.

3. Preliminary Interview: The purpose of preliminary interview is to eliminate unfit, unqualified or less qualified applicants. It is also a sort of screening test. It provides additional information about the candidates to judge their suitability for the job. It should be brief to have an idea of general education, experience, appearance, personality, and salary requirements of the candidates.

4. Application Bank: The successful candidates in the preliminary interview are given printed standardized application form. Application blank is used to obtain information in the applicant's own handwriting. These forms can provide more factual information about the applicant. The application blank should incorporate questions having bearing on the fitness of the applicant for the job. Application blank gives a written record of identification (family background, date and place of birth, age, sex, citizenship, marital status, height, weight etc.), education, experience, references, salary expected etc.

5. Employment Test: Many large firms use employment tests in conjunction with interviews, for selecting, placing, and training personnel. Employment test enables to know the level of ability, knowledge, the pattern of interest and aptitude of the candidate in details. A properly developed and administered employment test programme can provide a more objective way of judging job applicant's and improving the accuracy of the selection process.

Some of the commonly used employment tests are as follows:

(i) Intelligence Tests: These tests measure the individual's capacity or learning ability to grasp or understand instructions and also ability to reason and make judgement. IQ tests can help to reduce misfits by identifying applicants who fall below minimum standards and those who have considerably more mental ability than is required for the job. These tests are very useful for certain high level jobs.

(ii) Trade Tests: Technical jobs require 'trade tests'. The purpose of a trade test is to judge the candidate with respect to his proficiency and skilfulness in a particular trade. For example, for recruitment of a stenographer, a test can be conducted to check his speed at dictation and typing. A turner may be asked to produce a job on a lathe with desired accuracy and speed or asked questions related to construction and operation of a centre lathe.

(iii) Psychological Tests: Psychological tests are designed to measure emotional stability introversion, extroversion, interest etc. These tests are generally expensive to design and administer for a specific job.

(v) Aptitude Tests: Aptitude tests are used to determine whether an individual has certain minimum natural abilities or talents that can be developed through proper training. These tests measure ability to learn specific jobs. Special aptitude tests measure specific patterns of abilities necessary to perform certain jobs, for example, mechanical aptitude tests are useful in selecting apprentices for skilled mechanical trades.

(v) Interest Tests: Interest tests identify patterns of interest that is areas in which the individual shows special concern, fascination and involvement. These tests will indicate what type of jobs may be satisfying to the employees. These tests also help the individuals in selecting occupation of their interest.

(vi) Personality Tests: These tests are used to judge personality traits of the candidate such as emotional balance, attempt to determine the ability of an individual to meet interpersonal and situational stress.

6. Employment Interview: It is the most important and widely used tool in the selection process. This type of interview must be conducted in a friendly atmosphere. The questions should pertain to job specifications. A verification of the information finished by the candidate in application blank may be made. The candidate should be given a chance to ask questions to satisfy himself regarding the history of the concern, future prospects, salary offered and nature of job etc. The interview should be conducted in a room free from any disturbance, noise and interruption, so that interview may be held confidentially and in a quiet environment.

The following principles should be followed to improve the quality of interviewing:

(i) Formulate the objective of the interview and the questions to be asked before seeing the applicant.

(ii) Conduct the interview in private and put the applicant at ease with some general remarks about the business and the job.

(iii) Encourage the applicant to talk by asking pertinent questions and listening attentively to the answers.

(iv) Avoid any suggestion of discrimination.

(v) Retain control of interview and keep the interview headed towards the objective without dominating.

(vi) Allow plenty of time without wasting it.

(vii) Record the facts obtained in an interview while they are fresh.

7. Reference Check: This is generally the last step before the candidate is offered a job in the organisation. An investigation is made on the reference supplied by the applicant regarding his past employment, education, character, personal reputation etc. Reports of the referees may be either open or confidential. Referees may be contacted on telephones, through mail or personal visit. It is a good practice to call the confidential reports in a standard form to ensure that the requisite information is furnished. Reports of the previous employer which are specific are given a lot of weightage by the potential employers.

8. Medical Examination: This is the final step in the selection process. It is essential to ensure that the candidate is physically fit and is able to handle the job efficiently. It screens out the applicants who are physically unfit to meet the requirements of the specific job for which they are being considered.

Physical fitness requirements vary from job to job. Ability to cope with the stress is a critical factor in selection of individuals for stress prone jobs. Medical examination is done with the following purposes:

(i) It serves to ascertain the applicant's physical fitness to meet the job requirements.

(ii) It serves to protect the organisation against unwanted claims under Worker's Compensation Act.

(iii) It helps to prevent communicable diseases entering the organisation.

(iv) It helps in selecting individuals with sound health, and in reducing the rates of accident, labour turnover and absenteeism.

9. Final Selection: The successful candidates are ranked in order of preference. Appointment letters are issued to the candidates depending upon the number of vacancies to be filled in. The appointment letter must indicate the post for which the candidate is selected, the terms and conditions of appointment, pay scale etc. The appointment letter must also indicate the date by which the acceptance of offer shall be communicated or the date of joining. If the offer of appointment is not accepted within the stipulated time, then other selected candidates should be considered in order of their ranks. Normally, in the initial stage the candidates are appointed on probation basis, because it is considered better to try them for a few months on the job itself.

Introduction and Follow Up:

Induction is the introduction of an employee to the job and the organisation. A planned induction properly welcomes a new employee, creates a good attitude, and reduces labour turnover. The information about the organisation history, its products, policies, rules, mission, philosophies etc. is given to the candidate. The candidate is introduced to his fellow workers, subordinates and other concerned, in a friendly atmosphere. It is the foreman's responsibility to help orient the worker, making him feel at home and part of the working team.

A good induction programme should cover:

1. Information about the company, its products, manufacturing processes and major tasks in his job.
2. Intricacies about the job including its hazards.
3. Organisational structure and functions of various departments.
4. Employee's own position in the organisation and department.
5. Personnel policy of the organisation.
6. Service conditions, amenities and welfare facilities.
7. Policies, objectives and rules and regulations of the company.
8. Grievance and discipline handling procedures.
9. Promotion, transfers, suggestion schemes etc.

Placement:

If the persons are not selected for specific positions, as in case of trainees, they are required to undergo training or work in different departments/sections for some time. Based on their performance and aptitude, they are finally assigned to specific jobs. This process of putting a person on the specific job is known as placement.

4.6 TRAINING AND DEVELOPMENT OF MANPOWER

Building an efficient labour force requires not only proper selection, but also effective training of employees. Therefore, after the selection of an employee in an organisation, the next step is to train him for better performance.

Training is a process which improves individual's ability through imparting knowledge, developing skills and changing attitudes, to perform their jobs more efficiently and effectively.

Training may be defined as "a well thought and well planned processes of conscious learning of new knowledge and skills for improving the learner's ability to perform certain tasks and activities, more efficiently and effectively, in immediate/near future, with active support of some other individuals".

Training can also be defined as "a short-term process utilising a systematic and organised procedure by which people acquire technical knowledge and skills for a definite purpose".

Training and Development

Training is the act of increasing the knowledge and skill for doing a particular job, the development means growth of individual in all respects. Development is a long term educational process utilising a systematic and organised procedure by which managerial personnel get conceptual and theoretical knowledge. An executive development programme aims at increasing the capabilities of the individuals to achieve the desired objectives.

The personnel department determines the training needs of various units and different individuals and schedule them. The type of training, the method of training, the duration of training and all such matters should be taken care of, by the personnel department.

4.6.1 Need for Training

(i) The need for a systematic training programme has been increased by rapid changes in the business:
- job changes.
- changes in processes, methods and procedures - rapid changes in technology.
- change in volume of business
- changes in products etc.

The changes are constantly taking place. They are also rapid. They demand modification and changes in skills, knowledge, attitudes and understanding on the part of workers and executives.

(ii) Training is necessary to impart knowledge to new recruits, to acquint them with the job to be done by them. Industry is frequently compelled, particularly during periods of business expansion, to employ unskilled labour and to train them for specific operations or tasks.

(iii) Many jobs in business consist of tasks which are unique and peculiar to the company and require systematic training.

(iv) Training is necessary to develop better behaviour patterns which are appropriate to their jobs and responsibilities.

(v) To achieve flexibility in the labour force versatility or multiskill training is necessary.

(vi) To provide remedial instructions to old employees to improve their workmanship.

(vii) Training helps to promote individuals for higher positions.

Training and development of personnel is therefore an ongoing and continuous process to meet and adopt changes effectively and quickly. In developing countries like India, there is a great demand for trained personnel at all levels.

4.6.2 Objectives of Training and Development

When any company undertakes training and development, it aims at fulfilling certain objectives. There are three broad objectives of training:

1. Disseminating of knowledge.
2. Development of skills.
3. Change of attitudes.

Normally, an organisation can have one or more objectives such as:

- better performance of employee.
- development of more economic working methods.
- greater job satisfaction or morale.
- harmonious team work.
- To familiarise the new employees with company rules, regulations, introduce him to his fellow workers and give him an idea of where his job fits into the total operation of the company. (Orientation cum induction training).
- Learning new techniques (refresher training).

Specific types of training programmes are conducted to carry out some particular objectives.

4.6.3 Benefits/Advantages of Training

The importance of training in an organisation is quite obvious from the following benefits resulting from properly trained personnel of the organisation. In fact, trained labour is an invaluable asset to the organisation.

1. Increased Productivity: A systematic training programme causes an increase in skill and efficiency of an employee. A trained worker gives better performance. Training of labour results in increase in quality, quantity and output. Machines and materials are carefully handled and they are more economically used.

2. Higher Employee Morale: Training helps the employee to acquire necessary skill and efficiency. This provides him job satisfaction and confidence, thus resulting in higher employee morale.

3. Reduced Accidents: Training develops safety attitudes in the workers and they can take necessary precautions to avoid accident. Machines and equipment are carefully handled and maintained properly.

4. Reduction in Spoilage, Wastage and Optimum Utilization of Resources: Training in improved method results in better utilization of materials, equipments and reduction in defective work, damage and spoilage and substantial reduction in the manufacturing cost.

5. Reduced Supervision: A trained employee shows a high degree of self-discipline and self supervision. He takes intelligent interest in his work. Proper training may enable him to contribute a lot to the solution of managerial problems through participation. When labour is trained, management can be democratic or participative. Management can concentrate on planning and encourage expert workers through motivation.

6. Increased Organisational Stability and Flexibility: Stability means the ability of the organisation to sustain its effectiveness, inspite of the loss of key personnel. This is because of the availability of a reservoir of trained replacement.

Flexibility means the ability of the organisation to adjust itself to the short term changes in the volume of work. Training helps to achieve this ability by developing multiple skills in employees so that they can be transferred to other jobs when the need arises. Job rotation enables the development of versatile employees for necessary adjustment in the personnel due to change in the volume of work.

7. Self-development Versatility and Adaptability: Automation, rapid changes in technology and increasing use of computerization, requires the employees to adopt themselves to changed situations (new work methods). Systematic training provides them an opportunity for self development, versatility and adopting to new work situations. Similarly, better security and greater opportunity for self-development within or without the present organisation are possible only for trained employees. Management has to take up the responsibility for continuous training and re-training of employees to update their knowledge, skills to meet the changed situations.

8. Reduced Turnover and Absenteeism: Training develops confidence and provides job satisfaction to employees associated with a sense of achievement. This results in lower complaints, reduced turnover and absenteeism.

9. Reduction in Machine Breakdown and Maintenance Cost: Training in preventive maintenance, improved methods, result in better care and handling of machines, minimizes the breakdown and maintenance cost of machines.

10. Increase in Earning of the Employees: In short, a systematic training programme improves the quality and quantity of work, safeguards machinery, reduces costs, raises employee's earning and morale, and provides an effective means for improving company policies and regulations.

4.6.4 Guidelines For Training Workers (NQN-Managerial Employees)

There are number of guidelines which must be borne in mind, while designing or imparting training to workers. A few of them are given below:

Craftsmen (Workers Training):

This is also called workers' training to achieve skill in their work. Up-to-date training is required for those who actually work on machines to increase their skill and also for new employees. A learned skill is an asset which cannot be taken away. It is, therefore, valuable to the employee in terms of better job security and greater opportunity for promotion within the organisation and if necessary in the outside world.

Guidelines for Training Workers:

There are number of guidelines which must be considered, while designing or imparting training to workers. A few of them are given below:

1. Motivation is the main factor in training employees. It is very important to decide which incentive will motivate the employee - money, status, recognition etc. Motivating a new employee is always easier than motivating the old employees. The training sessions should be planned to meet the need of trainees and factors motivating different employees, should also be considered by the trainer.

2. A job should be broken down in requirements of the skill necessary to perform it successfully. Training should be planned and provided for each skill (physical, sensory, and mental). Carefully spaced practice periods, are essential for effective learning.

3. Individual differences should always be remembered. Individuals vary in intelligence, interest and skills or capability.

4. The trainee should also gain personal benefit from training. Management should see that successful trainees are rewarded.

5. The trainee should be provided with the report of his progress.

4.7 TYPES OF TRAINING

The various methods of training workers are:
1. Demonstration.
2. On-the job training.
3. Vestibule training.
4. Apprenticeship.

1. Demonstration: This method is especially applicable where some physical process is to be learnt, particularly one that involves use of machinery or equipment. In this method, the supervisor/instructor actually demonstrates how to do a certain task. For example, the instructor actually shows how to perform a certain job on a centre lathe.

This type of training can be seen in very small concerns e.g. workshops, auto repair shops etc. where there is no established training programme.

2. On-the-Job Training: This method provides training to new employees by experienced, skilled workers or foreman/supervisor, while the trainee works at a specific job in the plant or office. In this method, the supervisor gives instructions to a new worker, explains the nature of work, the use of machine and tools, safety precautions etc. and shows, how it is being done by an experienced worker.

The new worker is then put on the job on a separate machine near the experienced and skilled worker. During working whenever the new worker feels any difficulty, he can take the help and guidance of the skilled worker near him and acquire proficiency in course of time.

Advantages:
1. This method of training is widely employed, because of its economy and convenience, no special training facilities and instructional staff are required.
2. The worker learns while doing. He gets introduced to the actual work situation.
3. The suitability of the worker for the specific job can be readily ascertained by the competent instructor/supervisor.

This method is particularly suitable, when the training period is short, because of the simplicity of the job and when the number of trainees is limited.

Limitations:
1. It takes long time for a worker to acquire mastery in his work.
2. A new worker is likely to pick up some of the defective method of his colleagues.
3. Every experienced worker may not have the ability to impart his knowledge.
4. Working of a trainee on the production floor, may increase chances of spoilage of material, damage to equipment, accident etc.
5. If the workers are paid on piece wage, the experienced worker may be reluctant to spend much time to guide the new worker.
6. The worker may not be able to learn efficiently, because of noise on the shop floor.

3. Vestibule School Training: It is a special training school for training the employees. An attempt is made to duplicate as nearly as possible, the actual equipment, material and conditions found in a real work situation.

The vestibule training is desirable, when the demand for training is large and when on-the job training, is not practicable.

Advantages:
1. The emphasis is on training, rather than on production. Hence, the training is properly planned and controlled.
2. A large number of trainees can be trained in similar skills, quickly and uniformly.
3. There is no disruption of production.
4. Wastage and spoilage of raw material, and damage to production machinery is eliminated.
5. The school atmosphere is calm, peaceful and conducive to efficient learning.
6. Specially trained and professional instructors can be employed for imparting instructions to trainees.
7. Full time instructors are able to apply good teaching techniques under controlled conditions and can increase confidence of the trainees.

Limitations:
1. Its major limitation is the expense of both, of providing costly equipment, and of maintaining a teaching staff and every industry cannot afford it.
2. If the demand of workers to be trained is uneven, usually a part of vestibule school is idle or trainees are rushed through it, without proper training.
3. Moreover, since the actual shop conditions cannot be reproduced, the completion of training often finds the trainee, still in need of adjustment to plant conditions.

Many big industries have their own special training schools on permanent basis for training the newly selected employees.

4. Apprenticeship: Apprenticeship is one of the oldest methods of training. It is used to develop all round skilled craftsmen (machinists, tool makers, mill wrights, fitters, welders). It is generally best suited to the large firm with a steady demand for skilled labour. In this scheme, young boys of 16 to 18 years of age are trained for 2 to 4 years.

The training course usually consists of a predetermined schedule of factory work assignments (which generally contributes to production) and some related classroom instruction in the underlying principles of trade. Under the agreement, the trainee candidate is required to give a bond of service, e.g. 5 years' service in the organisation, after completion of training. An apprenticeship agreement, drawn up between the firm and the trainee stipulates the training period, wage rate (stipend), bonus and other conditions.

In order to provide training to the unskilled workers in the industries and workshops, an Apprentices Act was passed in 1961. The apprenticeship training programmes now adopted in different concerns, both private and government, include classroom instructions in blueprint reading, study of machine tools, shop mathematics, trade theory etc. in addition to the practical training in the related trade.

All big concerns like Hindustan Machine Tools, Heavy Electricals, Oil and Natural Gas Commission, Fertilizer Corporation of India, Bhilai Steel Plant, Tata Iron and Steel Company, Indian Railways, Godrej, Escorts etc. have their own training schools for imparting training to their new employees and apprentices.

Apprentice training aims to provide broad training to enable the trainee to take up a wide variety of tasks within his field of specialization.

4.7.1 Foreman or Supervisory Training (Lower Level Management Training)

Lower level management consists of Foremen, Supervisors, Inspectors etc. They are just above the operational staff and their function is to get the work done from the operational staff.

The foreman/supervisor is in close contact with the workers and interprets the firm's plans to them and conveys the workers' views to the management. He is a key man in the organisation. He is in direct charge of labour and controls the activities of his section. The training of foremen is therefore of paramount importance and should be a continual process, especially in expanding industry.

The aims of foreman training can be listed as:

(i) Bring his impact to the standard, where he can handle interactions with others effectively.

(ii) Develop in him the necessary skill to impart instructions to the workers under him.

(iii) To develop in him the qualities of leadership.

(iv) To impart adequate knowledge of management methods to deal with other people.

(v) Impart to him deep knowledge about the work, so that workers should feel that he is superior to them.

(vi) Develop in him the skill to improve upon the existing method of work.

(vii) To provide him the knowledge of labour problems and legislation.

(viii) Make him qualify for advancement to positions of greater responsibility.

(ix) Develop the ability to plan, co-ordinate, control and build up efficient team in order to obtain best result.

(x) Train him about safety rules and practices to be followed in the shops.

Foremen are best trained through planned conferences, (or discussions) which may be supplemented by lectures and carefully selected text books. A homogeneous group of twelve to fifteen men from the plant constitutes an ideal conference group.

Foremanship training should first deal with the immediate problems of supervision and then cover such topics, such as, the techniques and responsibilities of shop management, company policies, production planning, methods of training workers, terms of union contract, job evaluation, merit rating, safety, and work study and other methods of cost reduction.

Methods of Training Supervisors

1. Induction and Orientation: Induction and orientation training involves familiarizing the new employee about the following:

(1) The enterprise which he has joined, its history, organisation structure, products being manufactured.

(2) Information about the authorities and responsibilities assigned to him.

(3) Safety and proper use of tools and equipments.

(4) Conditions of employment, disciplinary rules and other aspects of personnel policy.

2. Lecture (Classroom) Methods: Under this method, lectures are delivered by experts within or outside the company. The lectures may cover such topics as the techniques and responsibilities of shop management, company policies, production planning methods,

methods of training workmen, job evaluation, merit rating, safety, time and motion study etc. The usefulness of this method can be enhanced by using audio-visual aids such as OHP, slides, technical films and other aids.

3. Conference: A homogeneous group of twelve to fifteen men from one plant constitutes an ideal conference group. People attending a conference, discuss the subject-matter of their interest, e.g. how to control absenteeism, how to reduce scrap etc. A conference helps in exchanging ideas and experiences of different persons and puts them open for discussion to arrive at a feasible solution of the problem in hand. A conference can uproot fixed ideas, change attitudes and develop analytical and questioning ability.

4. Written Instructional Method: This method is used to give to trainees the important information in permanent form for immediate or future use, e.g. standard practice instructions on how to perform various jobs.

5. Training within the Industry (T.W.I.): This was developed basically, as a supervisory training programme to make up for the shortage of civilian supervisory skills during World War II. In our country, the organisation like National Productivity Council, Small Industries Service Institute, Government of India and the Institution of Industrial Engineers, are running T.W.I. Scheme. T.W.I. courses are based upon group conference method, and supervisors attend on a part time basis. In this scheme for imparting training, 10 supervisors (trainees) and one instructor is the usual ratio. In this scheme the supervisors meet informally in the session and they apply the basic principles to their own jobs and thus they learn by doing.

T.W.I. Scheme Imparts Training in:

(a) Job Instructions: The supervisor develops the ability to impart clear instructions to the workers, regarding the work to be done and the procedure to be followed.

(b) Job Relation: The programme helps to develop the following qualities in a supervisor - Leadership qualities, Ability to analyse and handle labour problems, Ability to develop good labour relations.

(c) Job Method: The programme increases the supervisor's skill to improve methods of doing work to make optimum utilization of human and material resources.

(d) Job Safety: Supervisor can anticipate the possible hazards and learns how to prevent accident, create safety awareness in employees etc.

4.7.2 Executive (Managerial) Training and Development

Training and development is a continuing process and it has to do at all levels of employees including executives. Executive development can be defined as "an attempt to improve managerial effectiveness, through a planned and deliberate learning process". It seeks to develop certain attitudes, skills and knowledge.

In a broader sense, executive development is one of the tools of organisational development and is aimed at increasing the effectiveness of the organisation.

The efficiency of any organisation depends directly on how well its managers are trained to plan and execute the plans effectively. An effective team of managers is of paramount importance for the survival of the organisation. Because, the managers have to bear the responsibility of running the organisation profitability and effectively. The executives must keep themselves up-to-date with latest development in their field of business activity.

Rapid industrial expansion after the Second World War and separation of management from ownership (as in corporate form of business) resulted in the necessity of evolving a system of executive training and development.

The vitality of business enterprise is largely dependent on the men who manage it. The generation of dynamic leadership, which can build great enterprises, is the need of the hour.

The first necessity of executive development is right thinking and develop their capacity to face challenge, assume responsibility and acquaint them with general business background.

Principles of Executive Development

1. The first principle upon which a management development programme should be based is given primary emphasis on self-development. There is no substitute for personal drive, initiative, inner motivation and basic abilities of an individual.
2. Individuals differ in their aptitude. The individual differences in aptitude and ability should form the basis of executive development.
3. It is more of an education rather than imparting a particular skill; because aim of executive training and development programme is to broaden the outlook of the people and their capacity of judgement and decision making ability.
4. An effective organisational climate should be provided.
5. The aim should be to ensure effective utilization of human resources by exploiting fully, their talents and potentials.
6. To provide an opportunity to the employees to prepare themselves for higher assignments.

Method of Training Executives

The methods of training and development of executives can be broadly classified into two categories:

1. On-the-job training.
2. Off-the-job training.

1. **On-the-job Training Methods:**

   (i) Understudies (Appointment as an assistant to): This method is used for training of young managers for general management positions. In this method, the trainee is appointed as an assistant to some senior manager. The trainee, while working as an assistant, learns the ways of working of his superior under whom he is appointed.

   (ii) Membership of the Committee: Under this method, the trainee is appointed on some committee consisting of executives (managers) of different departments. The trainee develops the necessary skill of solving problems in a group situation. He also learns from the experience of senior persons. Committee assignments improve understanding and very well imparts the necessary general background.

   (iii) Job Rotation: The major objective of job rotation is to broaden the employee's exposure, as well as experience in the organisation. In this method, the trainee is rotated periodically from one job to another.

   The advantages of planned rotation are:

   - It stimulates a more co-operative attitudes by exposing a man to the other fellow's problems and viewpoints.
   - It provides a general background of the organisation to the executive and broadens his outlook.
   - It makes the executive (trainee) versatile.

   (iv) Job Enlargement, Job Enrichment: Job enlargement means adding some related tasks to the existing job, without increasing level of responsibility. It is a horizontal expansion of the job.

   Job enrichment means, increase in level of the responsibility of the executive. This is vertical expansion of the job.

   (v) Management by Objectives (MBO): MBO is a process of joint setting of objectives by superior and subordinate. The joint setting of objectives facilitates learning through interaction with the senior.

2. **Off-the-job Training Methods:**

   (i) Lecture Method (Refer supervisory training).

   (ii) Case Study Method: A case is real life illustration for studying a problem. In this method of training, a real life or hypothetical problem is given to a small group of trainees for analysis and finding out the solution. This method was developed in Harvard Business School and is one of the first deviations from the standard teaching method. In this method, learning occurs through participation, discussion and problem analysis.

This method is best suited to small groups of twenty or less. The trainer, in this method plays a relatively passive role and the trainees learn from their own discussion. They learn to look objectively at the facts, analyse them, find out various alternative solutions and support the best solution. Great care is taken in the preparation of case study material and in case writing. The trainer assists the participants of the group through the use of questions, to draw out, guide or direct the thinking of the group. He helps in sharpening their analytical ability to enlarge their capacity, to take a broader look at the situations.

The **advantages of case study method** are:
- It develops analytical thinking.
- It gives problem-solving ability.
- It broadens their outlook to look at the problems from different angles.
- It develops decision-making skills, verbal communication skills and inter-personal relation skills.

Business Games:

In this method, groups of participants are formed. The participants from each group may be from different departments within an organisation or from different organisations. The participants discuss and arrive at certain decisions concerning subjects, such as, production, planning, research and development, cost control, inventory control, sales forecasting etc. In management games, each group would be given data, relevant to the subject assigned to the particular group. The trainer also provides them with simulated data regarding results arising out of decisions made by them which in turn, lead to fresh decisions. At the end of the game, each group of participants is in a position to evaluate the performance of the group.

The advantages of this method are, that it develops decision-making abilities, a team work and an awareness on the effects of interaction between different groups. The participants would, as a result, develop talents to deal with their environment in the real life situations. The most important advantage is that, it gives opportunity to learn from experience, without paying the price that would result from wrong decisions made in real life. These games are powerful educational tools with numerous applications in problem-solving, anticipating the problems in advance, managerial decision-making and executive testing and selection.

Role Playing:

Role playing is widely used for human relations and leadership training. It is a supplementary training method, usually combined with the lecture or the conference. The trainees are provided with either written or oral descriptions of a situation and the role they are to play. Two or more trainees are given parts to play, before other participants. They play their parts spontaneously, before the group. The role players and the other participants in the group watching the behaviour, analyse and criticize the behaviour of the role players. The situation is described as fish-bowl exercise, where the participants in the centre of the arena, become the object of observation for the rest of the participants.

Typical examples of role playing are: Manager conducting interview, a salesman presenting sales talk on a product to customers, a superior discussing a grievance with an employee, method study engineer stressing the importance of new method of doing the work etc.

The **advantages of role playing method** are:
- It generates tremendous enthusiasm and interaction among the participants.
- The trainee gets a chance to observe different patterns of behaviour.

They get a chance to act out behaviours, different from their own and develop insight into interpersonal problems.

The participants get a fair idea about the kind of behaviour, which is likely to be a success or failure in real life.

It helps to develop human relation skill and brings about attitudinal change.

Conference:

Refer methods of supervisory training.

4.8 LEADERSHIP

Introduction

Leadership represents the abstract quality in a man. It is the ability of influencing other's behaviour and welding their efforts for the attainment of common purpose. Thus, a manager in this context, can be seen as a leader of his group and his basic task is to co-ordiante the activities of the individuals under him and direct them towards the attainment of organisational goals. Leadership may take place at any level in the organisaitonal hierarchy. Moreover, the formal position and status enjoyed by a manager does not necessarily ensure his domianance as a leader. In fact, in an organisation, an informal leader might exercise greater influence than the manager himself. The formal leadership is used through command and authority while informal leadership is used through personal traits and courage.

The essential qualities and skills involved in leadership can be learned and developed through education and experience. People can learn to communicate clearly, to make effective decisions, to motivate and inspire, to maintain and show respect for the trust in subordinates, to be just in making judgements, to instruct clearly and to be Patient with mistakes, to be loyal to followers and tough in their behalf, to be humble and open to new ideas and different opinions, to keep a sense of humor, and to know how to relax.

The leader: According to James McGregor-Burns, leaders are described as "those who first go forward". It is those who break ranks to show others what direction to take off. Leading almost always involves initiating and usually requires risk taking.

Definition of Leadership

"Leadership is like moving a string, you can't move it by pushing from behind, what you have to do is to get ahead and pull".

According to *Koontz* and *O'Donnel*, "Leadership is the ability of a manager to induce subordinates (followers) to work with confidence and zeal."

According to *Peter F. Drucker*, "Leadership is the lifting of man's visions to higher sights, the raising of man's performance to higher standard, the building of man's personality beyond its normal limitations."

"Leadership is largely the art of getting things done through mobilizing people."

It is the ability to get others to work enthusiastically and competently towards accepted objectives.

As *George R. Terry* has said, "Leadership is the activity of influencing people to strive willingly for group objectives."

According to *Alford* and *Bettay*, "Leadership is the ability to secure desirable actions from a group of followers voluntarily whitout the use of coercion."

As *Ordway Team* has said, "Leadership is the name of that combination of the qualities by the possession of which one is able to get something done by others, chiefly because through his influence they become willing to do it."

According to *Haimanu Theo*, "Leadership may be defined as the process by which an executive imginatively directs, guides and influences the work of others in choosing and attaining specified goals by mediating between the individual and the organisation in such a manner that both will obtain maximum satisfaction."

Thus, leadership is a process of purposive behaviour. It is an important instrument of motivation. It is considered as an important ingredient of management. The success of any industrial concern is dependent upon the quality of its leadership. An organisation, howsoever good it is, cannot be run effectively without effective leadership. Organisation without an effective leadership is nothing but a muddle of men, machines and materials. Unless they are directed, motivated and engaged in a co-ordinated manner to produce more and better towards the accomplishment of organisational objectives, all these elements of production are useless and inactive. An effective leader alone can pull out the organisation from darkness to light and push it to the path of development by resolving the various genuine difficulties tactfully.

4.8.1 Functions of Leadership

For successful leadership to happen, we need two things

(a) Better understanding of human psychology i.e., a basic knowledge of group behaviour, human relations, and managerial skills.

(b) Training in applying these skills.

The important functions of leadership can be stated as:

1. Integrating and directing: The leader directs and integrates the efforts of group towards the attainment of objectives of the organisation. By his personal conduct and behaviour, a good leader develops confidence in his followers by directing them to work, giving them advice and getting good results in the organisation through them.

2. Develops team spirit: An effective leader believes in team spirit. He, therefore, seeks and gives suggestions, develops team spirit and sense of co-operation in his followers to obtain good results. This is essential to have group cohesiveness as members feel a sense of participation.

3. Arbitration: When a group decision is made, the group members may disagree with each other at the problem identification stage or at the problem solving stage. In such cases, the leader will provide his services and arbitrate between them to resolve the difference by providing guidance.

4. To develop environment conducive to work: By ensuring a supportive face-to-face relationship and developing a positive attitude, the leader develops an environment conducive to work. By providing a sense of security and belongingness, he motivates the group to work effectively.

5. Acts as a healthy link between top management and the work group: Leaders represent the work group before the top executives and also represent the management before the work group. The effectiveness of an organisation depends upon how effectively the leader works as a link between top management and the workers.

6. Acts as a counsellor: A leader is often required to encourage his group members to work effectively. He is supposed to remove all barriers and stumbling blocks to effective performance. He works as a catalyst and spurs his subordinates to action. A leader not only sets his own objectives but also helps his sub-ordinates in setting realistic objectives.

7. Use of power: A leader must use power and authority in a manner that will stimulate a positive response from the subordinates. Depeding upon the situation a leader uses different types of power, i.e. reward power, coercive power, legitimate power and expert power. A leader may be effective only when his sub-ordinates obey him willingly. Hence, he must use the power in the best interest of the group he leads. He must apply an appropriate leadership style which is most suited to the organisation in given situation.

8. Motivation: Leadership influences the performance of the workers. Higher the motivation better would be the performance. By exercising his leadership a leader motivates the employees at work for better performance. He develops the talents of the individuals and utilises it for the benefit of organisation.

Thus, we can conclude that effective leadership must be able to successfully raise the group to high organisational level. He has to perform a dual role in the organisation. His effectiveness is enhanced when he acts as a formal agent of higher management and also an informal leader of the sub-ordinates. Leadership must facilitate interaction and provide the mechanism of communication. The leader creates an environment in which a large number of people work for a common purpose. He inspires, praises, guides and represents the group.

4.8.2 Qualities of Leadership

Leadership qualities or traits of leader are as follows

(1) Physical Traits, (2) Psychological Traits, (3) Intellectual Traits and (4) Traits of character.

(1) Physical Traits: A good leader must possess a sound health, good vitality and endurance so that he may perform his duties most effectively.

(2) Psychological Traits: Some of the psychological traits required by a good leader are (a) Enthusiasm, (b) Co-operativeness, (c) Tactfullness, (d) Ability to inspire, (e) Emotional Resilience (to cope with the emotional stress).

(3) Intellectual Traits: Intellectual traits are very important for the successful running and growth of business organisation. These are:

(a) Creativity, (b) Intelligence, (c) Capacity for sound judgement, (d) Communication skill. (e) Problem solving and decision making skills, (f) Clear vision, (g) Self awareness etc.

(4) Traits of Character: Strong character of a leader will set an example for the followers / subordinates.

These are:

(a) Integrity: Leadership lies in an individual's (or group of individuals') ability to give rise among others a feeling of trust and respect by the coherence and continuity of his actions and ideas. When the individual's integrity is doubtful, he will not succeed in bringing others to want to do what he and they believe should be done. Good leaders consider leadership as a responsibility and not a privilege. A leader must obtain the trust of his staff. This implies agreement between word and action.

(b) Self discipline.

(c) Physical and moral courage.

(d) Humanism: These traits of character will create confidence among workers and will help the organisation to achieve the objectives.

4.9 LEADERSHIP STYLES AND TYPES

4.9.1 Leadership Styles

A leader's typical way of functioning in the organisation is often referred to as "leadership style". Leadership style, thus, denotes the manner in which the leader behaves while using his power and influence in relation to the group and the task situation. It is the result of leader's philosophy, personality, experiences, traits and value system. It also depends upon the type of followers and the organisational atmosphere prevailing in the enterprise. Leaders and their styles affect everyone and everything within an organisation. There exists a direct relationship between leadership styles and the behaviour of the people they lead and the organisational climate.

The following are some of the leadership styles that have emerged as a result of research on leadership:

1. Autocratic Style or Authoritarian Style
2. Democratic Style or Participative Style
3. Free Rein or Laissez Fair Style (Self dispensing style)
4. Benevolent Style etc.

1. Authoritarian Style (Autocratic Style):

In this style of leadership decisions are made by leader (boss). The subordinates are directed to follow these decisions obediently. All policies are determined by the leader without consulting the subordinates. The leaders who follow this style never like to delegate subordinates as they fear they may lose their authority in this way. The leader dictates to the subordinates, the techniques and activity steps, he does not inform them about future plans.

The leaders of this style possess the following characteristics:
1. They are generally strong willed, domineering, and to some extent aggressive.
2. Ordinarily they are not ready to listen to views and suggestions of others if they offer difference of opinion.
3. They do not encourage equal relationship. As a rule they do not allow themselves to get close to employees.
4. They do not like to see employees get close to one another.
5. The best subordinates in their opinion, follow directions without question.
6. They do not give subordinates the freedom to influence his thinking, decision or behaviour.

Advantages:
1. Permits quick decisions.
2. In case of less competent subordinates, it is effective.
3. It facilitates speedy implementation of plans.
4. Highly satisfied leader.
5. In case of extreme crisis, this stage may be the only solution.

Limitations:
1. Creativity of sub-ordinates remains untapped.
2. There are no changes of development for the sub-ordinates.
3. High turn-over of subordinates due to frustration.
4. Low moral of workforce.

Suitability:
1. When there is unskilled, submissive, untrained workforce.
2. When there is inexperienced workforce.

Autocratic style is not preferred these days as the workforce is more educated, trained and organised.

2. Democratic Style (Participative Style):

A democratic leader believes in maintaining good human relations with his subordinates and encourage participation at all levels. An important advantage` of this type is that it gives the sense of belongingness to the members of the group.

The characteristics of democratic supervisors are:
1. They discuss and consult their subordinates, draw ideas from them and supervise.
2. They follow the majority opinion as expressed by their group after discussion with them.
3. They promote participation of subordinates and develop strong team work.
4. They give their decisions only after consulting their subordinates and follow the majority decision.
5. They also communicate the long term plans to their subordinates and the subordinates are kept well informed.

Advantages:
1. Participative style motivates the subordinates to think and work. Hence, there is high job satisfaction and moral among employees.
2. It promotes healthier relations between workers and supervisors.
3. Chances of good decisions are more because of involvement of followers.
4. Decision making ability in subordinates is cultivated.
5. Labour turnover is quite less.

Disadvantages:
1. Time consuming process of decision making.
2. In case of uneducated / unskilled or untrained workers it is not very effective.
3. Evasive employees, who prefer not be involved, may create problems.

Suitability:
1. General industrial scenario, R & D organisations, project work.
2. Consultancy firms, software industry, quality circle etc.

3. Free-rein or Laissez-fair Style:

Under this style, managers give employees almost total authority in all matters. He assigns the work and then let employees decide how they will complete the job.

In other words, the involvement of managers is quite less and there is little guidance, motivation and control. This is useful when qualified sub-ordinates are willing to accept responsibility.

Advantages:
1. Effective if sub-ordinates are competent and extremely responsible.
2. It allows the employees to develop themselves by giving them chance to think and take decisions.

3. High job satisfaction and moral of employees.
4. Labour turnover is reduced.

Limitations:
1. Chances of misdirected followers, doing unwanted activities.
2. Lack of guidance and support.
3. Chances of confusion and chaos.

Suitability:

R & D organisation, highly talented and responsible group.

4. **Benevolent Style:**

The leader of this style is more of a "big brother". Human relationship is more important in this style. The group, not the individual is the key unit in the organisation and friendliness and harmony among its members create the desired atmosphere. The leader encourages and builds up moral of the employees. Such a leader influences his followers by his personal contact. He gives directions personally, hears their difficulties, grievances and tries to overcome them. The whole of the group responds to his call because they love and respect him and have full confidence in him.

Suitability:

Suitable for small organisation with less number of employees.

Leadership involves an inter-relationship among three elements:
1. The qualities, skills and needs of the leader.
2. The needs and expectation of the group (employees)
3. The demand or requirements of the situation.

The inter-relationship suggest that no one style of leadership serves best for all situations. The best style is one most appropriate in a given situations.

A good leader will change his style from group to group and from situation to situation. Exercising strong directive power provides effective leadership when group lacks a sense of direction or purpose. Groups sometimes need orientation. At the other times they need encouragement. The two major parts in the leadership process are (i) Task oriented (ii) Relationship oriented. Leaders need to strike a balance between them. To over-emphasize the task, results in short term effectiveness and longer-range human problems. Over-emphasize on maintenance of relationship results in groups so involved with their feelings that they neglect the task.

4.9.2 Leadership Types

System theory of leadership suggests that leadership is an emergent phenomenon in the form of integrative leadership out of interaction of leaders and follows within the contextual variables lying within the organisation and outside it. Because of these interaction four types of leadership patterns emerge in organisation in stages.

These are :

1. Formal Leadership
2. Emergent Leadership
3. Shared Leadership
4. Integrative Leadership

Brief characteristics of these types are as follows:

1. **Formal Leadership:**
   (a) Types of leadership: Transformational and transactional
   (b) Influence: Authority / position based
   (c) Control: Top down
   (d) Communication: Vertical
   (e) Content: Large number of people in predictable and stable context.

2. **Emergent Leadership:**
   (a) Types of leadership: Emerging
   (b) Influence: Based on skills and knowledge of an individual and his acceptance by the group.
   (c) Control: Individual accountability.
   (d) Communication: Vertical and horizontal
   (e) Context: Comparatively small number of people fluctuating between different attractions.

3. **Shared Leadership:**
   (a) Types of leadership: Self managed team
   (b) Influence: Shared among participants
   (c) Control: Collective self - regulation
   (d) Communication: Horizontal
   (e) Context: Relatively small number of people in an open-ended dynamic context.

4. **Integrative Leadership:**

   (a) Types of leadership: Interdependent

   (b) Influence: Irregularly oscillates between the formal leader, several individuals (emergent leaders) and collective.

   (c) Control: Collective self regulation (for policy making) and individual accountability (for operations).

   (d) Communication: Multidirectional – Vertical, horizontal and diagonal.

   (e) Context: Can deal with complex and unpredictable contexts.

4.10 MOTIVATION

Definition

Motivation means "inspiring people to intensify their desire and willingness to perform their duties effectively and co-operate for the achievement of common objectives of the business".

Motivation is the mental preparation of an individual to do a specific job. It is a desire to do something. According to *Michael J. Jucius*, "Motivation is the act of stimulating some one or oneself to get a desired course of action, to push the right button to get desired action".

As put forth by *Brech*, motivation is a gentral inspiration on process which puts the members of the team to do their work effectively, to give their loyalty to the group, to carry out properly the tasks they have accepted and generally to pay an effective part in the job that the group has undertaken.

As mentioned by *Dalton Emcfarland*, "The concept of motivation is mainly psychological. It relates to those forces operating within the individual employee, or subordinate which inputes him to act or not act in certain ways".

Motivation and leadership are the master keys to successful management of any enterprise. They are also responsible to ensure productivity of human resources. Motivation can set into motion a person to carry out certain activity. Motivation assumes unique importance in modern business management. Democratic leadership heavily relies on motivation of employees, through financial and non-financial incentives. Effective communication and participation enhance the power of motivation. Feedback of information (upward communication) is necessary for effective motivation and direction.

Fundamentals of Motivation

The first fundamental thing is that a peron wants to exist and survive and for this he needs basic necessities of life e.g., food, cloth, shelter, education and medical aid etc.

The second fundamental of motivation is the desire to achieve a goal, for satisfaction or bliss. Basically people are motivated to put in sincere efforts if they are assured of fulfilling their needs such as psychological needs, social needs, security needs, ego (needs for self-respect) etc.

4.11 Intrinsic and Extrinsic Motivation

Motivation can be classified into two categoreis:

1. Intrinsic or Internal motivation
2. Extrinsic or External motivation

1. Intrinsic Motivation: The inner urge of a man for achieving a goal is called "Intrinsic or internal motive". There is no outside complusion for doing a wok in such cases. A person who works with internal motive is a self-motivated person. He is mentally prepared to do job and hence intrinsic motivation is more effective.

Employees are intrinsically motivated when they genuinely care about their work look for better way to do it. An intrinsic motivation emerges from work performance when the employee experiences sense of accomplishment on doing good work. It is achieved when people experience feeling of choice competence, meaningfullness and progress. Thus, job satisfaction emerges out of the performance associated with these features.

Examples of intrinsic motivation are interests, emotional attachments, burning desires, fighting spirit for some noble cause. For example, a patriot sacrifices his life for the sake of motherland, a scientist may be totally absorbed in his research work due to his inner desire mental satisfaction.

2. Extrinsic Motivation: An extrinsic motivation is in tangible form that is provided to employees after the work performance. Extrinsic motivation results from some material benefit in the form of pay increase salary, bonus, praise and so on; which motivates the workers to do their jobs more effectively and efficiently.

Some times extrinsic motivation may also emerge from fear of loss of job, punishment etc. which will motivate the workers to do their jobs more effectively.

Functions of Motivation:

Motivation performs the following three functions:

1. It originates action.
2. It directs activities in the direction of goal.
3. It helps to continue the activities till the goal is achieved.

Importance of Motivation

Motivation is needed to create interest, initiative, enthusiasm, loyalty and willingness to work. As a result of this, motivation helps to improve the productivity. The importance of motivation could be seen under these heads.

1. Arouse desire to work: Person may be capable of doing a work, be efficient, possess the necessary skill etc., still he cannot do the work allotted to him in right time, in right quantity and of right quality unless he is motivated to do so.

Workers not properly motivated may not mentally accept the orders or directions with the result the objectives of the company may not be achieved efficiently and effectively.

2. Appropriate use of factors of production: An organisation may have best instruments, equipments, tools, raw materials in sufficient quantity. But these factors can only be used appropriately (effectively) through sound motivation system.

3. Reduction in labour turnover: Labour does not try to go to another organisation if properly motivated. Not only this, the talented personnel from other organisations are also attracted to join the organisation in which motivation schemes are utilized.

4. Increase in production and productivity: Motivation increases the desire to work whole-heartedly and hence leads to increase in production and productivity.

5. Basis of co-operation: Motivation increases job satisfaction, so the workers' interest, loyalty for the organisation increases. This helps to maintain good employer-employee relations and develops the sense of co-operation.

Thus, without motivation the workers will not discharge their duties efficiently. There will be high rate of absenteeism, poor quality of production, higher degree of turnover. Effective motivation is the secret of improved quantity and quality.

Theories of Motivation:

Various theories have been developed by eminent authors on motivation. The following is one of the important theory of motivation.

4.12 Maslow's Theory of Motivation (Need Hierarchy)

Maslow advanced three important propositions about human behaviour:

(1) Men are wanting being: Their needs are unlimited and continuous. As soon as one need is satisfied, another appears in its place. The process is unending. It continues from birth to death. It keeps man to work continuously.

(2) Fresh needs can motivate persons to work: A satisfied need is not a motivator of behaviour, only the needs which are not satisfied are capable of motivating individuals.

(3) Man's Needs have a Hierarchy of Importance: According to Maslow man's needs are arranged in a series of levels. He classified the needs into five ascending levels, in which each level must be satisfied before going on to the next. The lower level needs have priority over higher level needs.

The following Fig. 4.4 shows the hierarchy of needs.

Needs	Description
Physiological (Basic)	Satisfying basic needs for food, shelter, clothing, water, air, sleep, sex etc.
└ Safety	Safety from physical harm. Protection against deprivation, danger, threat etc.
└ Social	Desire to be accepted, liked and loved.
└ Ego	Recognition and need for self-respect, status, independence etc.
└ Self Realisation	Ability to realise one's capabilities and to work for one's interest, (self-development, self-advancement).

Needs can be broadly classified into two categories as follows:

1. Primary Needs
   - Physiological (basic) needs
   - Safety needs

2. Secondary Needs
   - Social needs
   - Ego needs
   - Self-realization needs

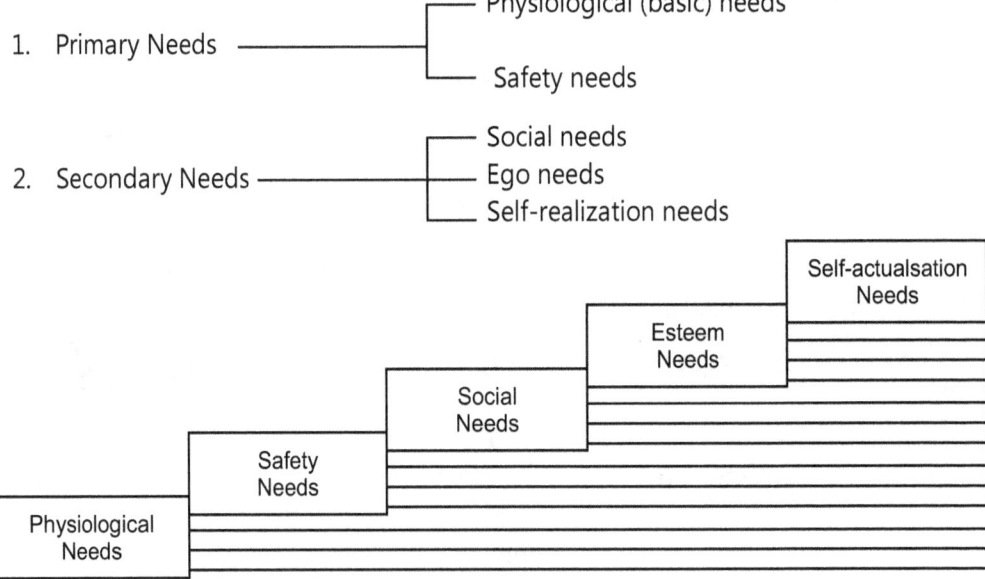

Fig. 4.4: Hierarchy of needs

4.12.1 Needs and Importance of Fulfilling Needs

Human needs are required to be satisfied. People are forced to work to satisfy their needs. This means people usually have reasons for doing what they do. They believe they can satisfy their needs by taking particular course of action. The needs, action, and satisfaction are closely inter-related and all these factors relate intimately to motivation.

1. Physiological needs: These are the basic needs in life. These are essential for everybody to remain alive, such as food, shelter, cloth, water, air etc. These needs motivate the person to do work and earn sufficient amount of money to fulfill them.

2. Safety needs: Security or safety needs arise only when the basic needs are fulfilled. These needs arise because most people think about future as much as they think about the present. Once people have sufficient food, shelter, cloth, rest, they will likely to direct their energies towards assuring these necessities in the future.

These are reflected in the desire for freedom from threat, potection against danger and accidents and security in the environment. In the workplace, individuals view these needs in terms of such aspects as safe working conditions, increase in salary, job security and an acceptable level of fringe benefits to provide for health and protection.

3. Social needs: When an individual's primary needs are relatively satisfied, then social needs, become an important motivator of his behaviour. Man wants to live with respect in the society. He wants that he should have relations with different groups of people. These needs are produced because man is a social animal, he does not like to live alone.

In the organisations, workers find satisfaction through frequent personal interaction and acceptance by others. Belonging to informal work group often satisfies his social needs.

When an individual finds that their social needs and even the security and basic needs are threatened, they may become resistant, violent and non-cooperative and thereby defeating the organisational objectives.

4. Ego, Status or Esteem needs: These needs have to do with self-respect and receiving respect from others for accomplishments as well as developing self-confidence and prestige. They are expressed in an individual's desire for strength, for achievement, for adequacy, for mastery, and competence for confidence to face the world and for independence and freedom. This involves others' opinions and includes such things as the desire for prestige, status, dominance, recognition, attention, importance and application. People value the esteem of others only when they believe they have earned it.

People exhibit ego needs when they seek opportunities for achievement, recognition, advancement, and greater responsibility. They work to earn skills. They take pride in maintaining high performance standards. They find better ways of doing their jobs. Like other needs esteem needs are rarely satisfied.

5. Self-Realisation needs: These are also called as self-actualisation needs. These are at the highest level. These needs are applicable to people having a sense of fulfillment by maximising their abilities, skills and potentials. Those who have strong self-realisation needs devote much of their energy to develop their creative potential.

Self-actualisation works differently in each individual ; for one person the desire may be to become an ideal teacher or an ideal leader. Another seeks to develop himself athletically, still others develop their potential through acting, painting, writing, dancing, singing, and research work.

In the workplace, people with dominant self-realisation needs have several characteristics. They like to perform work that: (i) challenges, (ii) permits them to use innovative approaches, (iii) provides for advancement and personal growth, (iv) allows them to set their own goals, (v) develops their creative potential, (vi) allows them to see change take place as a result of their personal efforts.

While higher needs never remain completely satisfied leaders can work with this concept of needs as a potential source of motivation. They must provide both the environment and job that enable people, at least to some degree, to have interesting, challenging work satisfying social relationship and self-realisation needs in carrying out their duties.

Maslow's theory of human motivation has been a land mark in the field of management. This hierarchical concept of needs is important for understanding the managerial task in relation of human resources working in organisation. Management at all levels must be sensitive to the changing needs of sub-ordinate groups and individuals to provide the best atmosphere for productivity and satisfaction.

4.12.2 Demerits or Weaknesses of Maslow's Theory

Although, Maslow's theory is accepted as a pioneering work in the study of motivation, it was criticized for the following reasons:
1. Most of the human needs are recurring and are never satisfied fully.
2. Most of the needs co-exist and there is no such hierarchy of. needs.
3. The levels of hierarchy are not rigidly fixed. The boundaries between them are hazy and overlapping.
4. This approach overlooks the interaction of needs. An act is seldom motivated by a single need. An act is more likely to be caused by several needs.
5. The concept of self-actualization is theoretical or academic. No person can ever know his maximum or best potentials.

4.13 SAFETY MANAGEMENT

Introduction

Technological development is taking place at a very fast rate in all the fields like mechanical, metallurgical, chemical, electrical and civil. These days every man is surrounded by automobiles, trains, aeroplanes, explosives, noise and air-pollution etc. which may cause accidents. The danger of life of human being is increasing with the advancement of scientific developments in different fields. The importance of industrial safety was realised because every year millions of industrial accidents occur which result in either death or in temporary disablement or permanent disablement of the employees and involve large amount of loss resulting from damage to property and wasted man hours and machine hours. Now-a-days serious attention is being paid to reduce the rate and severity of accident. Safety rules have been devised for each and every field to safeguard the interest of society. Hazard control and accident prevention have been considered as a basic need. Health and safety are basic desire and instinct. We believe in concept of safety, human protection and protection of nature. The benefits of accident prevention have been well-understood and accepted by industries throughout the world.

Safety: Safety is the state of being safe.

S – Spot the hazard

A – Assess the risk

F – Find a safe way

E – Every body

4.13.1 Industrial Safety Management

Any method, technique or process which can minimize unwanted events (accidents) in industrial concern may be referred to as a method, technique or process of Industrial Safety.

Industrial Safety management is mainly concerned with minimizing hazards in the industries ; and safety of people's life and property. Hazard is a state, physical or chemical having potential to injure the person or impairment of health. Risk or danger arises out of hazards.

Industrial Safety management is a branch of management which is concerned with identifying, evaluating, reducing, controlling and eliminating hazards from the industrial units. Safety management designs safety rules and makes the employees safety conscious.

Problem of Industrial Accidents

Accident may be defined as "an unforeseen, uncontrollable and sudden mishap which may result in minor injuries or death of the person involved, loss of property and interruptions in activities or functions in industry".

- As per Factory Act 1948, industrial accident has been defined as ; "*An occurrence in an industrial establishment causing bodily injury to a person which makes him unfit to resume his duties in the next 48 hours*".
- An unexpected, uncontrolled event which cannot be anticipated in advance.

4.13.2 Causes of Accidents

It is an established fact that accidents are caused, they do not just happen out of nothing. Whenever there occurs an accident, there must be some cause, which may be obvious or difficult to trace.

It is therefore necessary to investigate the causes and then take steps to prevent them in future.

The causes of accident may be classified as:

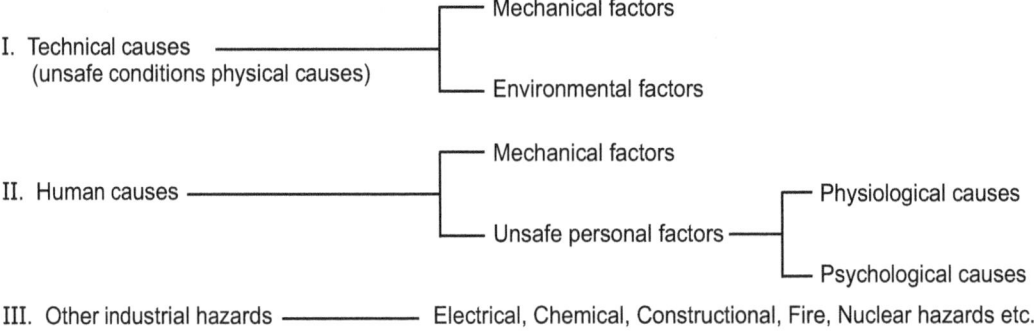

Fig. 4.5: Causes of accident

[I] Technical Causes

A. Mechanical Factors:

1. Continued use of old, poorly maintained or unsafe equipment. This is generally accompanied by failure to have regular plant safety preventive inspection of all production facilities in accordance with a properly designed time schedule. For example:

   (a) If crane elevator cables are not regularly inspected and promptly replaced when dangerously worm.

   (b) Power lines may be poorly insulated and worn insulation may be repaired with adhesive tape.

2. Unguarded or improper guarded machines or equipment, guards of improper height, strength, mesh etc.
3. Unsafe process, mechanical, chemical, electrical, nuclear etc.
4. Unsafe design and construction of building structures etc.
5. Improper material handling system.
6. Improper plant layout.
7. Untested boilers or pressure vessels.
8. Violation of prescribed safety practices.
9. Unsafely clothed, no goggles, gloves or masks, smoking in non-smoking areas, wearing high heal shoes etc.

B. **Environmental Factors:**
   1. **Temperature and humidity:** Low temperature cause shivering. Too high temperature cause headache and sweating, this also causes fatigue to the operator. Too high humidity (as in textile industry) may cause uncomfort, fatigue drowsiness especially when the atmosphere is too hot.
   2. **Defective and inadequate illumination:** It causes glares, shadows, eye strain etc.
   3. Presence of dust, fumes and smoke (e.g., in foundry or welding shops).
   4. **Overly fatigued worker:** Excess fatigue may arise out of work assignment that may tax the worker's physical and mental powers (excessive overtime, inadequate rest pauses).
   5. Unsafely arranged, poor house keeping, congestion, blocked exits, bad plant layout or arrangement of machines.
   6. Harsh or dominating behaviour of management or supervisors towards worker.
   7. The type of leadership style adopted by the management in the organisation.
   8. Excessively long duration of work, shift duty.
   9. Annoying outside noise and vibrations.

[II] **Human Causes**

A. **Unsafe Acts:**

Unsafe act may be defined as "the deviation from the normal and correct procedure or practice". It results in unnecessary exposure to hazards, or conduct minimizing the degree of safety. Any human action is manifestation of mental or psychological set up. Hence unsafe act is related to the psychological aspect of the workers.

The following are unsafe acts:
1. Operating without authority.
2. Operating or working at unsafe speed.
3. Making safety devices unoperative (removing, misadjusting, disconnecting etc.).
4. Using unsafe equipment or using equipment unsafely.
5. Taking unsafe position or posture (standing or working under suspended loads, lifting with back bent etc.).
6. Unsafe loading, placing, mixing, combining etc.
7. Working on moving or dangerous equipment.
8. Failure to use personal protective devices.
9. Improper use of tools.

B. The Unsafe Personal Factors:

The unsafe personal factors are the mental or bodily characteristics which promote unsafe act. These may be classified as (a) Physiological causes, and (b) Psychological causes.

(a) Physiological Causes: These causes of accidents are related to the bodily defects or health of the worker. Following are some of the physiological causes:
(i) Reduced hearing capacity of the worker.
(ii) Poor eye sight.
(iii) Arms or legs or any other part of the body may be defective or damaged.
(iv) Sleepiness due to fatigue or over eating.
(v) Poor health in general.
(vi) Old age or to young age.
(vii) High blood pressure and other diseases.
(viii) Colour blindness.

(b) Psychological Causes: These causes are related to the mental processes of the workers. Some of the psychological causes are:
(i) Improper attitude (disregard of instructions, failure to understand instructions, nervousness, excitability, depression etc.).
(ii) Ignorance, forgetfulness, carelessness, day dreaming etc.
(iii) Lack of knowledge and skill (unaware of safe practices, unskilled).
(iv) Home environment.

(v) Mental worries.

(vi) Feeling of job insecurity among workers

(vii) Over confidence

(viii) Accident proneness etc.

[III] Other Industrial Hazards

Hazards may be defined as "a potential condition which might be converted into an accident". Hazards may be broadly grouped under the following head:

(i) Mechanical   (ii) Electrical

(iii) Chemical   (iv) Fire

(v) Nuclear   (vi) Constructional.

A. Electrical Hazards may include:

(i) Ungrounded machine tools, casings and structures.

(ii) Uncovered switches and switch boards.

(iii) Poorly insulated powerlines which may cause fire and may give shocks.

(iv) Fuses of unsuitable capacity.

(v) Exposed resistances, rheostats etc.

(vi) Over confidence in working on the live circuits etc.

B. Fire Hazards: The main sources of fire are:

(i) Matches and smoking.   (ii) Heating and cooking.

(iii) Poor house keeping.   (iv) Electrical wiring and apparatus.

(v) Open flames and sparks.

(vi) Flammable liquids, explosive materials.

(vii) Welding and cutting torches etc.

C. Constructional Hazards:

(i) Faulty structural design.

(ii) Improper repair and maintenance.

(iii) Substandard and defective material of construction which do not satisfy the relevant standards and specifications.

(iv) Improper planning or layout.

(v) Lack of supervision during construction.

(vi) Ignoring the norms of sound engineering practice etc.

D. Chemical Hazards:

Industrial processes involve use of chemicals and hazardous materials. The raw materials used in industries could be hazardous due to toxicity inherent to materials. The products both intermediate and finished as well as the bye-products (including industrial wastes can pose serious problems of chemical safety. Hence storage, handling, manufacture and use of chemicals call for strict surveillance on the part of managers, supervisors and workmen. Some of the toxic chemicals are Carbon Monoxide, Carbon disulphide, Chlorine, Chromium, Mercury, Lead, Naptha, Sulphur dioxide etc.

4.13.3 Effects of Accidents

The adverse effects of accident can be summarized as under:

Effect on the Industry or Owner: An accident can be very costly to the industry as well as to the employees. The costs associated with accident can be classified as:

- Direct costs
- Indirect costs

Direct cost of an accident

1. Compensation has to be paid to the worker for temporary or permanent disability caused by accident.
2. Money paid for treatment and cure of workers disabled by on job accident.
3. Money value of damaged equipment and materials, expenses towards repairs, replacement of damaged machines and equipment.

Indirect cost of an accident

4. Cost of lost time of injured worker.
5. Cost of time lost by other employees who stop work
   (a) Out of curiosity
   (b) Out of sympathy
   (c) To assist injured employee
   (d) For other reason.
6. Cost of time lost by foreman, supervisors, safety engineers or other executives as follows:
   (a) Assisting injured employees.
   (b) Investigating the cause of accident.
   (c) Arranging for the injured workers production to be continued by some other workers.

(d) Selecting and training a new worker to replace the injured man.

(e) Preparing the accident report.

7. Cost of interruptions and delays in production due to accident.
8. Cost of lowered production due to substitute worker.
9. Cost of subsequent injuries that occur in consequence of the excitement or weakened morale due to original accident.

Effect on Worker: In addition to the industry the injured worker suffers financially as under:

1. If the worker dies in the accident, the family loses the bread earner.
2. Injury compensation never equals his earnings.
3. Accident also affects the morale of employee.
4. If the worker gets injured, he loses his efficiency and the workmanship. His rating gets lowered due to handicapness and therefore loses the incentives due to not performing at higher level.
5. After the accident, the worker is psychologically hesitant to work at the same place and even reluctant to exert himself in the job.

Cost to Society

Work connected injuries also put a considerable burden on society as a whole as under:

1. Even though a victim receives compensation, he may require additional helps from the society.
2. Obviously, for those who do not come under Compensation Act, the need for help from society is much greater.
3. Loss of production hours cause less products in market.
4. Employers necessarily include the costs of accident to the selling prices of their products. Therefore, the society has to pay more price for the products.
5. If the worker is involved in social activities, then his replacement is difficult to achieve.

4.13.4 Types of Industrial Accidents (Classification of Accidents)

There are several methods of classifying accidents. Some of them are as follow:

1. According to the nature of injuries
2. According to the event
3. According to place of accident

4. According to damage caused
5. According to length of recovery

1. **Nature of Injury (based on seriousness of injuries caused)**

    (a) Fatal Accident: In which case a worker losses his life due to an injury by the machine, electric shock, inhalation of poisonous chemicals fumes, fire and fall etc.

    (b) Accident which Cause Permanent Disablement (total or partial): In these type of accident, the worker receives permanent injuries because of which he looses his earning capacity. The employee is not capable of earning that much money which he was capable to earn before the accident. He losses his efficiency and workmanship consequently, his earning gets reduced. The employee may cut his finger, arm or hand, damage his eyes etc. due to accident.

    (c) Accident which cause Temporary Disablement: Less serious injuries are caused in this type of accidents and the worker becomes temporally unfit and looses his earning capacity for a short period of time. The worker starts work after receiving first aid in workshop or factory hospital when he suffers from minor injuries. Fracture of arm is an example of temporary disablement.

2. **According to the Event**

    This type of accidents are classified as
    - Machine Accidents
    - Non-Machine Accidents

    (a) Machine Accidents: These include
    - Accidents caused because of catching of tools, breaking of guides, metals chips flying from the machine.
    - Catching of fingers, arms, legs, clothing etc. in machine.

        These accidents are mainly caused by loose cloths or body parts of the worker being caught in the moving parts of the machine.

        These accidents are more serious because the work is suddenly stopped and it may cause damage to the machinery, body of the worker and material etc.

    (b) Non-Machine Accidents: Nearly 80 % of the accidents are non-machine accidents. These may include accidents caused by
    - flying objects striking the workers overhead,
    - metallic portion of the hammer becoming loose and flying away from the wooden handle and striking against someone.

- objects on the floor, unsafe house keeping facilities (unsuitable shelves, bins, racks, no aisle marking etc.)
- oily, slippery floor etc.

3. **Accidents According to the Place**

   These may include:
   - Accidents occurred in stores, foundry, machine shop, installation and building etc.
   - Accidents occurred on the road, traffic accidents, passenger accidents etc.

4. **Accidents According to the Damage Caused**

   In this type, accidents are classified according to the extent of damage caused as:
   - Damage to plant
   - Damage to machinery, material handling equipment.
   - Damage to materials
   - Damage to factory building etc.

5. **According to the length of Recovery**

   According to the length of recovery after the worker is injured in an accident there are following three types of accidents
   - First Aid Accidents
   - Home Cases Accidents
   - Lost Time Accidents

   (i) In case of *first aid accidents* the injuries are minor. After first aid treatment the workers are ready to work, no time is lost except the time of first aid treatment.

   (ii) In *home case accidents*, medical treatment is first given at factory hospital and the worker is allowed to go home for a maximum of 3 days. No compensation is paid to the worker.

   (iii) In *lost time accident*, the injuries are serious. The worker is admitted to the hospital. He is advised to take rest for a certain period. Compensation has to be paid to the worker for lost time accidents according to the "Workmen's Compensation Act".

4.13.5 Preventive Measures (Accident Prevention)

"An injury prevented is a benefaction, an injury compensated and apology". Accident prevention is the work of eliminating the mechanical hazards of environment and the unsafe actions of persons before the accident and the injury occurs.

It is concerned with the control of man performance, machine performance and physical environment. Accident prevention is a vital factor in every industrial enterprises; if it is ignored or practised unskillfully, leads to needless human suffering and business bankruptcy.

Accident prevention brings about a spectacular achievement in the saving of life, compensation, continuity of services, increased production, decreased labour turnover and improved labour management relations.

To be effective in hazard control programme, it must be planned and should be logical. Programme objectives and safety policies need to be established. Responsibility to the hazard control programme needs to be determined.

Accident prevention consists of four major steps. These are:

- Discover the causes
- Control environmental causes
- Control behaviouristic causes
- Supplementary activities

(a) Discovering Accident Causes

Before any steps can be taken it is essential to find out:

1. The causes of previous accidents and
2. The existing hazards that may cause accident unless corrected.

These activities are necessary not only before starting the actual procedures of accident prevention but also afterwards, for they must be given continuous never ending attention ; otherwise the real efforts of accident prevention will get out of hand. The supervisors report of accident investigation is the basis of all analysis of past accidents.

After finding the potential hazards by survey and inspection, analysis must be made to select most important hazards to be attacked. The reasons for existence of hazards must be found when these do not yield to corrections. Knowing and finding the hazards is only the beginning. These must be corrected/controlled.

(b) Controlling Environmental Causes

All the environmental causes have something to do with machinery and equipment, with the things one can see and feel. A good layout and working conditions play a major role in preventing many accidents. Improper physical and mechanical environment such as space, light, heat, arrangement, ventilation, materials, tools, equipment, procedures, company policy, routing etc. make it awkward, difficult, inconvenient or impossible to follow safe practice rules:

1. The layout should be such that: (a) Every employee has enough space to move and operate. (b) Passageways between working places, roads, tracks etc. must never be obstructed.
2. The working area should prevent the inrush of cold air, hot air and draughts to the working place.
3. For adequate lighting, ventilation etc. the heights of working room should be about 3 metres.
4. Floors must be non-skid type satisfactorily plane and should have capacity to absorb sounds, vibration etc.
5. Doors and windows should be of adequate dimensions in order to make full use of natural day-light.
6. Select, purchase and make use of machines and process which will produce little noise.
7. Isolate and keep noise producing machines in separate close cabin.
8. Use suitable machine mounts to damp-down the vibration.
9. Use proper material handling equipment, it should also be promptly repaired and adequately maintained.

If there are two or more different ways to prevent certain types of accidents, select proper way for example. If there is a hole in the floor and if there is any danger of worker falling in it and get injured, it is much wiser and cheaper in the long run to eliminate the hole than to place a guard rail around it or to try to teach the worker to stay away. Trying to teach a man to avoid hazard is never ending job requiring constant supervision and discipline. But the elimination of a hazard is an immediate and permanent cure.

Environmental Causes of Accident — How to eliminate them ?

Sr. No.	Environmental Causes of Accidents	Corrective Action
1.	Improper guarding (unguarded, inadequately guarded, guard removed by some one other than injured worker etc.)	(a) Inspection (b) Provide guards for existing hazards.
2.	Substances or equipment defective through use, or neglect (worn out cracked, broken etc. through no fault of injured worker).	(a) Inspection (b) Proper maintenance.

Contd...

3.	Substances or equipment defective through design or construction, (too large, too small, not strong enough, made with flaws etc.)	(a) Source of supply must be reliable. (b) Inspection for defects. (c) Correction of defects before operating.
4.	Unsafe procedure, hazardous process, management failed to make adequate plans for safety.	(a) Job analysis. (b) Formulation of safe procedure. (c) Job training.
5.	Unsafe housekeeping facilities (unsuitable shelves, bins, racks, no aisle marking etc.)	(a) Provide suitable layout and equipment necessary for good housekeeping.
6.	Improper illumination (poor, none, glaring, headlight etc.)	(a) Improve the illumination.
7.	Improper ventilation (poor, dusty, gaseous, high humidity etc.)	(a) Improve the ventilation.
8.	Improper dress or protective devices (management's failure to provide or specify use).	(a) Provide safe dress or personnel protective devices. (b) Specify the use of certain protective devices on certain jobs. .

(c) Controlling Behaviouristic Causes

These can be controlled through the application of

- Job analysis
- Job training
- Supervision
- Discipline
- Personal work
- Physical examination

Proper Placement of Workers: In general, it is much more difficult to control behaviouristic causes than it is to control environmental causes. It can neither be seen nor felt. It is the result of such complicated factors as heredity, emotion, diet and habits etc. For example, a wrong attitude is an important behaviourstic cause that is more closely induced by worry. Many workers worry about current finance problems or the possibility of poverty in old age or the expenses on medical care. The activities such as pension plans, group health and accident insurance and employee credit union have helped to relieve thousands of workers from some of these worries and problems and helped in improving the company's accident record.

Behaviouristic Causes of Accidents — How to eliminate them ?

No.	Behaviouristic causes of Accidents	Corrective Action
1.	Improper attitude (deliberate chance taking, disregard of instructions, absent-mindedness etc.)	(a) Supervision (b) Discipline (c) Personnel work
2.	Lack of knowledge of skill (New on the job unpracticed, unskilled etc.)	(a) Job analysis (b) Job training (c) Proper placement of men
3.	Physical or mental defect (one arm, deaf, partially blind etc.)	(a) Pre-employment physical examinations (b) Periodic physical examinations (c) Proper placement of men
4.	Operating without authority, operating at unsafe speed.	(a) Supervision (b) Discipline
5.	Making safety devices unoperative, not using safety devices.	(a) Supervision (b) Training
6.	Taking unsafe position or using equipment unsafely. Improper use of tools.	(a) Supervision (b) Training

Only discovering the corrective action or remedy is not enough. Unless the remedy is successfully applied, all the previous steps will be useless.

The safety engineer has to direct authority for implementation of the remedies.

Hence he must:

(i) prepare and present his recommendations and suggestions to management so that management is convinced of the importance, and thus obtain active support.

(ii) establish safety organisation.

(iii) create enthusiasm and co-operation at all levels.

(d) Supplementary Activities

The workers should be properly trained to observe safety rules. If necessary, discipline is to be strictly enforced.

Wide publicity should be given through:

1. Posters,
2. Booklets and other literature,
3. Movies,
4. Film strips,
5. Contests,
6. Meetings,
7. Committees,
8. Suggestion system,
9. Employee magazines, Bulletins
10. Safety books, safety training

4.13.6 Safety Procedures

In every organisation, safety procedures or safety rules must be formed to promote safety of employees and to prevent the direct and indirect costs of accident.

The safety procedure consists of:

- Investigate the causes of accident that have already occurred.
- Control the physical, physiological and other causes of accidents.
- Promote safety consciousness amongst the employees.

A. Investigation of Accident

1. Record the causes of accidents.
2. From this dates try to locate various hazards which may cause similar accidents and make the persons concerned aware about them.
3. Try to locate accident prone workers and take suitable action.

B. Controlling Causes of Accident

1. Check all designs, blue prints and order etc. and develop means of making them safe.
2. Personnel protective equipments like safety glasses, respirators, aprons, shoes and gloves must be provided and used depending upon type of work.
3. Everything in plant should be in proper order i.e., good housekeeping is must.
4. There should be proper maintenance (Preventive maintenance).
5. Procedure and methods of work should be devised keeping safety in mind.
6. Electrical connections and insulation should be checked at regular intervals.
7. Safety guards must be provided on all rotating parts such as pulleys, gear-boxes etc.
8. Loose dress must never be used while working on machine.
9. Material handling equipment should have unobstructed path for movement.

10. Lighting arrangement and ventilation should be improved.
11. Jobs should be properly analyzed and evaluated. Most suitable and trained people should be put on a particular job.
12. Factory atmosphere, temperature and humidity should be controlled so as to improve the conditions of work place.
13. Any oil or coolant spills on the floor should be wiped off immediately to avoid slipping and falling.
14. Smoking should be strictly prohibited particularly near chemical or combustible materials.
15. Inflammable materials should be stored separately and away from the general stores.
16. Pressure vessels and their components must be periodically tested and defective parts should be promptly replaced.
17. Fire extinguishers should be kept in proper condition and at key places, and employees should be trained to operate fire fighting equipment.

C. Promotion of Safety Habits and Consciousness

(i) Promote safety consciousness amongst the employees.

(ii) Train the workers to observe safety rules.

(iii) In every plant, small or big, a definite planned safety programme is necessary for reducing the hazards to minimum and for developing safe and adequate behaviour for every employee.

(iv) A safety organisation should be set up by which interest is created and maintained and all safety activities are co-related and directed.

4.13.7 Welfare and Safety

Welfare activities are associated with economic and psychological growth of employees. In certain areas welfare and safety activities are closely linked together.

These areas of activities may include the following:

(i) Provision of compensation in case of accidents.

(ii) Precautionary measures for maintaining industrial health such as: Reasonable hours of work, rest pauses, housing facilities, education facilities, lunch room and cafeteria, medical facilities, recreational facilities, provision of rest rooms, financial assistance etc.

(iii) Fencing and covering of machines.

(iv) Proper layout of machinery and plant.

(v) Provision of first aid appliances.

(vi) Temperature and humidity control in the work places.

(vii) Proper ventilation.

(viii) Provision of fire, extinguishers.

(ix) Provision of personal protective devices.

(x) Good working conditions etc.

General Safety Rules

It is necessary to frame a set of rules to promote safety of employees and to prevent the direct and indirect costs of accident. These safety rules should be strictly followed and administered as a part of safety programme.

While framing safety rules following points should be taken into consideration:

1. The safety rules should be such that it does not cause annoyance to an employee.
2. Safety rules must be clearly defined without any ambiguity.
3. The safety rules must keep pace with changing environments and industrial situations.
4. Safety rules should be such that they should be acceptable to the employees without resistance.

Some of the general safety rules which may serve as a guideline to workers and supervisors are as follows:

1. Power should be switched off before repairing the equipment.
2. Smoking should be strictly prohibited, particularly near chemical or inflammable materials.
3. Personal protective devices like safety goggles, aprons, shoes, must always be used depending upon the type of operations involved.
4. Wire mesh and safety guards must be provided on all rotating parts such as pulleys, gear boxes etc.
5. High voltage equipments and other machines which cannot be properly guarded should be fenced.
6. Pressure vessels and their component parts must be periodically tested, the defective parts should be promptly replaced.

7. Mischievous acts should never be tolerated and defaulter should be punished.
8. Electrical connections and insulation should be checked at regular intervals.
9. Inflammable materials should be stored separately and away from the general stores.
10. Material handling equipments should have unobstructed path for their movement.
11. Defective tools such as hammers, spanners should not be used.
12. Only authorised employees should operate the equipment.
13. Loose dress must never be used while working on a machine.
14. Prompt first aid attention must be paid to any injured person, and remedial measures thereof must be taken.
15. Fire extinguishers should be kept in proper condition and at key places.

First Aid

Inspite of taking all safety precautions and measures, accidents cannot be avoided. An injured worker needs immediate proper treatment. Hence, every establishment should have adequate provisions for first aid treatment. The primary function of implant first aid facilities is to give prompt treatment to those who suffer injury at the work place (before his condition may become critical).

A First Aid-Box must be provided in the charge of a responsible person who must be always available in working hours and should be trained in first aid treatment.

The specified contents of first aid-box in workshops employing more than 60 persons (as per Factory Act) are:

No.	Contents of First Aid-Box	
	Item	Numbers
1.	Small sized sterilized dressings	24
2.	Medium sized sterilized dressings	12
3.	Large sized sterilized dressings	12
4.	Sterilized cotton wool packets	10 gm
5.	Snake bite lancet	1
6.	Pair of scissors	1

Contd...

7.	Large size burn dressings	12
8.	25 gm bottle of $KMnO_4$ crystals	2
9.	100 gm bottle containing 2% alcoholic solution	1
10.	First aid leaflet	1 copy
11.	Rolled bandages 10 cm wide	12
12.	Rolled bandages 5 cm wide	12
13.	Adhesive plaster	2 rollers
14.	100 gm bottle of salvolative having dose and mode of administration indicated on lable	1
15.	Safety pins	2 packets
16.	Eye drops	One bottle
17.	Some burn ointment like burnol	One tube

In addition, it may contain other medicines as recommended by doctor for first aid treatment.

QUESTIONS

1. Define personnel management. State its objectives.
2. Describe the functions of personnel management in brief.
3. What is staffing? Explain the importance of staffing in an organisation.
4. State and describe the factors affecting staffing.
5. Define manpower planning. Explain its importance in overall planning of business orgnisation.
6. State and describe the steps involved in human resource planning.
7. Define recruitment. Describe the various sources of recruitment.
8. Describe the internal sources of recruitment with its advantages and disadvantages.
9. Describe the various sources of external recruitment of employees.
10. What is scientific selection? State the major factors in individual fitness for a job.
11. Describe the steps involved in recruitment are selection of employees.
12. Describe the various tests commonly used for employment of personnel.

13. Explain the importance of training in business/industrial organisation.
14. State the need of training of workers (craftsmen training). Name the various methods of training workers.
15. Define training. What are the objectives of training and development.
16. Describe the benefits of training.
17. Name the various methods of training workers and explain any two of them.
18. Describe on-job training with its advantages and limitations.
19. State the objectives of foreman or supervisory training.
20. State and describe the various methods of training supervisors.
21. Describe the importance of executive training.
22. Describe the various methods of executive training in brief.
23. Describe any two of the following methods of executive training.
    (a) Case study method
    (b) Business games
    (c) Role playing.
24. Define leadership. Justify the statement "The essence of leadership is followership".
25. State and describe the important functions of leadership.
26. Describe the desirable qualities of leadership.
27. Describe the various styles of leadership in brief.
28. Describe the following styles of leadership with their advantages and limitations. (any two).
    (a) Authoritarion style
    (b) Participative style
    (c) Free-rain style
29. Describe in brief the various types of leadership.
30. Define motivation and explain its importance.
31. Differentiate between 'Instrinsic motivation' and 'Extrinsic motiviation' with suitable examples.
32. What do you understand by human needs? Explain the classification of needs as given by Maslow.

33. Explain the Maslow's theory of motivation with its significance.
34. What is safety management? Describe its need in industries.
35. Define accident. Describe the following causes of accident.
    (a) Mechanical factors
    (b) Environmental factors
36. State and describe unsafe personal factors which may cause accident.
37. State the effects of accident on:
    (a) Industry or owner
    (b) Worker
    (c) Society
38. Justify the following statements:
    (a) "An injury prevented is a benefaction, an injury compensated is an apology".
    (b) "Accidents are accidental, but their rate can be minimised by taking safety measures".
39. Write short notes on any two of the following:
    (a) Safety procedures
    (b) Welfare and safety
    (c) Safety rules.

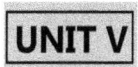

ETHICAL AND LEGISLATIVE MANAGEMENT

5.1 INTRODUCTION

Prof. Amartya Sen has expressed that economics as it has emerged can be made more productive by greater attention to the ethical considerations that shape human behaviour and judgment.

Ethics is intrinsic in our daily life and should be expressed in all our actions, speech, thought and attitude. We are consciously or unconsciously evaluating the actions of people around us, as well as ourselves and we frequently ask ourselves the question: It is right or wrong? Is it good or bad? Does it give us happiness or sorrow? We are all moral being in the sense we are gifted with an acute sense of right or wrong, a sense of pride, contentment and gladness is behaving properly, and sense of shame, inadequacy and unhappiness when we behave unproperly.

Business is a socio-economic activity flourishing in a special cultural ethos. Businessmen are rational human being who hold themselves accountable and responsible for their action. Business cannot function unless certain moral pre-requisites are fulfilled. A strong sense of leadership ethics and responsibility is asked of business today. Business people should be guided by concepts not only related to profitability and efficiency but also of professional integrity, responsibility and fairness. In other words, morality governs the way we should live with each other and with ourselves.

5.2 MEANING AND NATURE OF ETHICS

5.2.1 Meaning of Ethics

The term 'ethics' comes from Greek word 'ethos' meaning character, guiding belief, standards, or ideas that pervade a group, community or people. In the present context ethics is used as a field of study. It is a branch of philosophy which is concerned with moral human character and conduct, it prescribes moral principles that define what out to be.

There are different branches of ethics like business ethics, medical ethics, legal ethics, etc. Business ethics is defined as follows.

"Business ethics refers to a set of moral principles which play a significant role in guiding the conduct of personnel in the operation of any business organisation.

Freeman views that business ethics includes people's rights as well as moral rules that people apply in making decisions. Thus, business ethics is concerned with what is right or wrong in human behaviour.

Definitions of Ethics

Following are some of the definitions of ethics.

1. As already stated, 'Ethics or moral philosophy' is the branch of philosophy which has morality as its subject matter. It means that the study of what is right or what is wrong, what is good or bad in conduct is called ethics.

2. Ethics means 'Moral Science' and involves the study of moral philosophy, human character, conduct, the sense of doing right or wrong, good or bad and other similar moral values.

3. *Churchill* defined ethics as "the application of moral values or codes or complex problems using a rational decision making process".

4. "Ethics is doing what is right to achieve, what is good. Ethics is concerned with the principles of good and evil, which are universal and eternal".

   Honesty, responsibility, just and fair dealing are universally recognized as right, and just, while, lying, cheating, stealing, cowardice and irresponsibility are recognized wrong.

5. "Ethics is concerned not only distinguishing right from wrong and good from bad but also with commitments to do what is right or what is good. The concept of ethics is closely linked to that of value that is enduring belief that influences the choices we make from among available means and ends." — *Keneth Kernagham*

6. "Ethics is the study of morals and moral choices". It focuses on standards, rules and codes of conduct that govern the behaviour of individuals and groups.

7. In the simplest terms, business ethics are moral principles that define right and wrong behaviour in the world of business. What constitutes right and wrong behaviour in business is determined by the public interest groups, and business organisations, as well as individuals' personal morals and values.

8. 'Ethics' refer to the code of conduct that guides an individual while dealing in a situation. It relates to the social rules that influence people to be honest in dealing with the other people.

9. Business Ethics is the process of evaluating decisions either pre or post, with respect to the moral standards of the society's culture.

10. According to *R. Wayne Mondy*, 'Ethics is the discipline dealing with what is good and bad, or right and wrong, or with moral duty and obligation.

11. Business ethics is the application of general ethical rules to business behaviour.

5.2.2 Nature of Ethics

The concept of ethics deals with human beings only. Only human beings are endorsed with the freedom of choice.

Ethics aims at systematic knowledge. So ethics is a science. As a science, ethics has its own particular sphere, it deals with certain judgements that we make about human conduct. It deals with systematic explanation of rightness or wrongness in the light of the highest good of man.

Ethics is a normative science. It differs from positive science (i.e. natural science or descriptive science). Positive science deals with fact. But ethics does not deal with fact. Rather it deals with value. It is concerned with judgements of 'what ought to be' but not with 'what is the actual case'.

Ethics deals with human conduct which is voluntary and not forced by persons or circumstances. For example, injuring or even killing a person who has come to kill you is not considered moral or legal offence, but a cold blooded murder is considered to be the highest kind of moral or legal crime. Ethics is basically an area dealing with moral judgement regarding voluntary human conduct.

Business ethics can be, and has been, ethical and can still make profits. But profit maximization and discharging of social responsibilities at the maximum limit con not be done simultaneously as they are at opposite ends (e.g. concern for task and concern of workers).

Following characteristics are needed for a decision to be ethical. These characteristics also explains nature of ethics.

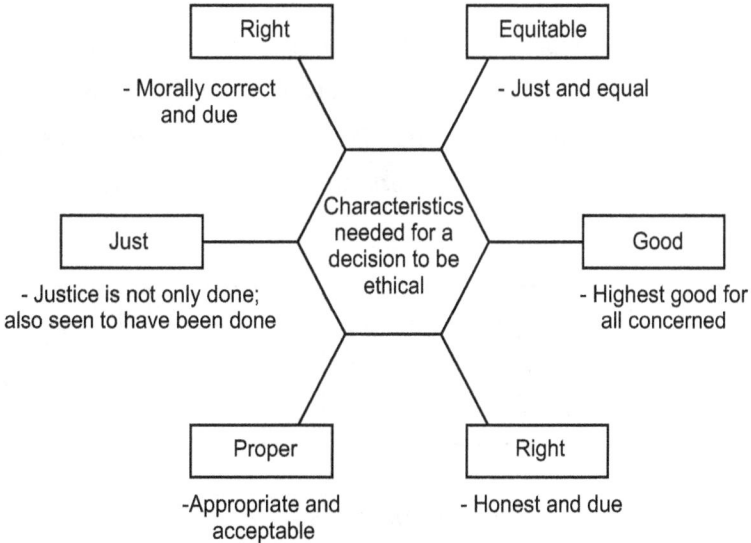

Fig. 5.1: Characteristics of ethical decision

Ethical decisions should express some obligations to others. If a decision helps in benefitting only to one self, then that is not an ethical decision. The very concept of being ethical means that results in some good for the larger society and not just for oneself.

Objectives of Ethics

The objectives of ethics are as follows:

1. Establish moral standards/ norms of behaviour; while establishing the standards it is necessary to consider ethics to deal with several interrelated and complex problems which may be of Psychological, legal commercial, philosophical, sociological and political in nature.
2. Study of human behaviour, making evaluative assessment about them as moral or immoral.
3. Establishing moral standards and norms of behaviour.
4. Making judgement upon human behaviour based on these standards/norms.
   - Prescribing moral behaviour and making recommendation about how to behave or vice versa.
   - Expressing on opinion or attitude about human conduct in general.

5.3 MORAL AND ETHICS

Ethics can be distinguished from 'morals' which are the rules or duties that govern our behaviour as persons to persons (such as "do not tell lies" or "do not hurt other person".) Ethics is an area dealing with moral judgement regarding voluntary human conduct. Moral judgement requires moral standards by which human conducts are judged. Ethics are the ultimate ends or the highest good to be pursued. Ethics covers wide area as compared to moral.

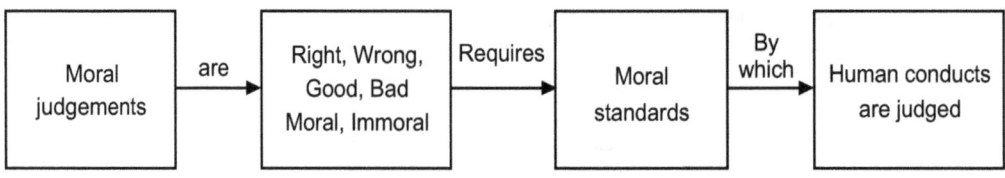

Fig. 5.2: Moral judgments

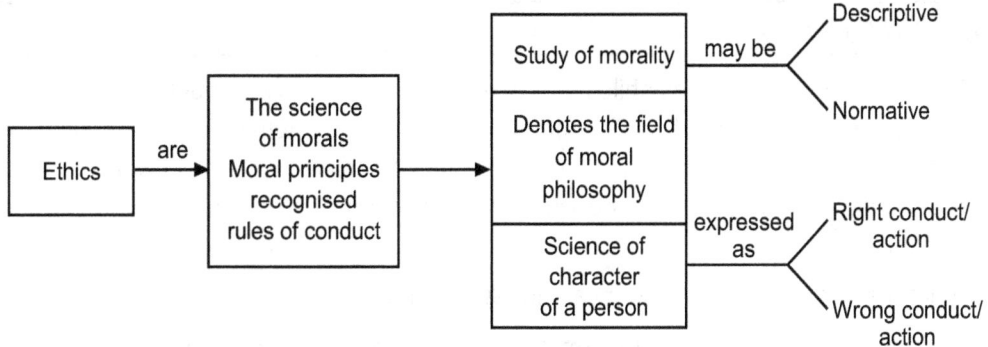

Fig. 5.3: Ethics cover wide areas

Comparison between Moral and Ethics

	Moral	Ethics
1.	Morals are principles or habits with respect to right or wrong conduct. It defines how things should work according to an individuals ideals and principles.	Ethics is the rule of conduct recognized in respect to a particular class of human actions or a particular group, culture, etc. It defines how things are according to the rules.
2.	Moral comes internally from within the individual.	Ethics comes from social system i.e. external.
3.	We behave morally because we ourselves believe something right or wrong.	We follow ethics in our conduct because society says it is the right thing to do.
4.	Doing something against ones morals and principles can have different effects on different people, they may feel uncomfortable, remorse, depressed etc.	It we do not behave ethically we may face peer/societal disapproval or even may be punished.
5.	Morals are usually consistent, although there may be some change according to individuals' belief.	Ethics are dependent on other for definition. They are more flexible than morals. They tend to be consistent within a certain context, but can vary between contexts.
6.	Moral comes from a Latin word "mos" meaning "Custom".	Ethics comes from Greek word "ethos" meaning character.
7.	Morality is governed by social and cultural beliefs or requirements.	Ethics are governed by professional and legal guidelines within a particular time and place.

5.4 TYPES OF ETHICS

Ethics sometimes known as philosophical ethics, ethical theory, moral theory, and moral philosophy, is a branch of philosophy that involves systematizing, defending and recommending concepts of right and wrong conduct. Philosophical ethics investigates what is the best way for human to live and what kinds of actions are right or wrong in particular circumstances.

Ethics may be classified into four categories as follows:

I. **Meta-ethics**, about the theoretical meaning and reference of moral propositions and how their truth values (if any) may be determined.

II. **Normative ethics**, about the practical means of determining a moral course of action.

III. **Virtue ethics**, describes the character of moral agent as a driving force for ethical behaviour.

IV. **Applied ethics**, draws upon ethical theory in order to ask what a person is obliged to do in some very specific situation or within some particular domain of action (such as business).

[I] Meta-Ethics:

Meta-ethics asks how we understand, know about, and what we mean when we talk about what is right and what is wrong. An ethical question fixed on some practical question, such as "should I eat this particular piece of a chocolate cake?" can not be a meta-ethical question. A meta ethical question is abstract and relates to a wide range of more specific practical questions. For example, "Is it ever possible to have secure knowledge of what is right or wrong?" would be a meta-ethical question.

Meta-ethic always accompanies philosophical ethics. For example, Aristotle implies that less precise knowledge is possible in ethics, than in other spheres of inquiry, and he regards ethical knowledge as dependent upon habit that makes it distinctive from other kinds of knowledge.

Studies of how we know in ethics divide into cognitivism and non-cognitivism. Non-cognitivism is the claim that when we judge something as right or wrong, this is neither true or false. Cognitivism can then be seen as the claim that when we talk about right and wrong, we are talking about matters of fact.

[II] Normative Ethics:

Normative ethics is concerned with practical means of determining a moral course of action. It is the study of ethical action. It is the branch of ethics that investigates the set of questions that arise when considering how one ought to act morally speaking. Normative ethics is distinct from meta-ethics. Meta-ethics, studies the meaning of moral language and the meta physics of moral facts. Whereas, normative ethics examines standards for the rightness and wrongness of actions.

Normative ethics is also different from descriptive ethics, as the descriptive ethics is an empirical investigation of peoples' moral beliefs.

For example, descriptive ethics would be concerned with determining what proportion of people believe that killing is always wrong, while normative ethics is concerned with whether it is correct to hold such belief. Normative ethics is thus, called as prescriptive, rather than descriptive.

Traditionally, normative ethics, (also known as moral theory) is the study of what makes actions right or wrong. These theories offers moral principles one could apply in resolving difficult moral decisions.

[III] Virtue Ethics:

Moral character rather than right action is fundamental in virtue ethics. It was originated with ancient Greek and received its fullest expression in Aristotles' Nicomachean ethics.

Virtue ethics theory does three things:

- It defines the concept of a virtue.
- It must offer some list of the virtues.
- It offers some justification of the list and explain how we define what are virtues and vices.

   e.g. Honesty is in the list of virtues.

Aristotle defines virtue as a character trait that manifests itself in habitual action. Honesty for example, cannot consist in telling the truth once. It is the tract of a person who tells the truth as a general practice.

For the Greeks, virtue means excellence and ethics was concerned with excellences of human character.

Virtue ethics = Excellences of human character

The list of possible virtues include.

- courage
- Tolerance
- Generosity
- Integrity etc

- Honesty
- Benevolence
- Self control

Role of Virtue Ethics:

1. Successful, rewarding lives (the kind of lives we would call the good life)
2. The good life in Aristotle's sense is possible only for virtuous person i.e. person who develop the traits of character that we call virtues.

Virtue ethics could be applied to business. Virtual ethics looks at moral issues from a very different perspective than action based ethics.

[IV] Applied Ethics:

Applied ethics attempts to apply ethical theory to real-life situations. The discipline has many specialized fields, such as engineering ethics, bio-ethics, geoethics, public service ethics and business ethics.

Applied ethics is used in some aspects of determining public policy, as well as by individuals facing difficult decisions. The sort of questions addressed by applied ethics include. "Is getting an abortion immoral?" "Is affirmative action right or wrong". "What are human rights and how do we determine them?" "Do animals have rights as well?"

A more specific question could be: "If some one else can make better out of his/her life than I can, is it then moral to sacrifice myself for them if needed?" Without these questions there is no clear fulcrum on which to balance law, politics, and the practice of arbitration. In fact, the ability to formulate questions are prior to rights balancing. However, in ethics the issues are most often multi faceted and the best proposed actions address many different areas concurrently.

Ethics can also be classified into following types:

1. Transactional Ethics
2. Participatory Ethics
3. Recognitional Ethics

1. Transactional Ethics: The transactional ethics is based on common interest. The common interest occur at one and the same time and place, without however, dependent on one another. All parties involved in the action pattern have interests that happens to coincide in time but that do not affect each other.

There is morality involved in this relation between the parties involved. In order to let each party's transaction run smoothly, all parties have to accept the principle of equality, i.e. every party/person should allow every other the same amount of freedom of action he claims for himself.

Interests can also be common in the stronger sense of being connected. The interests of both connot be realized without the interest of the other being satisfied as well.

Both parties are needed to arrive at intended result (for mutual benefit). Every party is indispensable, every party is equally entitled to an appropriate share in the outcome of the arrangement.

All market transactions fall within the category of transactional ethics.

Example: One person need vegetables from vegetable vendor. The vendor wants customers for survival, so both are dependent on each other, as long as both contribute appropriately.

In order to let things run smoothly in this type of transactions two specific moral principles are required.

- Principle of honesty, i.e. one should operate in good faith fairly and equitably.
- Principle of reciprocity i.e. one should avoid free riding on somebody else's efforts.

In short, the transactional ethics covers the transactions that are performed on the basis of simultaneous or connected interests and that are general by the principles of equality, honesty and reciprocity.

2. Participatory Ethics: Participatory ethics is a privileged part of business ethics. Within this category, the actions of the parties involved are not on the basis of simultaneous or connected interest but by shared interest. Parties co-operate in order to produce a more distinct common good that has three characteristic features.

- The goods can only be realized through the participation of all parties.
- Participation cannot be enforced (no explicit moral obligation to take part in the project.
- Though participation may be profitable by participating parties as well as the community at large, none of the parties have to participate in order to survive.

The important thing is that the parties join the alliance voluntarily, committing themselves to a self imposed and non-enforceable obligations. This results a specific type of social relations that is guided by two more principles, namely, 1) Principles of decency and 2) Principle of emancipation.

Principle of decency (a specimen of moral aesthetics) where a real opportunity to contribute to the general welfare presents itself and no obstacles arise.

Principle of emancipation – It means special attention is given to the least powerful who deserve measure for development.

On the basis of decency, corporations voluntarily contribute to a city development project that aims for benefit of all. By participating on a regular basis, in common projects on behalf of general welfare, a corporation demonstrates that it can take seriously its corporate citizenship.

3. Recognitional Ethics: From moral point of view it is necessary to protect the interest of weaker section of the society and to give them recognition. In such situations, the positions of the parties involved would be claimant on one side and that of a duty bound actor on the other, the former being entitled to the recognition of his claims and interests whereas the latter is obliged to recognize these claims (i.e. one party's moral right and other party's corresponding moral duty.)

In terms of interest we may face a situation of conflicting interests and unequal claims. The rights of the party affected have a great moral weight than the freedom to act of the acting party. The domain of ethics will be at stoke here as the domain of 'recognitional ethics'.

Basic moral principles which characterize the field of recognitional ethics are:

1. The principle of recognition of the claimant (weaker section of the society)
2. Principles of beneficence or the principles of non malificence (no harm should be done to others, that harm done should be compensated. Everybody to a reasonable extent has the moral duty to avoid harm being done by others)

The domain of recognitional ethics covers a large part of traditional ethical interventions. Ethics in fact is about asymmetrical relations about the rights of interest of one generating a duty of another.

For example, employees aged 57 to 60 years morally obliged to retire to give way to some younger colleagues who, being in the midst of their careers can raise a more weighty claims to a job.

Recognitional ethics clarifies and support this type of moral action.

5.5 IMPORTANCE OF ETHICS IN ORGANISATIONS

Ethics are the principles and values an individual uses to govern his activities and decisions. In an organisation, a code of ethics is a set of principles that guide the organisation in its programmes, policies and decisions for the business. The ethical philosophy an organisation uses to conduct business can affect the reputation, productivity and the image of the organisation.

Leadership Ethics: The ethics that leaders in an organisation use to manage employees may have an effect on the moral and loyalty of workers. The code of ethics used by the leaders determines discipline procedure and the acceptable behaviours for all workers in an organisation. When leaders have high ethical standards it encourages workers in the organisation to meet the same level. Ethical leadership also enhances the company's reputation in the financial market and community. The leaders of a business may create an ethical culture by exhibiting the type of behaviour they would like to see in employees. A solid reputation for ethics and integrity in the community may improve the company's business.

Employee Ethics: Ethical behaviour among workers in an organisation ensures that employees perform their work with honesty and integrity. Employees who use ethics to guide their behaviour adhere to employee policies and rules while striving to meet the goals of the organisation. Ethical employees also meet standards for quality in their work, which can enhance the company's reputation for quality products and service.

The organisation can reinforce ethical behaviour by rewarding employees who exhibit the values and integrity that coincides with the company code of ethics and displining (punishing) those who do not behave ethically and disobey company's code of ethics.

Benefits to the Organisation

A positive and healthy corporate culture improves the moral among workers in the organisation, which may increase productivity and reduce labour turnover, this in turn, has financial benefits for the organisation. Higher levels of productivity improve the efficiency in the company, while increasing employee retention reduces the cost of replacing employees.

5.6 ETHICS IN MANAGEMENT

Now, business organisation have recognized that mere social responsibility is not just a sufficient concept for serving the society and its various constituents. They are inculcating ethics in all aspects of their functioning. Though ethical issues are relevant for all segments of the society in different forms, ethical issues in management are in the form of business ethics.

The crucial role of top management is prime in a business asset. To achieve results, the management need to be strongly committed to ethical conduct and give constant leadership intending and rewarding the values of the organisation. Management play a crucial role in creating, maintaining and changing ethical culture. Leaders at every level should serve as role models for ethical behaviour.

Ethics managing in organisations is not just managing formal ethics or compliance programmes, Ethical climate or culture in an organisation is more important than specific ethics compliance programme goals. The elements of ethical culture that guide employee thoughts and action covers:

- Leadership
- Perceived fairness
- Employee authority structure

- Reward system
- Ethics as a topic of conversation in the management
- Code of conduct
- Ethics training programmes etc.

Depending on the size of the organisation certain roles may prove useful in managing ethics in the work place. These can be full time functions assumed by some one already in the organisation. The following roles are important for ethics management, particularly in big organisation.

1. Top management attitudes: The top management must fully support the ethical programme and aspire to lead in ethical manner.
2. Establishing an ethics committee, and opening up corporate culture to broad ethical standards.
3. Carry out organisational charges that help employees at all levels.
4. Building ethical safe guards into the company, such as:
   - Code of ethics
   - Ethics management committees.
   - Ethics training progammes.
   - Ethics audits.

Ethics in business management enables the company to adhere to society's basic rules that define right and wrong behaviour, and the business meets.

- Public expectations
- Prevents social harm.
- Protects itself from abuses by employees and other firms and stake holders.
- Reduces labour turnover.
- Preserves the dignity and integrity of individuals who work in the organisation.

5.7 Qualities and Social Responsibilities of Manager

Qualities of Manager:

Ethics management benefits the managers in the following ways.

It develops moral imagination and sharpens his analytical and critical skills. It helps the managers in decision making. Moral standards are the yard sticks of business ethics. They provide basis for judging whether an act is right or wrong. It thus, guides the managers to take decisions with respect to moral standards of the society's culture. Ethics plays an important role in decision making consciously or un-consciously.

As decision makers, managers have more opportunities than others to set an ethical tone for the company. They are the key people to act ethically or unethically. The qualities and values held by the managers are important in promoting ethical activities.

Values and qualities must likely to influence management at work are:

- Service to customers
- Ability
- Company loyalty
- Logical thinking
- Integrity
- Honesty
- Benevolence
- Self control
- Capability
- Imaginative power
- Achievement
- Responsibility
- Courage
- Generosity
- Tolerance

A manger possessing these qualities and virtues exhibits the excellences of human character and behaviour and able to take decision ethically.

Social Responsibilities of Managers / Management

Social responsibility contends that management is responsible to the organisation itself and to all the groups with which it interact. Other interest groups to which the management is responsible are employees, customers, creditors, suppliers, and society in general.

Its responsibilities go beyond mere production of goods and service at a profit, but extends to putting some of the resources at the service of society in order to help to solve the pressing problems of the society in which it operates.

The pursuit of mere economic growth produced several detrimental side effects and they imposed significant social costs on certain segments of society (which are the burden without any gain) or on the society as a whole. For instance, environment deterioration, unsafe workplaces, avoidable exposure to toxic substances, discrimination against certain sections of society, urban decay, industrial wastes, unhealthy labour practices and such other social ills could be traced to business organisations. Hence, a new thinking of the role and responsibility of business came about which insisted that business has an obligation to work for social as well as economic betterment.

The business was, thus, asked to assume greater responsibility to society than ever before. It was asked to serve a wider range of human values. Business enterprises were expected to contribute more to the quality of human life than just supplying quantities of goods and services. Those who work for, buy from, sell to, live near, or otherwise get affected by the activities of the corporation need to be served and cared for Fig. 5.4 shows Archie – Corroll's Social Responsibility model.

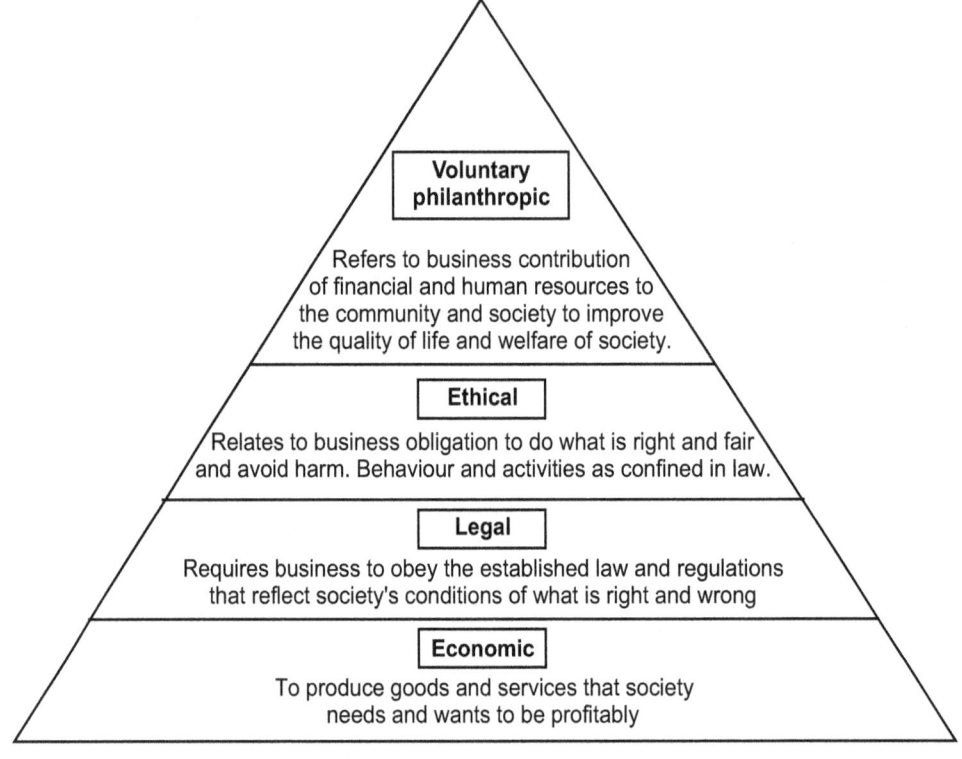

Fig. 5.4: Archie Corroll's social responsibility model

In addition to responsibilities toward society the managers/ management discharge their responsibility towards shareholders, employees, customers as follows:

Responsibilities Towards Shareholders:

1. Protecting and safe guarding their investment and
2. Ensuring them a fair return.

Responsibilities Towards Employees:

1. By a realistic and general understanding and acceptance of their needs and rights and enlightened awareness of the social responsibilities of industry.
2. By providing adequate wages, good working conditions, job security, effective machinery for speedy redressal of grievance, and suitable opportunities for promotion and self development.

3. By promoting feeling of trust and loyalty through a human and purposeful awareness of their needs and aspirations, and

4. By creating a sense of belongingness and team-spirit through their closer association with management at various levels.

Responsibilities Towards Customers:

1. By products of proven quality at a fair price.

2. By fulfilling its commitments impartially and courteously in accordance with sound and straightforward business principles; and

3. By bearing their confidence in its productive ability and its technical competence to keep improving the quality of its products.

The company management may undertake number of programmes for the benefit of the community and country such as:

The city development, pollution control, community development and social welfare programme, rural development programme etc.

5.8 Introduction, Objectives and Features of Industrial Legislation

Introduction

Industrial legislations (Acts) are the laws enacted by the Government to provide economic and social justice to the workers in industries. These laws provide guidelines to the industrialists in dealing with the matters of wages, incentives, facilities and other working conditions of the workers. Mr. V. V. Giri explained industrial legislation as, "A provision for equitable distribution of profits and benefits occurring from industry, between industrialists and workers and affording protection to the workers against harmful effects of their health safety and morality."

Industrial legilsation may be classified into two categories:

(a) General legislation and (b) Specific legislation.

General legislation looks after the general labour problems like social welfare, insurance and industrial disputes, while specific legislation looks after the work of specific industries, transport, mines, electricity, waste disposal, boilers etc.

Objectives of Industrial Legislation

1. Improves industrial relations and minimises industrial disputes.

2. Protects workers' interest and avoids their exploitation by the employer.

3. Helps to pay fair wages to workers.

4. Minimises unrest among the workers.
5. Reduces conflicts, strikes etc.
6. Helps to protect the larger interests of society by aiding in the improvement of trade and industry.
7. Provides job security for the workers.
8. Promotes good environmental conditions in the industry.
9. Fixes hours of work, rest pauses etc.
10. Provides compensation to workers suffered from industrial accidents.

Features of Industrial Legislation

Industrial/labour legislation is based upon the following principles:

1. Social justice.
2. Social equality.
3. National economy.
4. International uniformity and solidarity.

1. Social Justice: Industrial laws provide social justice to the employees by ensuring suitable distribution of profits and benefits between the employer and employees. It also ensures better working conditions in industry. Industrial acts based on social justice are

- Factories Act
- Minimum Wage Act
- Workmen's Compensation Act, etc.

2. Social Equality: Another objective of industrial legislation is to ensure social equality or social welfare of workers. These laws make the employers to improve social status i.e. material and morale conditions of the workers by ensuring adequate wages, working hours, health and safety of the workers.

3. National Economy: It ensures normal growth of industry for the development of nation. It satisfies the workers' need and increases their efficiency. Efficient industry finally contributes a lot to improve national economy and makes the country self-sufficient.

4. International Uniformity: International Labour Organisation (ILO) has been set up to safeguard the interest of labour. The main objective of ILO is to secure minimum standards on uniform basis in respect of all labour matters. Uniformity of standards can be maintained only by enforcing various industrial laws.

Some of the important industrial acts are discussed briefly in this chapter.

5.9 THE INDIAN FACTORIES ACT, 1948

The Factories Act was passed by the Governer General of India on 23rd Sept. 1948 and it came into force on 1st April 1949. The Act was further amended in 1950, 1951, 1954 and 1976 which came into force on 26th November 1976. This act is applicable to any factory in India that employees 10 or more than 10 workers.

Aims and Objectives

The major objectives of the factories act are:

(i) The main object of the act is to provide protection to the workers employed in factories against industrial hazards and to ensure safe and better working conditions.

(ii) It regulates and properly maintains various safety health and welfare activities in the factories.

(iii) It also regulates and properly maintains working hours and rest hours of workers, employment of children and adolescents, employment of women, annual leave with wages etc.

Some Important Definitions

Factory: A working place under one management wherein 10 or more than 10 persons are normally working with power aid or 20 or more persons working without power aid.

Manufacturing process: A manufacturing process is a process for:

- Making, altering, repairing, ornamenting, finishing, packing, oiling, washing, cleaning, breaking up, demolishing, or otherwise treating or adopting any article or substance with a view to its use, sale, transport, delivery, disposal etc.
- Pumping oil, water or sewage or any other substance, or
- Generating, transforming or transmitting power, or
- Composing types of printing, printing by letter press, lithography, photography or other similar process or bookbinding, or
- Constructing, reconstructing, repairing, refitting, finishing or breaking up ships or vessels or
- Preserving or storing any article in cold storage.

Adult: A person who has completed 18th year of age is called adult.

Child: A person who has not completed 15th year of age.

Adolescent: A person who has completed 15th year, but has not completed 18th year of age.

Worker: Any person employed directly or through any agency for any manufacturing process or for cleaning any part of machinery, or premises, or other identical work connected with manufacturing process is called worker.

Machinery: Machinery means different appliances used in a factory like prime movers, plants, machines, transmission machinery or any other appliances whereby power is generated, transformed or transmitted.

Occupier: A person who has ultimate control over the affairs of factory.

Hazardous Process: Hazardous process means any process or activity in relation to an industry where, unless special care is taken, raw-materials therein or the intermediate or finished products, by products, wastes or effluents thereof would:

(a) cause material impairment to the health of the persons engaged in or connected therewith or

(b) result in the pollution of the general environment.

Approval, Licensing and Registration of Factories

The act specifies that before starting a factory:

(1) It is necessary to take permission of the state government or chief inspector for the site on which the factory is to be situated or for the construction or extension of the factory.

(2) The plans and specifications have to be approved by the factory inspector.

(3) The factory has to be registered and the license obtained after paying the necessary fees. The application for permission should be sent to the Chief Inspector, it should contain name and address of occupier, and factory, nature of manufacturing process, nature of power to be used, name of factory manager, number of workers required etc.

If after submitting the application to the State Government or the Chief Inspector, nothing is communicated to the applicant within 3 months, the permission is deemed to have been granted.

If a State Government or a Chief Inspector refuses to grant permission to use a particular site, the applicant may appeal to Central Government in this connection with 30 days from the date of refusal.

Inspection Staff

The act permits the State Government to appoint a Chief Inspector and other inspectors who

(a) may enter the factory and

(b) may make examination of premises, plant, machinery and any documents related to factory.

Certifying Surgeons

The act also permits the State Government to appoint qualified medical practioners as qualifying surgeons for

(a) the examination and certification of young workers and

(b) the examination of workers engaged in dangerous occupation or processes.

The factories act makes detailed provisions in respect of the following:

1. Health
2. Safety
3. Welfare
4. Working hours of adults
5. Employment of young persons
6. Employment of women
7. Leave with wages
8. Special provisions
    (a) Dangerous Operations
    (b) Accidents and Diseases
    (c) Penalties and Procedure.

[I] Health Provisions

The factories act makes the following provisions for maintaining the health of workers and for reducing the possibilities of injuries:

(1) Cleanliness:

(a) All dirt and refuse from floors, benches etc. should be removed daily.

(b) The floors of the work-room should be washed at least every week, using disinfectant.

(c) All inside walls, partitions, ceiling, sides and tops of passages and staircases should be whitewashed or varnished at least once in every 14 months. If they are painted, they should be repainted at least once in 5 years.

(d) Effective means of drainage should be provided to avoid collection of water etc. on the work floor.

(2) Disposal of Wastes and Effluents:

Effective and suitable arrangements should be made for the disposal of wastes and effluents due to manufacturing process.

(3) Ventilation and Temperature:

Effective and suitable provisions should be made for securing and maintaining in every workroom

(a) Adequate ventilation by fresh air circulation.

(b) Suitable temperature to provide conditions of comfort and prevent injury to the health of workers.

(4) Dust and Fumes:

Effective measures should be taken for the prevention of inhalation or accumulation of dust and fumes in the work-room.

(5) Artificial Humidification:

In factories (e.g. textile) where artificial humidification is used

(a) Prescribed method should be used for achieving humidification and the artificial humidification should be maintained within the prescribed limits.

(b) The water employed for humidification should be from a source of drinking water.

(6) Over-Crowding:

(a) No work-room should be over-crowded so as to be injurious to the health of the workers.

(b) The minimum space provided for a worker should be 14 m^3. To arrive at this figure, a height above 4.2672 metre from floor level should not be taken into consideration.

(7) Lighting:

(a) Light whether artificial or natural or both, should be sufficient and suitable in all work places.

(b) Sky lights and glazed windows for lighting the workplaces should be kept clean and unobstructed.

(c) Glares and shadows which may cause eye strain and increase the chances of accidents should be prevented.

(8) Drinking Water:

Drinking water should be made available at suitable points. All such points should be legibly marked "Drinking Water". No such points should be located within 3.5 metres from urinal or latrine.

(9) Latrines and Urinals:

(a) Sufficient latrine and urinal accommodation of the prescribed type should be provided.

(b) Separate enclosed accommodation should be provided for male and female workers.

(c) Latrines and urinals should be adequately lighted, ventilated and maintained clean at all the times.

(10) Spittoons:

Sufficient number of spittoons should be provided at convenient places. The spittoons should be maintained in clean hygienic condition.

[II] Safety

(1) Encasing and Fencing of Machinery:

Every prime mover like engine or motor, moving part of the machinery and every dangerous part of the machinery should be fenced properly.

(2) Work on OR Near Machinery in Motion:

(a) Examination of any part of the machinery in motion should be carried out only by a specially trained adult male worker, wearing tight fitting clothes.

(b) No woman or young worker should be permitted to clean, lubricate or adjust any part of a moving machinery which may involve a risk of injury.

(3) Employment of Young Persons on Dangerous Machines:

No young person should be allowed to work on a dangerous machine unless he is properly trained and carefully supervised.

(4) Hoists and Lifts:

(a) Every hoist and lift should be of good mechanical construction, adequate strength and must be protected by enclosures and fitted with gates.

(b) Every hoist and lift should be adequately maintained and periodically (at least once in six months) examined.

(5) Lifting Machine, Chains Ropes and Lifting Tackles:

Lifting machines such as cranes, crab, winch, pulley block etc. should be of good construction, adequate strength. They should be properly maintained and thoroughly examined at least once in a year by a competent person.

(6) Pressure Plants:

It should be ensured that the working pressure of pressure vessels such as boilers does not exceed the safe limit.

(7) Floors, Stairs and Means of Access to different Places:

All floors, steps, stairs, passages and gangways should be of sound construction and free from obstructions.

(8) Pits, Sumps, Opening in Floors etc.:

Every pits, sumps, opening in floors, fixed vessels, tanks etc. should be securely covered or fenced.

(9) Excessive Weights:

No person should be asked to lift, carry or move any load so heavy that is likely to cause him injury.

(10) Protection of Eyes:

To protect the eyes of workers from the flying particles (such as in grinding, fitting, rivet cutting, chipping etc.) or from exposure to welding rays, each worker should be provided with effective screens or suitable goggles.

(11) Precautions against Dangerous Fumes:

(a) Adequate protection should be provided against dangerous fumes. No person should be allowed to enter confined space, chamber, tank pit etc. in which dangerous fumes are likely to be present.

(b) If a manufacturing process is producing dust, gas, fumes or vapour which can explode on ignition, the plant should be effectively enclosed; and such dust, gas, fumes etc. should not be allowed to accumulate.

(12) Precautions in case of Fire:

(a) Effective fire warning signal.

(b) Unlocked doors and opening towards outside the workroom as a means of escape in case of fire.

(c) A free passageway and easily openable windows.

[II] Welfare Provisions

(1) Washing Facilities:

In every factory separate and adequate washing facilities must be provided and maintained for male and female workers.

(2) Facilities for Sitting:

Suitable sitting facilities should be provided for all workers obliged to work in standing position so that they may take rest if an opportunity occurs in the course of their work, without affecting the work.

(3) First Aid Appliances:

First aid boxes equipped with prescribed contents and not less than one in number for every 150 workers at any one time must be provided and maintained at accessible places.

(4) Canteen:

A canteen should be provided and maintained in every factory employing more than 250 workers.

(5) Shelters, Rest-rooms and Lunch-Rooms:

Every factory in which more than 150 workers are ordinarily employed, adequate, suitable, clean, sufficiently lighted and ventilated rest and lunch rooms should be provided.

(6) Creches:

In factory, wherein more than 50 women workers are employed, suitable rooms (creches) must be provided for the use of the children under the age of 6 years of such women.

(7) Welfare Officers:

Every factory employing 500 or more workers should employ prescribed number of welfare officers.

The State Government may prescribe the duties, qualifications and conditions of service of welfare officers employed.

[IV] Working Hours

Hours of Work for Adults: No adult worker should be required or allowed to work in a factory for more than 48 hours in any week ; or 9 hours in any day. Moreover, no worker should work for more than 5 hours before he had an interval of half-an hour.

Holidays: No adult worker should be required or allowed to work in a factory on the first day (i.e. Sunday) of the week, unless the factory manager substitutes Sunday by a holiday one or three days immediately before or after Sunday. If he is required to work on Sunday, he shall be entitled to the compensatory holiday for the same.

Extra Wages for Over-time: Where a worker is required to work for more than 9 hours in any day or for more than 48 hours in any week, he shall be entitled for an overtime at the rate of twice his ordinary rate of wages as specified in the act. The manager of every factory should maintain a register of adult workers to be available to the inspector at all times during the working hours.

Restriction on Double Employment: No adult worker should be allowed to work in a second factory on any day on which he has already been working in one factory.

[V] Employment of Young Persons

A young person means a person who is either a child or an adolescent. A "Child" means a 'person who has not completed his 15th year of age. An "adolescent" means a person who has not completed his 18th year.

No child who has not completed 14th year should be required or allowed to work in a factory. But a child who has completed his 14th year or an adolescent may be allowed to work in a factory if:

(1) A certificate of fitness for such work granted by certifying surgeon is obtained by the manager of the factory.

(2) Such a child or adolescent carries a token giving a reference to such certificate while he is at work.

Working Hours of the Children

(1) No child should be employed or permitted to work in any factory for more than 45 hours in any week and during the night hours.

(2) The period of work for all children employed in a factory should be limited to two shifts which should not overlap or spread over more than 5 hours each. The manager of every factory in which children are employed should maintain a register of child workers, showing the details such as name ; nature of work the group in which he is situated, the number of fitness certificate etc. of the child worker.

[VI] Employment of Women

No women should be allowed to clean, lubricate or adjust any part of the machinery while that is in motion. Every factory must provide for the creches wherein more than 30 women workers are ordinarily employed. No woman should be permitted to work in any factory except between the hours of 6 a.m. and 7 p.m.

[VII] Annual Leave with Wages

Every worker who has worked for a period of 240 days or more in a factory during calendar year should be given leave with wages for a number of days calculated at the rate of;

(a) One day for every 20 days of work performed during the previous calendar year by an adult worker.

(b) One day for every 15 days of work performed by a child worker.

(c) If a worker does not in any one calendar year take the whole of the leave allowed to him, any leave not taken by him shall be accumulated and allowed to him in the succeeding calendar year subject to a maximum of 30 days in case of adult or 40 days in case of the child.

(d) A worker interested to take leave should apply 15 days in advance (30 days in case public utilities). A worker can not take leave more than 3 times during a year.

[VIII] Special Provisions

(a) Dangerous Operations:

If any operation carried out in the factory is likely to cause bodily injury, poisoning or disease to the worker, the State Government, may declare such operations as dangerous and make the following rules:

(a) Stopping the employment of women and children in such operations.

(b) Provision of proper safeguards of all concerned with that operation.

(c) Periodical medical check-up of all concerned with such operation etc.

(b) Accident and Diseases:

(1) If an accident causes death or bodily injury due to which the worker cannot work for a period of 48 hours or more immediately after the accident, it should be reported to the factory inspector within the prescribed time.

(2) If a worker is suffering from any disease specified in the schedule, a report to that effect should be immediately send to the chief inspector. Such a report should include the particulars of the worker and the disease from which he is suffering.

Power to take Samples: Any inspector, during working hours, after informing the manager may take samples of any substance or materials being used in the factory.

(c) Penalties:

No court shall take cogniance of any offense made under this act except on complaint by or with the previous sanction in writing of an inspector.

If in any factory, there is any contravention of any of the provisions of the act or of any rules made there under, the occupier and the manager of the factory shall each be guilty of an offense and punishable with imprisonment for a period upto 3 months or with fine upto ₹ 2,000 or both. If the contravention is continued after conviction, they shall be punishable with further fine which may extend to ₹ 75 for each day on which the contravention is continued.

5.10 THE EMPLOYEES' STATE INSURANCE ACT, 1948 (ESI ACT)

The Employees' State Insurance Act was passed in 1948 because it was experienced that, in many cases the benefits provided to the workers under the Workmen's Compensation Act, 1924 did not reach them. This was due to the following reasons:

(1) The Workmen's Compensation act did not cover many diseases.

(2) It involved much delay in payment of compensation.

(3) In many cases it is difficult to prove that the accident occurred due to the negligence on the part of employer.

The Employees' State Insurance act is the first attempt in India for introducing a broad based scheme of health, maternity and accident insurance.

The Object: The object of the act is to introduce social insurance through the compulsory state insurance by providing for benefits like sickness, maternity and employment injury.

The Scope of the Act: The act applies to all factories running with power and employing 20 or more persons except seasonal establishment. This act extends to the whole of India, except Jammu and Kashmir.

Contribution: The act makes provision for creation of fund called Employees' State Insurance Fund. Contribution towards raising the fund is mainly from the Employer and Employees of the undertaking. The Central and State Government also give grants and donations to the State Insurance Fund. The employer deducts employees' contribution from their salaries and the same along with employer's share is submitted in a bank nominated for the purpose by the Employees' State Insurance Corporation set up under this act. The employees' share depends on the rate of the emoluments.

The E.S.I. corporation may appoint inspectors to check the particulars about the amount of fund submitted by the employer.

Benefits:

The workers getting not more than ₹ 1000 per month are entitled for the six types of benefits:

1. Sickness benefits.
2. Maternity benefits.
3. Disablement benefits.
4. Medical benefits.
5. Dependents benefits.
6. Funeral benefits.

1. **Sickness Benefits:** For sickness, cash benefits are available to a insured person for a period of 56 days in a year at the rate of roughly 50% of the average daily wages. In special cases of sickness like tuberculosis, sickness benefits at reduced rates are extended upto a period of one year, provided that the concerned person has completed continuous service of 2 years in the establishment.

   An insured person is entitled to sickness benefit only if his sickness is certified by a duly appointed medical practioner.

2. **Maternity Benefits:** An insured woman employee is entitled to periodical payment in case of confinement or miscarriage or sickness arising out of pregnancy. These benefits are granted for 12 weeks.

3. **Disablement Benefits:** An insured person suffering from disablement as a result of injury in course of employment is entitled for disablement benefits. Disablement benefits vary according to the nature of injury.

   For temporary disablement lasting for more than 7 days, the insured worker is entitled to get half of his average daily wages for the period of disability. For permanent disablement, the insured worker is entitled to a pension for life in accordance with the proportionate loss in his earning capacity. The injured employee has to obtain a medical certificate from Medical Insurance Officer from whom he gets treatment.

4. **Dependents Benefits:** If the insured person dies as a result of an injury his dependents are entitled to get benefits as under;

   (1) The widow of the person will get $3/5^{th}$ of the rate at which the employee would have been paid under disablement benefit scheme had he survived the injury.

   (2) Each legitimate or adopted son is entitled to an amount equal to $2/3^{rd}$ of the full rate until he attains the age of 16 years.

   (3) Each legitimate unmarried daughter is entitled to an amount equal to $2/5^{th}$ of the full rate until she attains the age of 18 years or is married.

5. **Medical Benefits:** An insured person or his family are entitled to medical treatment if necessary. The medical benefit is available in either of the following terms:

   (a) As an outdoor patient attending a hospital dispensary or clinic.

   (b) Treatment as an indoor patient.

   (c) Treatment given at the home of the insured person visiting physician.

   The standard and rate of such benefits are determined by agreement between the EPHIC (Employees' State Health Insurance Corporation) and the State Government.

6. Funeral Benefits: In the event of death of the insured employee the expenditure on his funeral can be claimed. An amount of ₹ 100 is payable to the eldest, surviving member of the family or such person who actually incurs funeral expenses.

Adjudication of Disputes and Claims

1. **Constitution of Employees' Insurance Court:** The State Government shall constitute an Employees' Insurance Court to decide all matters, questions and disputes arising from the insurance of workers.

2. **Matters to be Decided by Employees' Insurance Court:**
   (i) Whether any person, is an employee with the meaning of this act or whether he is liable to pay the employee's contribution.
   (ii) The rate of contribution to be paid by principle employer in respect of any employee.
   (iii) The rate of wages or average daily wages of an employee for the purpose of this act.
   (iv) The right of any person to any benefit and to the amount and duration thereof.
   (v) Any dispute between the employer and ESI corportion in respect of any contribution or benefit or other dues payable or recoverable under the act.

3. **Power of Employees' Insurance Court:** The employees' insurance court shall have all the powers of a civil court for the purpose of summoning and enforcing the attendance of witnesses, compelling the discovery and production of documents and material objects, administering oath and recording evidence and such court shall be deemed to be a civil court.

4. **Penalties:** Whosoever knowingly makes or causes to be made any false statement or false representation shall be punishable with imprisonment upto six months or fine not exceeding ₹ 2000 or both.

5. **Punishment for Failure to Pay Contributions:** If any person:
   (i) fails to pay any contribution which under this act he is liable to pay, or
   (ii) by reason only of his liability for any contributions reduces the wages or any priveleges or benefits admissible to an employer, or
   (iii) dismisses, discharges, or otherwise punishes an employee during the period of sickness or
   (iv) obstructs any inspector or other officials of the corporation in the discharge of his duties, or
   (v) is guilty of any contravention of or non-compliance with any of the requirements of this act or the rules or regulations in respect of which no special penalty is provided.

He shall be punishable with imprisonment exceeding upto 3 years or a fine upto ₹10,000. Prosecution shall be instituted only with the previous sanction of the Insurance Commissioner. No court inferior to that of Presidency Magistrate or First Class Magistrate shall try any offence under this act.

Miscellaneous: The appropriate Government may exempt certain factories or employees from the operation of this act, under certain conditions.

Central Government, State Government and the Corporation has powers to make rules and regulations consistent with this act.

5.11 WORKMEN'S COMPENSATION ACT

The Workmen's Compensation Act, 1923 came into force on 1 July, 1924. The act was amended in 1926 and 1929 to introduce certain changes and to rectify the International Labour Convention on occupation disease. In 1933, a consolidating and amending act was passed to incorporate the recommendations of the Royal Commission on Labour. The Workmen's Compensation (amendment) act, 1976 is the latest amendment which became effective from 1st October 1976. Main provisions of the act amended in 1976 are as follows:

Workmen's Compensation Act provides compensation to certain categories of workers for the loss of working capacity due to accidents. This act prevents the exploitation of workers in case of payment of compensation. It safeguards the workers and their families in case of death or disablements of workers arising from accidents. The object of awarding compensation is to replace the actual loss suffered by the worker.

Important Definitions in the Act

1. **Dependent:** 'Dependent' means any of the following relatives of the deceased worker

   (i) A widow, a minor legimate son, an unmarried legimate daughter or widowed mother.

   (ii) An infirm son or daughter who has attained the age of 18 years and who was wholly dependent on the earning of the workman at the time of his death and

   (iii) If wholly or partly dependent on the earning of the workman at the time of his death a widower, a parent other than widowed mother, a minor legitimate son, an unmarried illegitimate daughter or a daughter legimate or illegimate if married and minor or if widowed and minor, a minor brother or an unmarried sister or widowed sister, if a minor, a widowed daughter-in-law, a minor child of a predeceased son, a minor child of a predeceased daughter where no parent of the child is alive or a parental grand parent if no parent of the workman is alive [Section 2(d)].

2. Partial disablement: Partial disablement means disablement of temporary nature that reduces the earning capacity of a workman in the employment in which he was engaged at the time of accident resulting in the disablement.

3. Temporary partial disablement: Disablement that temporarily reduces the earning capacity of a workman.

4. Permanent partial disablement: It means any disablement that permanently reduces the earning capacity of the workman in every employment.

5. Total disablement: Total disablement means such disablement whether of a temporary or permanent nature, which incapacitates a workman for all work which he was capable of performing at the time of accident resulting in such disablement. The Act also specifies certain injuries which are to be deemed to result in permanent total disablement. These include:

- Loss of both hands or amputation at higher sites.
- Loss of hand and a foot.
- Double amputation through leg or thigh or amputation through leg or thigh on one side and loss of other foot.
- Loss of sight to such an extent as to render the claiment unable to perform any work for which eye-sight is essential.
- Very severe facial disfigurement and
- Absolute deafness.

Besides permanent total disablement shall be deemed to result from any combination of injuries where the agreegate percentage loss of earning capacity (as specified in schedule I) (Table 5.1) amounts to one hundred percent or more. (Refer Table 5.2).

Application of the Act:

The act applies to all workers employed in Railways, Factories, Mines, mechanically propelled vehicles, construction work and other hazardous occupations except persons employed in a clerical or administrative capacity or in Armed forces.

Employer's Liability for Compensation: If a personal injury is caused to a workman by accident in the course of his employment, the employer shall be liable to pay compensation in accordance with the provision of this act if:

(a) injury has been caused by accident.

(b) during the course of employment.

(c) and has resulted in workman's death, permanent or temporary disablement.

The employer is not liable to pay compensation if:

(a) the injury disables the workman for less than 3 days.

(b) the injury is caused by an accident which occurred while the workman was under the influence of drink or drugs.

(c) the injury is caused by wilful disobedience of the safety rules by the worker ; or

(d) the injury is caused owing to the wilful removal or disregard of any safety guard by the workman. But, if the worker dies of an accident due to the above reasons the employer has to pay compensation.

Amount of Compensation: Amount of compensation depends upon the following factors:

(1) Average monthly wages of the worker concerned which should not be more than ₹ 1000.

(2) The extent of injury e.g.

    (a) Death.

    (b) Permanent total disablement.

    (c) Permanent partial disablement.

    (d) Temporary disablement.

(3) Type of work of the worker (clerical, industrial, administrative).

(4) Causes of accidents (whether it occurred due to negligence of the worker etc.)

Amount of compensation payable in case of different injuries can be ascertained from Schedule IV as given below (as amended upto 1976)

Table 5.1: Rate of Compensation

Sr. No.	Monthly wages	Amount of Compensation for		
		Death	Permanent Disabled	Temporary Disabled
1.	Upto ₹ 60	7,200	10,080	50% of Monthly Wages
2.	More than 60 upto 90	9,720	14,608	36.00
3.	More than 90 upto 120	11,520	16,128	42.00
4.	More than 120 upto 150	13,500	18,900	48.75

Contd...

5.	More than 150 upto 200	16,800	23,520	60.00
6.	More than 200 upto 300	18,000	25,200	82.50
7.	More than 300 upto 400	19,200	26,880	100.00
8.	More than 400 upto 500	21,000	29,400	118.75
9.	More than 500 upto 600	21,600	30,240	135.00
10.	More than 600 upto 700	23,100	32,340	148.75
11.	More than 700 upto 800	24,600	33,000	160.00
12.	More than 800 upto 900	27,000	37,800	168.75
13.	More than 900 upto 1,000	30,000	42,000	175.00

Notice of Accident: A worker injured in an accident should first of all give in writing a notice of the accident to the employer.

Every such notice should include:

- Name and Address of the injured worker.
- Cause of accident.
- Date of accident.

Medical Examination: An injured worker who has submitted a notice, must present himself for the medical examination, if the employer wants. The employer must offer the medical examination free of charge and with 3 days from the time at which service of notice has been affected.

If the worker does not present himself for the medical examination then he will not have the right for compensation.

Distribution of Compensation: Payment of compensation in respect of death of workman or under legal disability shall be depicted by the employer with the commissioner. Employer should not make payment of compensation directly.

However, in case of deceased workman an employer can give an advance upto ₹ 100 to dependents of the deceased worker for meeting the immediate expenses. The commissioner, after deducting this advance, may allot the entire amount of compensation to the dependent of the deceased workman.

Occupational Diseases: If a worker suffers from any of the specified occupational disease (the list of which is given in schedule III of the act) and he worked in the factory for at least six months, then the employer has to pay compensation. Some of the occupational diseases are compressed air illness, poisoning by lead, phosphorous, mercury, arsenic, radium and other radioactive substances, x-rays etc.

Appointment of Commissioner: The State Government, may by notifications in the Official Gazette appoint any person to be commissioner for workmen's compensation for the areas specified in this modification. Every commissioner is deemed to be a public servant within the meaning of the Indian Penal Code.

Table 5.2: Schedule I: Percentage of loss of earning capacity

Sr. No.	Description of Injury	Percentage loss of earning capacity
1.	Loss of both hands	100
2.	Loss of a hand and a foot	100
3.	Loss of sight to an extent that renders the claimant unable to perform any work for which sight is needed	100
4.	Very severe disfigurement of face	100
5.	Absolute deafness	100
6.	Double amputation to leg or thigh and other foot	100
7.	Amputation through shoulder joint	90
8.	Amputation of both feet	90
9.	Loss of a hand or a thumb and four figures of one hand	60
10.	Loss of 4 fingers of one hand	50
11.	Amputation below knee	40
12.	Loss of one eye	40
13.	Loss of all toes of both feet	40
14.	Loss of thumb	30
15.	Loss of three fingers of one hand	30
16.	Loss of two fingers of one hand	20
17.	Loss of vision of one eye	30
18.	Loss of index finger	14
19.	Loss of middle finger	12
20.	Loss of index finger	7
21.	Loss of right or left great toe	14
22.	Loss of any other toe	3
23.	Two toes of one foot excluding great toes	5
24.	Three toes of one foot excluding great toes	6
25.	Four toes of one foot excluding great toes	9

Illustrative Example for Calculating Compensation:

A worker getting ₹ 1000/- per month, meets an accident and loses one eye and three fingers of his right hand and also one of his great toes. Determine the compensation to be paid to the worker. What would be the compensation if the poor worker also loses his thumb?

Solution

(i) Percentage loss of earning capacity due to loss of one eye   40%
   (Schedule I. Table 5.2)

(ii) Percentage of loss of earning capacity due to loss of three fingers   30%
    of right hand

(iii) Loss of earning capacity due to loss of his one great toe.   14%

   Therefore, the total loss due to above = 40 + 30 + 14 = 84%

   Amount of compensation payable to the worker

   = 84/100 × 42000 = ₹ 33768/-

(iv) If the worker also loses his thumb, then the percentage of loss   84 + 30 = 114%
    of earning capacity would be

But it cannot be more than 100% loss and therefore, the compensation payable would be ₹ 42000/-.

5.12 THE INDUSTRIAL DISPUTE ACT, 1947

The Industrial Dispute Act was passed in 1947. The act makes provision for settlement of industrial disputes between employees and the employers. The main object of the Act is to secure industrial peace by settling the industrial disputes through negotiations and conciliations rather than on the strength of strikes and lockouts.

Important Definitions

1. **A ward:** A ward means an interim or final determination of an industrial dispute by a labour court or industrial tribunals.

2. **Average Pay:** Average pay means the average of wages payable to the workman:

   (a) In 3 calendar months for monthly paid workman.

   (b) In 4 completed weeks, in case of weekly paid workers.

   (c) In 12 full working days for daily paid workers.

3. **Industry:** Industry means any business, trade, undertaking, manufacture etc. It includes calling service, employment handicraft or industrial occupation or a

vocation of workman. The educational and the professional firms of solicitors, chartered accountants are not treated as industry under this act. But municipality, Government, run hospitals are treated as industry.

4. **Industrial Dispute:** Industrial dispute means any dispute or difference between:

   Employers and Employers

   Employers and Workmen

   Workmen and Workmen and which is connected with:

   the employment or

   non-employment or

   the conditions of labour of any person.

5. **Lay-off:** Lay-off means failure, refusal or inability of an employer, on account of shortage of coal, power, raw-material, accumulation of stock, breakdown of machinery or for any other reason to continue to employ workers (in his industry) whose name is borne on the muster-rolls and who have been retrenched.

   Lay-off is a temporary phase, the employer-employee relations do not come to an end but are simply suspended for some period (of emergency).

6. **Lock out:** Lock out means closing at place of employment or suspension of work or the refusal by an employer to continue to employ any number of workers employed by him.

7. **Retrenchment:** Retrenchment is the termination of the services of a worker for any reason whatsoever, other than due to disciplinary action.

   Retrenchment does not include,
   - Voluntary retirement of the worker,
   - Termination of service on the ground of continued ill-health.

8. **Strike:** Strike means refusal to work under a common understanding of any number of workers. It is the weapon of the workers to compel the employer to accept their demands.

9. **Settlement:** Settlement means a settlement arrived at during the course of conciliation proceedings. It includes a written agreement between the workers and the employer.

10. **Workman:** Workman means any person (including an apprentice) employed in any industry to do any skilled or un-skilled, manual, supervisory or clerical work for hire or award.

11. Suspension of Workman: A workman may be suspended during pending inquiry and disciplinary action. If after inquiry misconduct is proved, the worker is dismissed and is not entitled to any wages of the suspension period. In case when a worker is fully exonerated after enquiry, he would remain in service and would be entitled to receive full wages of the suspension period.

Main Provisions

The main provisions of Industrial Disputes Act are:
1. Constitution of formation of machinery for settlement of industrial dispute.
2. Strikes and lock-outs.
3. Compensation for lay-off and retrenchment.
4. Notice for change of service conditions.
5. Penalties for break of provisions of Act.

The act provides for the prevention as well as settlement of the industrial disputes. It has provided for an extensive and effective machinery for establishing industrial peace. The provisions are made in the act for establishing the following machineries for the prevention and settlement of industrial disputes.

Works Committee: Any industry in which 100 or more workers are employed or have been employed on any day in the preceding 12 months, shall constitute a works committee. The works committee shall consists of the representatives of the employer and workmen employed in the unit. The number of the representatives of the workman shall not be less than those of the employer. The representatives of the workman shall be chosen from among them in consultation with the trade union, if any.

The duties of the works committee are:

(i) to secure and preserve the unity and good relations between employer and the workman,

(ii) to comment upon the matters affecting the interest of all the workman,

(iii) endeavour and to compromise any material difference of opinion in respect of such matters.

Conciliation: Conciliation officers are appointed by the appropriate Government, for any specified area or for one or more specific industries, either permanently or for a limited period. The duty of the conciliation officer is to mediate in and to promote the settlement of the industrial disputes.

If he fails in this he shall report to Government, The appropriate Government, in case of need, will refer the dispute to Board of conciliation, Labour Court, Industrial Tribunal or National Tribunal.

Board of Conciliation: A Board of conciliation is constituted by the appropriate Government, by notification in the Official Gazette. The Board consists of a chairman and two or four other members, chairman is an independent person and other members are representatives from employer and employees, in equal numbers.

Powers of the Board

(i) A member of a board can enter the premises of the establishment for the purpose of inquiry into any industrial dispute after any reasonable notice.

(ii) Every board inquiry is treated to be judicial proceeding within the meaning of section 193 and 228 of the Indian Penal Code.

(iii) The Board will try to settle the industrial dispute. If it fails in this then, it will send its report within two months from the date of reference to the appropriate Government, regarding the steps taken by it and the reasons why the settlement could not be sought.

Court of Enquiry: Court of Enquiry may also be appointed by the appropriate Government, by notification in the Official Gazette. Such a court may consist of one or more independent persons appointed by the Government The duty of the court is to enquire into the matter referred to it and report thereon to the Government, within 6 months from the commencement of enquiry.

Labour Court: The appropriate Government, may constitute labour court for adjudication of the disputes relating act. It consists of only one person who possesses a high judicial standing as specified in the act. The matters within the jurisdiction of labour court as per second schedule are:

(i) The propriety or legality of an order passed by employer under the standing orders.

(ii) The application and interpretation of standing order.

(iii) Illegality or otherwise of a strike or lock-out.

(iv) Dismissal of workers including reinstatement of or grant of relief to workers wrongly dismissed.

(v) Withdrawal of any customary concession or privilege.

(vi) All matters other than those specified in the third schedule.

Presiding officer of one man labour court shall have the following qualification:

(a) A judge of a high court, or

(b) A district judge who has worked for more than 3 years.

Industrial Tribunals: Appropriate Government, may also constitute one person Industrial Tribunals for the adjudication of Industrial disputes relating to matters specified in:

(i) Schedule II (as mentioned in jurisdiction of labour court)

(ii) Schedule III. The schedule III includes matters such as,

1. Wages including the period and mode of payment.
2. Compensatory and other allowances.
3. Hours of work and rest pauses.
4. Holidays and leave with wages.
5. Bonus, provident fund and gratuity.
6. Rules of discipline.
7. Classification by grades.
8. Rationalisation.
9. Retrenchment of workman and closure of establishment.
10. Shift working otherwise than in accordance with standing orders.

Presiding officer of the tribunal shall have the same qualification as that of Labour court.

National Tribunals: The Central Government, may constitute one or more National Tribunals for the adjudication of the industrial disputes which may involve questions of national importance. It can also take up industrial disputes which are of such a nature that industrial establishments situated in more than one state are likely to be interested in or affected by such disputes.

The presiding officer of the National Tribunal shall be:

(i) an independent person

(ii) less than 65 years of age, and

(iii) an existing or retired judge of a high court.

Strikes and Lock-outs

1. **Strikes:** No employee of a public utility service shall go on strike,

    (i) without giving a notice of strike to the employer within 6 weeks before strike OR

    (ii) within 14 days of giving such notice, OR

    (iii) before the date mentioned in the notice, OR

    (iv) during the pendency of proceeding before a Labour court, Tribunal or National tribunal and two month after the conclusion thereof.

2. **Lock-outs:** No employer of any public utility service shall lock-out,
   (i) without giving a notice of lock-out within six weeks before locking out,
   (ii) within 14 days of giving such notice,
   (iii) before the date specified in the notice,
   (iv) during the pendency of conciliation proceeding.

The employer shall send information of strike or lock-out to the specified authority on the day on which it is declared.

Penalty for Illegal Strikes or Lock-outs: A strike or lock-out is illegal if it is declared in contravention of points 1 and 2 above (i.e., section 22 and section 23 of the act, respectively):

(i) Any worker who commences or continues strike which is illegal, shall be punishable with imprisonment upto one month or a fine upto ₹ 50 or both.

(ii) Any employer who commences or continues lock-out, which is illegal, shall be punishable with imprisonment upto one month or fine upto ₹ 1000 or both.

(iii) Instigating others for strikes or lock-outs is punishable upto a period of six month or ₹ 1000/- or both.

(iv) Any person held responisble for breaking the term of settlement of award is punishable upto a period of six months.

Compensation for Lay off and Retrenchment: If a worker who has completed not less than one year of continuous service under an employer is laid-off, he shall be paid for all days during which he is so laid-off. The compensation applicable is 50% of basic wages plus dearness allowances that would have been payable to him had he not been laid off or retrenched.

No worker who has been in a continuous service for not less than one year under an employee shall be retrenched by that employer until:

(a) The workman has been given one month's notice in writing indicating the reasons for retrenchment and the period of notice has expired or the worker has been paid in lieu of such notice wages for the period of the notice provided that no notice shall be necessary if the retrenchment is under an agreement which specifies a date for the terminations of service.

(b) The worker has been paid, at the time of retrenchment, compensation which shall be equivalent to 15 days' average pay for every completed year of continuous service or any part thereof in excess of 6 months.

(c) The workman who is employed last in particular category will be retrenched first.

The following persons are not entitled for any benefit from the employer:

(i) Who does not present himself at the appointed time during the laid off period at least once a day.

(ii) Who refuses to accept an alternative job on the same wages and of the same nature within a radius of 8 kilometers.

(iii) The enterprise is seasonal or employees less than 50 workers.

Notice for Change of Service Conditions: According to the provisions of Industrial Disputes Act, an employer can not introduce any change in service conditions of a worker until and unless the worker is served with a notice of 20 days in advance for effecting such change. The conditions under which notice for change in service can be given are: Wages, contribution towards provident fund, compensatory or other allowances, leave with wages, hours of work and rest intervals, gratuity, holidays, modernisation of plant and equipment etc.

Closing Down the Undertaking: An employer who intends to close down an enterprise shall serve, atleast 60 days before the date on which he intends closure to become effective, a notice to Appropriate Government, stating clearly the reasons for closing the undertaking. Compensation by reference to section 25-FFF of the act is provided to workers who are in continuous service for not less than a year with the undertaking.

The Industrial Disputes Act was amended in 1976.

This amendment deals with the special provisions relating to following:

(a) Prohibition of Lay-off and conditions precedent to retrenchment of workers in certain undertakings with 300 or more than 300 workers.

(b) Restarting of establishments closed before the commencement of the Amendment Act 1976.

(c) Penalty for lay-off and retrenchment without prior permission.

(d) Penalty for closure.

The Industrial Disputes Amendment Act (1976) has provided for reasonable restrictions put on employer's right to lay-off, retrenchment and closure.

The act also provides for restarting the undertakings which have already been closed down on account of unavoidable circumstances.

Penalty for illegal lay-off or retrenchment is one month's imprisonment or fine upto ₹ 1000 or both (Section 25).

In case of illegal closure of an establishment the workers shall be entitled to all the benefits from the date of closure under any law in force as if no notice has been given [Section 25-0 (3)].

QUESTIONS

1. Define ethics, and explain the nature of ethics.
2. What do you mean by ethics? State the objectives of ethics.
3. Compare between 'Moral' and 'Ethics'.
4. Sate and describe the various types of ethics in brief.
5. Write short note on any two of the following:
   (i) Meta Ethics
   (ii) Virtue Ethics
   (iii) Applied ethics
   (iv) Transactional ethics
6. Describe the importance of ethics in a business organisation.
7. Describe the social responsibilities of management.
8. Define ethics. Why the business needs to be ethical? Explain.
9. What is the necessity of industrial acts?
10. Describe the principles of industrial legislation (in brief).
11. Define the following as per Factories Act:
    (a) A manufacturing process (b) Adolesent
    (c) Worker (d) Machinery
    (e) Occupier (f) Factory.
12. Explain briefly the different health provisions mentioned in the Factories Act.
13. Describe the welfare provisions under Factories Act. Explain how it will affect productivity.
14. Describe the following in connection with Factory Act:
    (a) Objectives of Factories Act.
    (b) Approval, Licensing and Registration of Factories.
15. Explain the following with respect to the provisions of the Factories Act:
    (a) Hours of work for adults, women, and young persons.
    (b) Annual leave with wages.
16. Explain the following in brief in connection with Factories Act:
    (a) Extra wages for over time.

(b) Employment of young persons.

17. Explain the importance of safety provisions in case of machinery, hoist and lifts and precautions in case of fire as mentioned in Factories Act.

18. Factories Act helps productivity. Justify the statement with reference to few relevant provisions of the Factories Act, 1948.

19. Explain the purpose and scope of ESI Act.

20. Name and explain the different benefits provided in ESI Act.

21. Describe the following terms with reference to the ESI Act.

    (i) Contribution   (ii) Disablement benefit

    (iii) Dependents benefit   (iv) Sickness benefit.

22. What are the penalties mentioned in the ESI Act?

23. Explain the purpose of Workmen's Compensation Act. Where is it applicable?

24. Describe the complete procedure for payment of compensation under the Workmen's Compensation Act.

25. Describe briefly the main provisions of Workmen's Compensation Act.

26. Define the following terms in accordance with the Workmen's Compensation Act:

    (i) Dependent   (ii) Partial disablement

    (iii) Temporary partial disablement   (iv) Permanent disablement.

27. Explain the following terms related to Workmen's Compensation Act:

    (i) Employer's liability for compensation.

    (ii) Notice of accident and medical examination.

28. State the factors which govern the amount of compensation paid to the worker in Workmen's Compensation Act.

29. What is an industrial dispute? State the aims of Industrial Dispute Act.

30. Define the following terms related to Industrial Dispute Act:

    (i) Average pay   (ii) Industry

    (iii) Strike   (iv) Lockout

www.ingramcontent.com/pod-product-compliance
Lightning Source LLC
Chambersburg PA
CBHW080243170426
43192CB00014BA/2545